The Lawyers
of the Last
Capetians

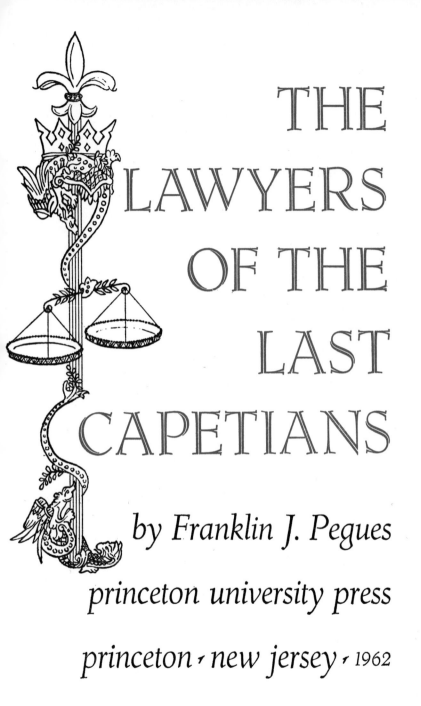

THE
LAWYERS
OF THE
LAST
CAPETIANS

by *Franklin J. Pegues*

princeton university press

princeton · new jersey · 1962

Publication of this book has
been aided by the Ford Foundation
program to support publication,
through university presses, of work in
the humanities and social sciences

Printed in the United States of America
by Princeton University Press, Princeton, New Jersey

for Nancy

CONTENTS

PREFACE

THE lawyers of Philip the Fair were an unusual group of men who were associated with an unusual reign and with two notable events, the struggle with Boniface VIII and the destruction of the Templars. So far as individual lawyers are concerned, only the names of Guillaume de Nogaret and Pierre Dubois are mentioned in textbooks although historians are also acquainted with Pierre Flote and Guillaume de Plaisians. I first became aware of the lesser known lawyers in 1952 when, in the process of reading through the Chancery Registers of the last four Capetian kings, such names as Raoul de Presles, Philippe de Villepreux, and Pierre de Latilly occurred with noticeable frequency. I was then engaged in a long-range study of the civil service of the feudal monarchies, and when I returned to France in 1956 to continue the study I carefully examined the careers of these men and the other lawyers who served the last Capetians. The present book has come out of that research.

What I have attempted to do here has little or nothing in common with Richard Scholz' *Die Publizistik zur Zeit Philips des Schönen und Bonifaz' VIII* (Stuttgart, 1903). Scholz was entirely concerned with the political ideas developed by the lawyers on both sides of the struggle between Philip and Boniface. He therefore dealt at some length with the ideas of Flote, Nogaret, and Plaisians while he omitted, in most cases, mention of the other lawyers of Philip the Fair. Furthermore, the church-state struggle is only one of many topics included in the present study. I have sought to draw to the center of the stage Presles, Villepreux, Latilly, and Gilles Aicelin and to compare them with the more familiar figures of Flote, Nogaret, Plaisians, and Dubois. The focus of this study is not on institutions or even on Philip the Fair but on the origins and rise of the Capetian lawyers, their conduct in power, and their significance in French history.

The technical problem of this study was the delimitation
of the term *légiste*. It has been used indiscriminately by
historians to refer to many civil servants who were supposedly influenced by the principles of Roman law and who
played leading roles in Philip the Fair's reign. I have applied
the term only to men for whom there is concrete evidence
that they were lawyers and had legal training. Not all of
the lawyers of the last Capetians are in this study. I have
selected about twelve who seem to typify the Capetian legist
and who appear most prominently in the reigns of Philip
the Fair and his three sons.

Throughout the text I have Anglicized the Christian
names of kings and popes while keeping other names in their
French forms. For *librae, solidi,* and *denarii,* or their French
equivalents, I have used the abbreviations *l., s.* and *d.* Where
there is a question of a particular kind of currency I have
used the French term.

Most American scholars who enjoy the privilege of study
and research in Europe owe a debt of gratitude to foundations and universities. For grants and financial aid, I wish
to thank the U.S. Fulbright Commission, the University of
Colorado, the American Philosophical Society, and the Ohio
State University. Most of the research was done in Paris
at the Archives Nationales and the Bibliothèque Nationale.
I am indebted to the staffs of those two institutions and of
the several Departmental Archives whose manuscripts are
cited in this work. I also wish to thank the librarians of the
following libraries for making my work easier: the Widener
Library of Harvard, the Sterling Memorial Library of Yale,
the University of Michigan Library, and the Ohio State
University Library.

My gratitude to the late Carl Stephenson and to the late
M. L. W. Laistner can never be adequately expressed. For
her interest and valuable assistance in research I owe much
to my wife.

*The Lawyers
of the Last
Capetians*

ABBREVIATIONS

A.N.	Archives Nationales, Paris.
B.N.	Bibliothèque Nationale, Paris.
B.E.C.	*Bibliothèque de l'Ecole des Chartes.*
Boniface VIII	*Les registres de Boniface VIII,* ed. G. Digard, M. Faucon and Antoine Thomas. Paris, 1884-1939.
Boutaric	*Actes du Parlement de Paris,* ed. E. Boutaric. First Series. Paris, 1863-1867.
Bull. Soc. Arch. Soissons	*Bulletin de la société archéologique, historique et scientifique de Soissons.*
Clement V	*Regestum Clementis Papae V ex Vaticanis Archetypis.* Rome, 1885.
Comptes royaux	*Comptes royaux (1285-1314),* ed. Robert Fawtier with assistance of François Maillard (Recueil des historiens de la France: Documents financiers. Vol. III. In Three Parts). Paris, 1953-1956.
Furgeot	*Actes du Parlement de Paris,* ed. H. Furgeot. Second Series. Paris, 1920.
H.F.	*Recueil des historiens des Gaules et de la France.* Paris, 1738-.
H.L.	C. Devic et J. Vaissete, *Histoire générale de Languedoc,* new edition by A. Molinier. Toulouse, 1885.
Jean XXII	*Jean XXII (1316-1334). Lettres communes,* ed. G. Mollât. Paris, 1905-1946.
Journ. Charles IV	*Les journaux du trésor de Charles IV le Bel,* ed. J. Viard (Collection de documents inédits). Paris, 1917.
Journ. Philippe IV	*Les journaux du trésor de Philippe IV le Bel,* ed. J. Viard (Collection de documents inédits). Paris, 1940.
Journ. Philippe VI	*Les journaux du trésor de Philippe VI de Valois,* ed. J. Viard (Collection de documents inédits). Paris, 1899.
Livre Rouge	Charles Victor Langlois, "Registres perdus des archives de la Chambre des comptes de Paris," *Notices et extraits des manuscrits de la Bibliothèque Nationale et autres bibliothèques,* XL (1916), 33-398.
Longnon	*Documents relatifs au comté de Champagne et de Brie, 1176-1361,* ed. Auguste Longnon (Collection de documents inédits). Paris, 1901-1914.
Mignon	*Inventaire d'anciens comptes royaux dressé par Robert Mignon,* ed. Charles Victor Langlois (Recueil des historiens de la France: Documents financiers. Vol. I). Paris, 1899.
Nicholas IV	*Les registres de Nicholas IV,* ed. Ernest Langlois. Paris, 1886.
Olim	*Les Olim ou registres des arrêts,* ed. A. Beugnot (Collection de documents inédits). Paris, 1839-1848.
P.T.E.C.	*Positions des thèses de l'Ecole des Chartes.*

INTRODUCTION

Capetian Lawyers
and French Historians

A T THE beginning of this century, Charles Victor Langlois restated the basic question of Philip the Fair's reign: Was the monarch or were his ministers responsible for the policies which made his reign the most unusual and perhaps the most violent of medieval Europe?[1] This problem had given little concern to historians in the early nineteenth century. For the most part, they pushed the king into the shadows and concentrated their attention on his ministers, whom they fondly and loosely called *légistes.* Writing in the wake of the French Revolution, they assigned to these lawyers a unique role in the history of France, and their interpretation of Philip's ministers has since influenced all writing on the subject. Langlois was interested in Philip's lawyers because he despaired of ever knowing the character and personality of the king. But Langlois believed that role and responsibility could not be discussed intelligently until the character and personality of the lawyers became clear. This, he felt, was the key to the solution of the basic question. Who were these lawyers? How did they come to power and what was their conduct in government? Not until these matters had been determined could one proceed to the question of responsibility. But the views of both Langlois and the early nineteenth-century historians differed radically from the position of the pre-Revolutionary writers. The historiography of the Capetian lawyers, as developed by these three groups of historians, demands the attention of any student who seeks to understand and to increase our present

[1] Charles Victor Langlois in Ernest Lavisse, *Histoire de France,* III, Part 2 (Paris, 1901), 119-126.

knowledge of the lawyers who served the last Capetian kings.

Apart from the contemporary chroniclers and annalists of Philip the Fair's reign, who are not our concern at the moment, French historians before the Revolution saw no significance or unusual character in the lawyers of the last Capetians, and did not think peculiar the work these men had done. This fact is all the more interesting because many historians between 1500 and 1789 were lawyers. With the understatement characteristic of the better known antiquarians, most of these writers simply chronicled the events of the Capetian reigns, or else devoted their efforts to the laborious compilation of lists of chancellors, presidents of the Parlement, and other royal officers of the late medieval and early modern French kings. The work of such erudites as Denys Godefroy, Abraham Tessereau, and Père Anselme will remain immensely valuable for all students of French history if only for the reason that these authors put into order and tabulated the holders of various royal offices, appending to their lists detailed genealogical discussions of their subjects.[2] But the verbal parsimony of these early writers gives us no living picture of the administrative officers of the medieval French monarchy, either individually or as a group. Stripped of the warmth and color of human life which lets us discern foible and strength, motive and significance, they appear immovably attached to offices, reigns, and a series of dates; they are so many stiff, elongated figures on a Romanesque portal.

[2] Denys Godefroy, *Histoire des connestables, chanceliers et gardes des sceaux, maréschaux, admiraux, etc.* (Paris, 1658); Abraham Tessereau, *Histoire chronologique de la chancellerie de France* (Paris, 1676); Père Anselme, *Histoire généalogique et chronologique de la maison royale de France, des pairs, grands officiers de la couronne, etc.* (9 vols; Paris, 1726). These are three of the antiquarian works which furnish basic information on the administrative personnel of the medieval French kings.

An occasional historian of the sixteenth century paused and looked more carefully at a particular person or event, and Etienne Pasquier (1529-1615), in his encyclopedic commentary on French life and culture, detected in the fate of one of Philip the Fair's ministers an item of more than routine interest. In the *Recherches de la France,* he dedicated a short dissertation to Enguerrand de Marigny, the minister of Philip IV who was closest to the king during the last years of his reign, and who was tried for malfeasance and hanged the year after the monarch's death in 1314.[3] Pasquier perceived the terrible uncertainty of royal favor in the example of Marigny, who for all of his arrogance and audacity was nevertheless worthy of compassion. But Pasquier moved to a more eloquent plane and placed Marigny against the background of classical antiquity. Parmenion had his Alexander, Sejanus his Tiberius, and Belizarius his Justinian. Marigny was worthy of their company; he gave similarly faithful service and received in like manner an undeservedly harsh fate. Pasquier chose this one great minister of the Capetian king and gave him almost lifelike dimensions. But he, like the other historians, saw no historical significance in the role played by Marigny or by any of the lawyers of Philip the Fair.

A contemporary and admirer of Pasquier was Antoine Loisel (1536-1617), who let his friend carry the burden of the conversation in the *Dialogue des avocats.*[4] The principals of the dialogue engaged in a historical discourse on great lawyers in French history, beginning with Pierre de

[3] *Les Recherches de la France,* Bk. 6, Chap. 43, pp. 669-672, in *Les Oeuvres d'Estienne Pasquier* (2 vols; Amsterdam, 1723). First published in 1560, the work continued to enjoy vogue long after the author's death. Pasquier is an excellent example of the sixteenth-century lawyer who wrote history. *Conseiller* and attorney-general of the king in the Chamber of Accounts, he knew well the ambitions and fortunes of royal lawyers.

[4] Antoine Loisel, *Pasquier, ou Dialogue des avocats du Parlement de Paris,* edited by André Dupin (Paris, 1844).

Fontaines and other prominent legists of the age of Saint
Louis. Loisel, speaking through Pasquier, noted that for
the reign of Philip the Fair he had found few men to whom
the name of *avocat* could be given. Three such candidates
were Guillaume de Nogaret, Raoul de Presles, and Pierre Dubois. But Loisel only mentioned their names. Regarding the
lawyers of Philip's three sons, he could do little more than
note that Jean d'Asnières had delivered the principal speech
against Enguerrand de Marigny in 1315 and that Guillaume
du Breuil was the author of the "*stile du parlement.*" If
there was a theme on which Loisel played, it was that of
the lawyers' role in making the French monarchy free of
papal control. Pierre de Cuignières was singled out for particular praise. When questioned by his nephew on the
identity of this person, Loisel had Pasquier reply that Cuignières was one of the most virtuous of wise men, whose
memory must be kept because he was the first lawyer bold
enough to defend the rights of the king and of the barons
against ecclesiastical usurpation.[5] Loisel was a Gallican lawyer and saw only the church as the enemy of the French
monarchy.

The treatment of medieval history by the seventeenth-
century historians was no more original than it had been in
the preceding century. For the most part, the writers repeated what had already been said. One interesting view
is found in the work of François Eudes de Mézeray (1610-
1683), whose first volume of his *Histoire de France* appeared
in the auspicious year of 1643.[6] Despite the fact that Pasquier was one of his sources, Mézeray had hard words for
the ministers of Philip the Fair and believed that Marigny
was the villain of the reign. Not only was he responsible for
the king's broken promises, and for the exclusion of Philip's
brother, Charles de Valois, from the government, but Mar-

[5] *Ibid.*, p. 22.
[6] François Eudes de Mézeray, *Histoire de France*, i (Paris, 1643).

igny was also guilty of treason in dealing with the Flemish. When he was hanged in 1315, Mézeray believed that it was not so much for peculation as for arrogance. Mézeray mentioned several of Philip's lawyers, Nogaret, Pierre Flote, Raoul de Presles, and Pierre de Latilly, but rendered no judgment on their character or careers.[7] Finally, Mézeray maintained that a degrading influence which emanated from the papal court at Avignon corrupted and debased the French lawyers and introduced into the practice of law calumny, malice and subterfuge.[8] There was in Mézeray's historical writing a distinctly aristocratic sympathy coupled with a Gallican partisanship.

The century of the *philosophes* was not a likely age for the composition of great histories of medieval monarchs or lawyers. The intellectual framework constructed by Voltaire and Diderot could well do without lessons or enlightenment from the years before 1500. We need little reminder that the author of *Le Siècle de Louis XIV* recommended the study of the Middle Ages only that they might be better scorned. On the other hand, the compilers of the historical dictionaries did treat the Middle Ages and its people in numerous biographical sketches. One of the better known examples of these compilations was *Le grand dictionnaire historique* of Louis Moreri. In the 1759 edition, this dictionary contained a biographical study of Raoul de Presles based on an article that Antoine Lancelot had submitted to the *Académie royale des inscriptions et belles lettres*.[9] Although the study covered three men who bore the name of

---

[7] *Ibid.*, p. 712.　　　[8] *Ibid.*, p. 706.

[9] Louis Moreri, *Le grand dictionnaire historique* (20th ed.; Paris, 1759), viii, 554-556. First published by Moreri as a one-volume work in 1674, the dictionary was so popular that successive editors continued to expand and reissue it until it consisted of ten volumes in the edition of 1759. For the original article on Presles, see Antoine Lancelot, "Mémoire sur la vie et les ouvrages de Raoul de Presles," *Mémoires de littérature de l'Académie royale des inscriptions et belles lettres*, xiii (1740), 607-624.

Raoul de Presles in the fourteenth century, it has remained the most complete study ever made of Philip the Fair's lawyer by any scholar. All subsequent comment on Raoul de Presles has been based directly or indirectly on Lancelot's work. This is unfortunate for, while Lancelot used many of the Chancery Registers in his study, he made numerous errors of fact. And like the historians who had briefly remarked on the lawyers of the last Capetians, Lancelot perceived no historical significance in the life and career of Raoul de Presles.

If pre-Revolutionary historians saw no significance in the lawyers of the last Capetians, that fact was altogether changed by the historians of the nineteenth century. The most illuminating example of this change is the difference in definition given by the dictionary writers before and after the Revolution to the term *légiste*. Diderot's *Encyclopédie* maintained that *légiste* was a term applied to the masters or students in law. "The appearance of the *légistes* in the Parlement, under Philippe de Valois, brought about great changes; these men, full of formulas and ceremony which they had imbibed in the (Roman) law, introduced procedure and thereby made themselves masters of the most complex matters."[10] This definition is interesting for the misplaced chronology and for the vague realization that "great changes" had been effected by the lawyers if only under the Valois kings. Nothing was hinted beyond that. But one hundred years later the classical interpretation of the role of the Capetian lawyers was fixed, and the *Dictionnaire historique* of André Chéruel explains the change which had been wrought in the course of a century. Chéruel maintained that French lawyers first assumed importance in the thirteenth century when the study of Roman law spread throughout France. Men like Pierre de Fontaines and Phil-

---

[10] *Encyclopédie ou Dictionnaire raisonné des sciences, des arts et des métiers*, IX (Neufchâtel, 1765), 363.

ippe de Beaumanoir, writers and practitioners in the new science, influenced the legislation of Saint Louis. But it was principally in the reign of Philip the Fair that the *chevaliers-ès-lois* came to dominate affairs of state. Enguerrand de Marigny, Guillaume de Nogaret, Pierre Flote, Raoul de Presles, and Pierre de Latilly were simply the most eminent of those lawyers who worked with energy and perseverance to raise royal authority upon the ruins of feudalism. Imbued with the maxims of Roman law, they coined the phrase and made it their own: *si veut le roi, si veut la loi.* Chéruel left no doubt as to his source for this new view of the lawyers; he noted that Thierry had vividly portrayed the role of the legists in his essay on the Third Estate.[11]

The prime quality of Augustin Thierry's life work (1795-1856), which gave flavor and color to all of his historical writing, was his obsession with the Third Estate. The Third Estate was the French nation, and the common man was the Third Estate. Only through their triumph could Frenchmen come to civil equality, political liberty, and human freedom. "We are the sons of the men of the Third Estate; the Third Estate came out of the communes, the communes were the refuge of the serfs; the serfs were those vanquished in the conquest."[12] Thierry not only searched the origins of the serfs, the rise of the communes, and the growth of the middle class, he lived, fought, and suffered with them. As far as he was concerned, the whole sorry drama of the failure of human freedom and civil equality was re-enacted before his very eyes in the France of 1820. Never was a man's soul so torn with anguish as Thierry's when he contemplated the imminent defeat of the noblest aspirations of the French

[11] André Chéruel, *Dictionnaire historique des institutions, moeurs et coutumes de la France* (5th ed.; Paris, 1880), II, 649f. The first edition appeared in 1855.

[12] Augustin Thierry, "Sur l'antipathie de race qui divise la nation française," *Dix ans d'études historiques* (Paris, 1834), p. 280. This article was first published in the *Censeur européen*, April 2, 1820.

nation, while the violent and savage debate went on between the liberals and the monarchists during the Restoration years. But he had no illusions about the Revolution; that, too, begun under most promising auspices, had been twisted and betrayed and finally struck down in ignoble defeat.

Thierry's earliest comment on lawyers in French history came in 1820, when his pen was fully engaged in the furious struggle with the Ultras. A new journal had appeared, the *Journal général de législation et de jurisprudence,* and the young liberal, then twenty-five years of age, took the opportunity to wish it well by writing a column in the *Censeur européen.* His remarks took the form of a dissertation on the role of lawyers in French history, which he entitled "On the Old Spirit and the New Spirit of French Lawyers."[13] He detected a new spirit among the present-day class of young legists; this was the spirit of law and liberty. For a long time in France the men who practiced the science of law had ignored the true nature of human rights. The representatives of justice had based their decisions on the capricious wills of the powerful or on the servile maxims of the civilians. But Thierry believed that this hateful discord was beginning to disappear. The French Revolution had been reawakened in 1814, the soul of France had been reborn and had passed into the schools of law, so long without color or life. The dogma of human liberty had been naturalized at the French bar; from there it would envelop the bench of the judges, and soon the character of jurists would no longer contradict their name; they would be truly the men of law. The old generation of French legists was disappearing and would give way to a generation as new in existence as in principle.

[13] Thierry, "Sur l'ancien esprit et sur l'esprit actuel des légistes français," *Dix ans d'études historiques,* pp. 259-267. This article first appeared in the *Censeur européen,* May 1, 1820. For recent comment on the political milieu in which Thierry wrote, see Stanley Mellon, *The Political Uses of History* (Stanford, 1958), pp. 9-12.

This old generation of lawyers is far more pertinent to our purpose, and now that Thierry had come to the subject of lawyers he was compelled to portray them within the framework of his obsession, the Third Estate, the communes, human liberty. Whatever role he ascribed to them had to fit the prearranged form. He realized first of all that the lawyers were of the Third Estate. But during the *ancien régime,* these lawyers of the Third Estate, advocates, judges, *conseillers,* were forced, under penalty of betraying their own maxims, to condemn juridically the liberty of the cities and communes, which had been the bulwark of their nation against all tyrannies. One lawyer in particular was singled out, Michel de l'Hôpital, chancellor of the last Valois kings, who signed the Ordinance of Moulins in 1570, which had destroyed with one blow the civil justice, the elective administration, and all the liberties of one hundred French towns and cities. This loyalty to the Third Estate, then, was the prearranged form and the acid test which lawyers must undergo to meet the rigid demands of that young revolutionary. And the lawyers of the *ancien régime* failed miserably.

But in speaking of l'Hôpital, who was after all one of the fairest jewels produced by French law, Thierry mixed sugar with his gall. The Chancellor was worthy of a measure of sympathy. He labored under the same yoke that weighed down the other lawyers of the *ancien régime.* They had spawned the legal maxims which had in turn created the absolute authority of the French king. Their work accomplished, they became the prisoners of the master whom they had raised, and were compelled to do his bidding. This was the yoke which had bound the lawyers from the fourteenth to the eighteenth century, and under which they destroyed in the name of absolute monarchy all of human liberty that had been born and nourished in the urban communities. Corruption was not among the sins of these men; they had

simply broken faith, and justice in their hands had descended to the level of a commercial transaction. But the
doctrine of natural rights soon came to do battle with the
principles of absolutism. From this point the Revolution
proclaimed the rights of the individual as superior to those
of society, the rights of society as superior to those of the
monarchy, and thereby destroyed the doctrines, the traditions, and the credit of the old lawyers. If the Revolution
had not been thwarted at its birth, there would have arisen
a new class of lawyers which would have defended the new
maxims of liberty and human reason. The security of the
citizen against the unjust aggression of private or public
force would have been assured. But two facts destroyed this
grand hope—the violence of the Revolution and the tyranny
of the Empire.[14]

Three decades passed before Thierry returned to the subject of lawyers. In the interval, he participated in the July
Revolution and continued historical research on the rise of
the communes, the Third Estate, and the growth of human
freedom. The result of these activities was the publication
between 1850 and 1870 of the *Recueil des monuments
inédits de l'histoire du Tiers Etat*. It was a fitting close to
a life of revolutionary writing and activity colored by deep
devotion to the ideals of human liberty and equality. Pre-
fixed to the first volume was a lengthy essay on the history
of the Third Estate, in which he once more reminded his read-
er that the Third Estate was not just the bourgeoisie; it was
the French nation. This introduction was published separate-
ly in 1853 with the title *Essai sur l'histoire de la formation et
des progrès du Tiers Etat*.[15] It was in the *Essai* that Thierry,
in discussing the medieval origins of the Third Estate, came

[14] Thierry, *Dix ans d'études historiques*, pp. 263-266.
[15] Thierry, *Recueil des monuments inédits de l'histoire du Tiers
Etat* (4 vols; Paris, 1850-1870). The references which follow are taken
from the *Essai sur l'histoire de la formation et des progrès du Tiers
Etat* (Paris, 1853).

once more to the subject of lawyers, and this time to the Capetian lawyers.

Thierry believed that for France the two great developments of the twelfth century were the renovation of royal authority and the rise of the communal revolution. In one, kingship was strengthened; in the other, common men became free. The thirteenth century contributed the decisive ingredient to this combination when the study of Roman law was introduced to France and an entirely new class of jurisconsults and political men, the head and the soul of the bourgeoisie, entered the royal service and began the battle of law and reason against feudal custom. The Parlement de Paris, supreme tribunal and council of state, became by the admission of these men the most active foyer of this new struggle. It was there that the new law was practiced and applied day after day, and the theory of public authority appeared, one and absolute, equal for all, the unique source of justice and law. These new lawyers who rose from the communes believed that in their society nothing was legitimate outside of kingship and the Third Estate. They seemed even to have a presentiment of the historical destiny of these two institutions; in almost every case, the legists of the Middle Ages, judges, counselors, royal officers, marked out the route of revolutions to come. Above all, they began the immense task which was consummated only after centuries of work: to unite in a single hand the parcelled sovereignty, to level toward the middle class all that was above it and to raise to its station all that was below it. In short, the Capetian lawyers, the intellectual leadership of the middle class, began the construction of an egalitarian nation united under a single public authority—the French king.[16]

The war of rational law against irrational feudal custom, which the Capetian lawyers fought, was a war of new ideas against ancient usage, and Thierry believed that, like all

[16] *Ibid.*, pp. 35ff.

such struggles, it had two quite different stages. The first phase was completed under Saint Louis when the agents of innovation moved cautiously but steadily, marking out in advance the limits of their sphere of action and tempering their every act with equity. In the vanguard of this new force were lawyers like Philippe de Beaumanoir and Pierre de Fontaines who, with measured step, began to restrict by royal act and legislation the feudal privileges of the aristocracy and to increase the area of the king's jurisdiction. The reign of Philip III was a period of transition, for the most part arid and unproductive with respect to the growing power of royal authority. But during the reign of Philip the Fair, grandson of Saint Louis, the grand program of rolling back feudal pretensions and strengthening royal power entered a new phase wherein license replaced restraint. Harsh, violent, and arbitrary, this second phase broke its bounds and destroyed all obstacles in its path. This new class of lawyers was represented by Guillaume de Nogaret, Raoul de Presles, Pierre Flote, and Guillaume de Plaisians.

These legists conceived their grand scheme in *froideur;* no popular fervor, no feeling of hope and joy accompanied their work. They dealt anguish and spoliation to the privileged classes and, at the same time, placed upon the mass of common men the weight of a rough-hewn administration that had more cunning than strength and lived on expedients and extortions, costing much and giving little. But this struggle, somber and foreboding, had the goal of a more just order for all, and above the pitiless ruin and suffering one voice alone was raised, that of the "absolute king who, in the name of natural law, proclaimed the right of liberty for all and, in the name of divine law, repressed the institution of serfdom."[17] These legists of the fourteenth century who, Thierry

---

[17] *Ibid.*, p. 38. Not all French liberals agreed with Thierry on this view. Frédéric Morin, *Origines de la démocratie: la France au moyen âge* (3rd ed.; Paris, 1865), pp. 226-229, attacked Thierry for idoliz-

maintained, were the founders and ministers of royal autocracy, inherited the fate common to great revolutionaries: the boldest among them perished in the reaction of those groups whom they had offended. But despite temporary defeats and feeble kings, the forces which had been set in motion continued to bring a growing class of free men under the protection and justice of one king until the egalitarian society of the new nation came into existence. Such was the contrast which Thierry drew between the reigns of Saint Louis and his grandson. He painted a panorama of a social and political revolution and, awesome in its grandeur, there was no doubt of its central theme. From all of the fire, heat, and hammering, stronger and purer steel was forged, and the smiths at the anvil were the lawyers of the last Capetian kings.

From Thierry's treatment of the Capetian lawyers emerged his final interpretation of French history for, with the passing of the age of Philip the Fair, the French nation moved beyond a mighty watershed. The historical destiny of the French people was therefore the construction of a one-class society in which the entire population would be identified with the Third Estate, and the ideal of absolute social and legal equality would become a reality. But this goal could be achieved only through the partnership of monarch and middle class, who would work together to destroy the aristocracy and all rank and privilege. Behind the creation of this partnership lay Thierry's eulogy of the Capetian lawyers: the intellectual leadership of the middle class, architects of revolutions to come, founders of absolute monarchy and of an egalitarian French nation. In this scheme of things the absolute monarch was necessary, for without him the

---

ing the medieval French monarchy. From the time of Philip Augustus, all French kings and lawyers, particularly those of Philip the Fair, had worked to suppress the common people and to destroy communal liberties.

lawyers could not subdue and abolish the privileged nobility.

Thierry had therefore to deal with a balance which was precarious at the outset. The lawyers of Philip the Fair, the great fourteenth-century levellers, did their work well enough. But Thierry found that his architects grew increasingly hard to live with. The lawyers of the *ancien régime* lost sight of their high calling, broke faith, and became subservient to the power they had created. Because of this failure, French history moved inexorably to a second great watershed, beyond which the liabilities of the old legists would be liquidated, and the nineteenth-century lawyers would proceed to the achievement of the ancient goal. If such a day had come, Thierry in 1853 did not care to point it out. He ended his *Essai* with the eighteenth century and left a dim light burning in the Parlement de Paris, original cradle of the legists and their last stronghold before the cataclysm of the Revolution.[18] Between the emergence of Thierry in 1820 and the close of his career in 1856, a multitude of young historians had come to the arena, and the volumes of Michelet, Martin, and Guizot had already been warmly received.

For Jules Michelet (1798-1874), the opening of the fourteenth century found the old world dying and a new world coming to birth; the transition began in France and was dominated by the odious figure of Philip the Fair. The old world was destroyed by the same men who founded the new one: the lawyers, the Lombard bankers, the false moneymen, and their master the French king. This was not an attractive new world, but it was certainly more legitimate than that of the Middle Ages, although no contemporary, save a Dante, recognized its virtues at that moment. But the modern system, particularly in France, its first representative, was weighted with a strange contradiction which worked

[18] Thierry, *Essai*, p. 251.

against the easy acceptance of the new order. This contradiction was the instinct for duplicity and the naïve hypocrisy
with which France alternately employed the two opposing
principles of Roman law and feudal institutions. France,
under Philip the Fair, was a lawyer in armor; she used feudal
force to execute Roman and canon law. From the moment
that Michelet set himself to describe the modern world, he
could not escape the fact that France, Philip the Fair, and
the Capetian lawyers played the dominant role in bringing
it to birth.[19]

Michelet, like Thierry, saw the contrast between the lawyers of Saint Louis and Philip the Fair, but he could not
draw the differences so sharply. The twin enemies of the
medieval French monarchy were the Church and the feudal
aristocracy, and the lawyers were the instruments used by
Louis IX and his grandson in reducing them to impotence.
They took the feudal principle of suzerainty and, overlaying
it with a veneer of Roman law, insisted that the king had the
right to make laws not only for his own domain but for the
entire kingdom. The key to understanding this new legislation lay in the class of men who came to be the councillors
of the last Capetian kings. Unlike Thierry, Michelet felt that
most if not all of the lawyers of Saint Louis and Philip IV
were of base origin; he even suspected the nobility of Pierre
de Fontaines and Beaumanoir.[20] Men who had recently ar-
rived were more willing servants of royal masters, and initial
success served only to make them bolder and more violent.
Michelet believed that the legists who had influenced
English kings in the twelfth century and Saint Louis, Alfonso
X, and Frederick II in the thirteenth, under Philip the Fair
came to be the tyrants of France. With souls of lead and
iron, they proceeded with the *froideur* detected by Thierry

[19] Jules Michelet, *Histoire de France* (rev. ed.; Paris, 1876), III,
265.
[20] *Ibid.*, p. 270f.

in servile imitation of Roman law and taxation. The Pandects were their Bible and evangel. And so, armed with the texts and citations of the civilians, they destroyed the Middle Ages, the papacy, feudalism, and chivalry.[21]

One final bit of common ground lay between Michelet and Thierry on the subject of the Capetian lawyers. Both men agreed that for all their violence, cunning, and dark deeds, these lawyers were the founders of civil order and that despite temporary defeats their work was destined to endure. For Thierry, as we have seen, this accomplishment was an important point in the progress of a much larger scheme that encompassed all of French history and the destiny of the French people itself. To Michelet it was the beginning of the modern world. The lawyers centralized monarchical power through the Parlement de Paris and the Chamber of Accounts and the Chancery, the great central administrative organs at Paris. They then proceeded to insure that centralization by sending into the provinces every conceivable sort of royal official—*baillis*, seneschals, provosts, proctors, *serjeants à cheval*, masters of money, and foresters—all with a zeal to do the royal will and, in the spirit of the legists, to destroy feudal pretensions and particularism and create a unified France under the rule of one man. Unfortunately, the creation and maintenance of this judicial and administrative army was unbelievably expensive, and the new society was soon stricken with the sickness which had destroyed the ancient world: it consumed without producing.[22] The only recourse was to invent one new tax after another until both noble and common man were locked in the stranglehold of fiscal exactions which bred hatred of the king and his lawyers. The stage was set for the vengeance which followed the death of Philip the Fair.

[21] *Ibid.*, p. 272.   [22] *Ibid.*, p. 273.

The fall of the lawyers provided Michelet with his concluding theme in treating the origin and rise of civil and political order in the modern world. He believed that the entire history of this period was contained in the fight to the death between the legist and the baron. But nothing was accomplished in hanging Marigny, imprisoning Raoul de Presles, and despoiling Nogaret. The lawyer was more tenacious than the noble supposed; Marigny was reborn with each reign, and always they killed him in vain. The old system, staggering under the blows of the lawyers, struck back with furious vengeance and each time destroyed an enemy: after Saint Louis, Pierre de la Broce; after Philip the Fair, Marigny; after Philip V, Géraud Gueite; after Charles IV, Pierre Remy. They all died illegally but not unjustly, for they died soiled with the violence of an imperfect system in which the evil still outweighed the good. But in dying they left to the king who let them be struck down his instruments of power, and to the people who cursed them their institutions of peace and order.[23] So Michelet conceived of the role played by the Capetian lawyers in the history of France. The Middle Ages had come to a mean death at the hands of the low-born lawyers, but the French monarchy which they founded had greater consolation when it ended under Louis XVI. It perished in the eternal glory of a young republic which conquered Europe and thereby carried abroad the seeds of the new order.

Any attempt to determine derivation and influence in the views of Thierry and Michelet is made difficult by the volumes of Henri Martin (1810-1883) which appeared contemporaneously with the work of the two men. Martin's treatment of the Capetian lawyers lay between that of Thierry and Michelet. He saw the lawyers of Saint Louis as noble men engaged in noble work, and while the legists of Philip

[23] Michelet, *Histoire de France*, IV, 130f.

the Fair were ruthless and even villainous their work was an important step in the construction of French national sovereignty and social equality.[24] Martin doubtless borrowed from Michelet; more especially, he acknowledged his debt to Sismondi and Guizot. But his greatest debt was to his "dear and illustrious master, Augustin Thierry, who has clarified so much of the Germanic settlement, the fusion of races and the communal revolution."[25] Thierry, Michelet, and Martin were certainly acquainted with each other's work, but it appears that all three were under the influence of some common inspiration. This common source is not difficult to find because each man admitted at one point or other his obligation to Guizot.[26]

For three years before the July Revolution, the lecture halls in the University of Paris were filled with listeners who came to hear the impassioned lectures of François Guizot (1787-1874) on the rise of French civilization. The lectures were published almost as rapidly as they were given, and Guizot's interpretation of French history came to be known to a large reading public.[27] To read Guizot's lectures on the age of Philip the Fair is to realize that the classic view of the Capetian lawyers was publicized in the classrooms of the Sorbonne almost a decade before Michelet composed his third volume, and a quarter of a century before the appearance of Thierry's *Essai*. Practically every major point of interpretation used by Thierry, Michelet, and Martin in their

[24] Martin's remarks on the lawyers of Saint Louis and Philip IV are found in his *Histoire de France* (4th ed.; Paris, 1855), IV, 290-296, 390-392.

[25] Martin, *Histoire de France*, I, xiii.

[26] In the sixth edition of Thierry's *Lettres sur l'histoire de France* (Paris, 1839), p. 3, he praised Sismondi, Guizot, and Barante, all of whose works had appeared since 1820. In Thierry's remarks on the lawyers of Philip IV in his *Essai*, he cited Guizot's work.

[27] François Guizot, *Histoire de la civilization en France depuis la chute de l'empire romain* in *Cours d'histoire moderne* (6 vols; Paris, 1829-1832).

treatment of the lawyers can be found in the pages of Guizot.

For Guizot, there were four stages in the growth of French royal power. Louis VI made himself master in his own domain, the Ile de France; Philip Augustus, through his wars against the foreigner, reconstructed the kingdom and gave to the French people a sense of nationality; Saint Louis consolidated the gains of his predecessors and, through his respect for rights and his love for justice and the public good, put the stamp of equity upon the French monarchy. The character of Philip the Fair's reign was contained in the metamorphosis of kingship into despotism.[28]

How was it that Philip IV was able to give such a radically different direction to the development of French kingship? Guizot believed that the judicial authority which had been formerly exercised by the great barons in conjunction with the royal *baillis* had passed in the course of the thirteenth century to the feudal seigneurs of lower rank. These yielded their power in turn to a new class of royal agents as legal process became ever more complicated and as the royal administration experienced a natural growth. These new agents were the legists, and they came finally to control the administration of justice. Drawn at first from the ecclesiastics, they ended by being taken almost exclusively from the middle class. In the hands of the monarch, these agents became a natural instrument against the two adversaries of the crown, the ecclesiastical and the feudal power, and in destroying them rendered an immense service to the French nation and brought to birth the idea of an indivisible public authority.[29]

But, at the same time, these Capetian lawyers of the early fourteenth century were from their origin "a terrible and wicked instrument of tyranny." Guizot believed that it was under Philip the Fair that the grand battle was engaged, the

[28] Guizot, *Cours d'histoire moderne*, v, 78f.
[29] *Ibid.*, pp. 100ff.

battle between the legists and their adversaries which was to hold so important a place in French history. These royal agents not only brushed aside ecclesiastical and feudal claims, but often enforced principles contrary to all liberty. This tendency was particularly noticeable as they became the executors of the royal will in the new "commissions" which appeared under Philip III and which Philip the Fair used with increasing frequency. But this battle between the legist and the baron, later dramatized by Michelet, was fought in two directions. In the time of reaction, the triumphant feudal lords also used lawyers and "commissions" to work their own arbitrary justice against those who, on behalf of the crown, had so recently persecuted them. That time came with the death of Philip in 1314, and Guizot introduced what followed with the words, *"Malheur aux parvenus légistes!"*[30]

To whom did Guizot owe his interpretation of the last Capetian lawyers? In his introductory remarks to his audience, he recommended that his students read some particular history of France for the facts and sequence of events which he would omit from his lectures. "Of all the histories of France which I can recommend, the best is doubtless that of M. de Sismondi."[31] At that moment, J. C. L. Simonde de Sismondi (1773-1841) had completed twelve of the thirty-one volumes in his *Histoire des Français,* and had passed well beyond the last Capetians. But to read Sismondi on the Capetian lawyers is to realize that Guizot could not have got his interpretation from this source. At the same time, in understanding Sismondi's view, we may come to realize how and why Guizot's interpretation came to be. Sismondi recognized that a new class of lawyers had arisen in the thirteenth century as a result of the revival of Roman law. But the age of Philip the Fair gained no particular signifi-

[30] *Ibid.,* pp. 103ff.
[31] Guizot, *Cours d'histoire moderne,* I, 40.

cance from this development. The onslaught against feudal
and clerical privilege had taken place under Saint Louis and
continued without break until Louis XIV crowned the work
begun by the thirteenth-century king.[32] The lawyers therefore helped to found the absolute French monarchy and
nothing more. Since he was not French, Sismondi was unaware that the Capetian lawyers had laid the foundations
of the French nation and of egalitarian French society. He
saw no necessity to make of the Capetian lawyers what
French liberal historians were compelled to make of them.

Sometime between the late years of the Restoration and
the very early years of the Second Empire, the outstanding
French historians fixed the liberal interpretation of the role
played by the last Capetian lawyers in French history. It is
scarcely necessary to say that the French Revolution was
the creative force in determining that interpretation. The
overwhelming purpose of that struggle was the destruction
of feudal and clerical privilege. Although historians might
later dispute the results of the Revolution, no one, certainly
no liberal or republican spirit, could argue about its purpose.
But the historian must dwell upon the unity of history and
not upon the isolated or particular instance. Thierry must be
regarded as the first who pointed the way to the historical
synthesis when in 1820 he published his article "On the Old
Spirit and the New Spirit of French Lawyers." His *Essai*
of 1853 was therefore the natural and logical completion of a theme on which he had begun work in 1820.
For him, and also for Guizot and Michelet, the question was simple: When for the first time in French
history did that revolutionary program appear which
was so evident in 1789? Under the influence of historical Romanticism Thierry, who admitted his debt to
Chateaubriand, sought the origin of the antifeudal, anticleri-

---

[32] J. C. L. Simonde de Sismondi, *Histoire des Français*, VIII (Paris, 1826), 64f., 80ff.

cal revolutionary spirit, not in the eighteenth century or even in the *ancien régime,* but in the darker recesses of the Middle Ages. In doing so, he dispelled the darkness and rediscovered the French Middle Ages. More than that, he discovered the original revolutionary in French history, the middle-class lawyer of Philip the Fair.

In wedding the Capetian lawyers to the French Revolution, Thierry and Guizot created a new legitimacy which opposed the legitimacy of the Restoration and the *ancien régime.* Indeed, they rediscovered the Capetian lawyers for the very reason that history was now brought to the political arena and made to serve the uses of politics. Pierre Flote, Guillaume de Nogaret, and Raoul de Presles were called forth from their medieval tombs, Flote with the lances of Courtrai in his breast, Nogaret with the stain of a papal condemnation on his soul, and Presles with the scars from the torture chamber of Louis X Hutin. The fourteenth-century lawyers were resurrected to point up once more the nature of the battle against the two historic enemies of the French nation, the aristocracy and the clergy, who had always fought against the establishment of an undivided public authority and an egalitarian nation. There was nothing illegitimate in resisting the aristocracy and the Church. And, if the monarch chose to protect these vested interests, he had in effect betrayed the Third Estate and thereby the French nation, for the king had been the ally of the Third Estate when its intellectual leadership, the lawyers of Philip the Fair, first led it forth against the enemies of the French nation.

Because of its ancient descent, the struggle was for Thierry a part of the unity of French history. The conduct of the French people in 1789 was not a political aberration but a glorious resumption of the historic struggle which, from its very infancy, had marked out the destiny of the French nation. Guizot, whose political vacillations are too well known to mention here, resigned himself to the violence of the battle just before 1830 and saw that the policy of blood and iron used by the lawyers of Philip the Fair could again be justified against such desperate enemies. Unlike Thierry, Michelet could not permit the lawyers of the last Capetians to be merely medieval founders of the revolutionary tradition. Because he detested the Middle Ages, he had to interpret the fourteenth-century legists as the founders of the modern world. The rising struggle to create an egalitarian French nation marked the end of medieval history and was in fact the cause of its death. As for Sismondi, he was not French and therefore had no need to see any marks of destiny in the program of the last Capetian lawyers.

The interpretation of the last Capetian lawyers, so vigorously propounded by Thierry, Guizot, and Michelet, had a profound influence on French historians during the remainder of the nineteenth century, and vestiges of this influence have reached into the twentieth century. Historians in this later period continued to make history serve the uses of politics, but as the Revolution receded in time, the passions which had accompanied the earlier writing of history also receded. A good example of dispassionate writing was Edgar Boutaric's *La France sous Philippe le Bel*, which appeared in 1861. Boutaric was conscious of the plebeian origins of Philip the Fair's lawyers; he was aware that these men had much to do with the progress of royal power in France; and he noticed the violent war Philip made on feudal and clerical privilege. But he put little accent on these developments, and in fact tried to show that Philip's council was not composed so much of *roturiers* as had generally been believed.[33]

[33] Edgar Boutaric, *La France sous Philippe le Bel* (Paris, 1861). This work, as its title indicates, was not a biography of Philip the Fair. But Boutaric was the first scholar to come to grips with the question of whether Philip or his ministers were responsible for the policies of his reign (pp. 417ff.). For comment on the lawyers, see pp. 55-59, 205f., 218-220.

Boutaric's work was the first book-length study of Philip the Fair's reign; the second such study was Jules Jolly's book, which was published in 1869. Jolly's work differed from Boutaric's both in spirit and in scholarship. Boutaric's book was a serious undertaking based on competent research, while Jolly's work had not the scholarship of Boutaric or of Thierry, Michelet, and Martin, whom he most often quoted. Jolly devoted a chapter of thirty pages to the lawyers of Philip the Fair, and his treatment of the legists was a veritable eulogy.[34] He heaped upon the heads of Flote, Nogaret, and Plaisians all of the praise which had been accorded them earlier by Thierry and his contemporaries. But unlike Thierry and the others, he saw no liabilities in the last Capetian lawyers that mitigated the virtues of their program and that would potentially lead to absolute monarchy without justice, liberty, or equality. He compared them to the nineteenth-century French revolutionaries and credited them with the birth of the French magistracy, "admired all over Europe for its independence and its disinterest."

A similar disparity in the treatment of the Capetian lawyers can be found in two studies of individual ministers. The first of these appeared in Pierre Clément's *Trois drames historiques*, published in 1857. Clément had earlier written a biography of Jacques Coeur in which he maintained that French kings (and French emperors?) seem to have used a policy of sacrificing faithful and capable ministers to public anger after these servants had advanced the cause of the crown by way of new taxation and other oppressive and unpopular measures.[35] His new work was a study of three

---

[34] Jules Jolly, *Philippe le Bel, ses desseins, ses actes, son influence* (Paris, 1869), pp. 335-364. Jolly's book was written in response to a question posed by the *Académie des sciences morales et politiques.* For his interpretation of the lawyers he probably owed more to Thierry than to any other historian.

[35] Pierre Clément, *Jacques Coeur et Charles VII* (rev. ed.; Paris, 1863).

French ministers, Enguerrand de Marigny, Beaune de Semblançay, and the Chevalier de Rohan. Marigny, Clément maintained, fitted perfectly the thesis he had earlier explained. But most of all, Clément's interpretation of Marigny was liberal and he did not see the minister's faults.[36]

Contrasted with Clément's portrait of Marigny is the picture of Guillaume de Nogaret that Ernest Renan presented in his well-known essay.[37] Renan conceded the classical interpretation of the Capetian lawyers and characterized Nogaret as a superior legist, a great minister, and one of the founders of French national unity. Like Michelet, he felt that Nogaret and the lawyers of the last Capetians led France into the modern world. In the sixteenth century, Nogaret would have been a Protestant; in the eighteenth century he would have been a *philosophe* and a reformer. Renan mentioned that "he was an excellent patriot and he was sometimes a revolutionary, but he was not sufficiently wise to see that one is a bad patriot when he builds the grandeur of his country without liberty, and his own power at the expense of justice and the independence of other people."[38] Renan, therefore, recognized Nogaret's role in the construction of French national unity, but as he wrote in the early years of the Third Republic he was careful to observe that Nogaret had nothing to do with the growth of justice and liberty.

The most interesting use made of the Capetian lawyers in the nineteenth century was by the nineteenth-century lawyers. While the historians were prone to make the Cape-

---

[36] Pierre Clément, *Trois drames historiques* (Paris, 1857), pp. 3-123. Clément's study of Marigny was perhaps the first extended work on any of Philip the Fair's ministers.

[37] Ernest Renan, "Guillaume de Nogaret," *Histoire littéraire de la France,* xxvii, 233-371. Also published without notes in *Revue des Deux-Mondes,* xcviii (1872), 328-349, 597-621, 764-797, and republished with his essays on Pierre Dubois and Bertrand de Got in *Etudes sur la politique religieuse du règne de Philippe le Bel* (Paris, 1899).

[38] Renan, *Histoire littéraire de la France,* xxvii, 369.

tian lawyers serve the political needs of the day, the nineteenth-century lawyers of liberal complexion believed that
all French lawyers at all times had been the defenders of
justice, liberty, and of whatever form of liberal government
they preferred at the moment. An example of this propen-
sity is found in the career and writings of André Dupin,
sometimes called Dupin *ainé*. A fervent defender of the principles of 1789, he played a large role in the events of 1830,
and rose to be *procureur-général* of the *Cour de Cassation*
and president of the Chamber of Deputies in the early part
of Louis-Philippe's reign. In 1843, he delivered before the
Cour de Cassation an *éloge* on the sixteenth-century
lawyer Etienne Pasquier. Pasquier had dared to condemn
kings who used their subjects and the means of government
to gain their own private profit. Dupin insisted that Pasquier had advocated a constitutional monarchy for France.
But most of all, Pasquier had spoken out against the Jesuits
and that pleased Dupin because he himself violently opposed
the Jesuits and Ultramontanism in nineteenth-century
France.[39]

The best example of a nineteenth-century Gallican lawyer
who eulogized the French legal profession throughout its
history was Agénor Bardoux, who published in 1877 a study
of the lawyers in French history.[40] While he insisted that the
medieval period was the golden age of the legists, he gave
more attention to the lawyers of the sixteenth, seventeenth,
and eighteenth centuries. Like Thierry, Bardoux felt that the
lawyers represented the middle class in French history. But
he went far beyond Thierry and maintained that the lawyers
gave to France the ideas of democracy, equality, unity of

[39] The *éloge* can be found in Dupin's edition of Loisel's *Pasquier,
ou Dialogue des avocats* (Paris, 1844), pp. 212-246.
[40] Agénor Bardoux, *Les Légistes. Leur Influence sur la société
française* (Paris, 1877). The chapters of this book were published
twenty years earlier as articles in the *Revue historique du droit français et étranger*.

the state, sovereignty of the people, and, after being educated by the eighteenth-century *philosophes*, liberty. Although his book was uncritical and based more on imagination than research, it is the only full-length study devoted to the role of the legists in the development of the French nation. When Bardoux published his completed work in the early years of the Third Republic, he believed that an era had passed, and he assigned to Dupin *ainé* the signal honor of having been the last of the legists.

This Gallicanism of Dupin and Bardoux can usually be found in the writings of nineteenth-century French lawyers who defended the liberal or republican cause. Heirs of the Revolution and fighters for the lay state, they delighted in memorializing any and all French lawyers who had ever shown traces of Gallicanism. As the historians had sought the first revolutionaries in French history, so the lawyers sought the first Gallicans; they found them in the men who planned and executed the strategy against Boniface VIII. This phenomenon was most pronounced during the last decade of the nineteenth century when the republican forces in France were desperately engaged in keeping education under lay control. At the opening of the *Cour d'Appel* of Riom in 1891 René Béchon delivered a discourse on Pierre Flote, a likely subject since he had been a native of the region about Riom.[41] For his historical comment Bechon depended heavily on Thierry, Michelet, and Martin; for his polemics he used the contemporary debate between clerical control and the lay state. So this lawyer of the Third Republic was easily led to infer that, since Flote began the struggle to make France free of papal control, he would be, if he were alive, a great fighter for the Republic. Because Flote was a laicist, Bechon—and other lawyers under the same conditions—could not afford to examine scrupulously his political stance. This theme was continued, but with a twist, when

[41] René Béchon, *Pierre Flotte, chancelier de France* (Riom, 1891).

Fernand Verdier in 1895 composed an essay on the origins and influence of the legists.[42] It was actually an essay on Saint Louis and his lawyers, who, Verdier insisted, initiated the principles of laicism. For Verdier, therefore, laicism was an ancient force extending across centuries of French history. He was oblivious to the lawyers of Philip the Fair, but he achieved a remarkable irony when he made of the sainted king the author of the French lay state and the instigator of the struggle against clerical control.

In 1885 a young scholar presented to his professors at the *Ecole des Chartes* a thesis on the reign of Philip III which won for him the diploma of *archiviste-paléographe* and first place in his graduating class. Charles Victor Langlois (1863-1929) had already proved that he was the most promising medievalist in France. During his studies for the diploma, he had received the *licence* in both the Faculty of Law and the Faculty of Letters and, most astounding of all, had received first place in the *Agrégation d'histoire* of 1884. For three years he taught at Douai and Montpellier, expanded his study of Philip, and presented it for the *doctorat-ès-lettres*. He was called back to Paris in 1888 and taught for the next twenty-five years in the Faculty of Letters. His publications were already impressive, and he had shown a special talent for medieval administrative and political history. But, most importantly, his thesis had not determined the chronological limits of his future work but had rather served as the point of departure for investigation into the administrative history of France in the late thirteenth and early fourteenth centuries. By the time he returned to Paris, he had discovered and published new material on the Parlement de Paris and had moved into the reign of Philip the Fair.[43]

[42] Fernand Verdier, "Origine et influence des légistes," *Mémoires de l'académie de Nîmes*, 7th ser., xviii (1895), 179-201.

[43] Charles V. Langlois, "Nouveaux fragments du *Liber inquestarum* de Nicholas de Chartres," *B.E.C.*, xlvi (1885), 440-471; "Rouleaux

Because Langlois had been trained in the scientific school, the earlier work of Thierry and Michelet had no crucial influence on him. Like all Frenchmen, he still considered their work as great history, but the time had come to treat history not as the servant of politics but as a discipline whose content consisted of a vast body of documentary material, published and unpublished, which had to be critically evaluated and from which the objective truth had to be extracted with no concern for political, social, or religious bias. He had been trained by exacting masters, Paul Meyer, Ernest Lavisse, and Adolphe Tardif, who realized that the Revolution was a hundred years in the past and that no critical or complete history could now be written until one had examined and exhausted all of the available evidence. It was on this premise that Langlois constructed all of his work, and it was also on this premise that he finally despaired of ever knowing enough about Philip the Fair or his lawyers to make a competent estimate of their role and importance in the history of France. It was precisely at this point that the work of Langlois, and of those who followed him, differed from the treatment that had been given to the last Capetian lawyers by the early nineteenth-century historians.

No one can say exactly what it was that led Langlois to make Philip the Fair and his lawyers the subject of his scholarship. Perhaps it was because they had been given a singularly important role in the histories of Thierry and Michelet. In his history of Philip III, he insisted at several points that the reign of Philip the Fair's father must first be studied before one could move to the succeeding period.[44] Above all, one must understand the administrative system and its per-

---

d'arrêts de la cour du roi au XIIIe siècle," *B.E.C.*, xlviii (1887), 177-208, 535-565; "Une réunion publique à Paris sous Philippe le Bel (24 juin 1303)," *Bulletin de la société de l'histoire de Paris et de l'Ile de France* (1888), pp. 13-134.

44 Langlois, *Le règne de Philippe III le Hardi* (Paris, 1887).

sonnel for the reign of Philip III, for this constituted the foundation of his son's work and determined the type of minister which became so famous after 1285. In the decade after Langlois came to Paris, he continued to lay the groundwork for a study of Philip the Fair's reign. He worked with Joseph Petit on the earliest documents of the Chamber of Accounts, edited with Léopold Delisle the very important inventory of Robert Mignon, and wrote short but valuable notices on various events of Philip's reign and on such figures as Pons d'Aumelas and Geoffroi du Plessis, two of the lawyers of Philip IV.[45]

It was in Langlois' study of Geoffroi du Plessis that he expressed most severely his pessimism about scholarly research on the lawyers of Philip the Fair. He chose first to quote Julian Havet, who had earlier commented that "the moment has not yet come to bring together the documentary information which we have preserved on each of the persons, famous or obscure, of the reigns of Philip the Fair and his sons; this work will be done only after the publication of the documents which are yet unedited."[46] But Langlois' caution surpassed that of Havet. If all the documents were brought together, Langlois believed, it might be possible to sketch the outlines of an administrative career under the last Capetians. But that would be all. "One will never know who these men were for the archival documents give only their names, their titles, their comings and goings, and their salaries and stipends. If, on the other hand, we want to construct hypotheses about these men whom we see assigned to tasks and roles, without knowing them or the precise roles which they played, and without knowing either their strength or their

---

[45] Joseph Petit, *Essai de restitution des plus anciens mémoriaux de la chambre des comptes de Paris* (Paris, 1899); Langlois, *Inventaire d'anciens comptes royaux dressé par Robert Mignon,* in Recueil des historiens de la France. Documents financiers, I (Paris, 1899).

[46] Langlois, "Geoffroi du Plessis, protonotaire de France," *Revue Historique,* LXVII (1898), 70.

weaknesses, we are merely engaging in child's play (*enfan-tillage*)."[47] But, in the face of such an admission, Langlois saw one saving grace. He felt that it would be possible to say something of value about those men who, like Guillaume de Nogaret, had left writings.

The time came, and perhaps too soon, for Langlois to write the history of Philip the Fair. Ernest Lavisse chose him as the author of the volume that covered France from 1226 to the end of the Capetians. One historian has remarked that it was not the book that Langlois had hoped to write, but that it has nevertheless become a classic.[48] On the ministers of Philip IV, Langlois repeated his earlier views. How did these men come to power? How did they conduct themselves? What was their character?[49] "The extent and nature of the role of the royal agents who had the most active roles is difficult to determine. Learned scholars have drawn up with great difficulty the list of missions with which they were charged, the salaries which they received and the properties which they acquired. Nothing more. Their faces have disappeared like those of the kings themselves. For the historian all of the councillors of Philip the Fair who have not left writings are, like Philip the Fair himself, enigmas."[50] Therefore, to be known, a lawyer would have had to leave literary evidence of his thought and ideas. Langlois seemed to forget that those Capetian lawyers who wrote the most, such as Pierre Dubois and Pierre de Belleperche, are the least known. Despite this pessimism, Langlois wrote not only a good history of Philip the Fair but a rather complete one, bringing together most of the information then available.

Since Langlois' work in 1901, the condition of studies on

[47] *Ibid.*, p. 71.
[48] See Langlois' necrology by R. Fawtier in *English Historical Review*, XLV (1930), 85-91.
[49] Langlois in Lavisse, *Histoire de France*, III, Part 2, 125.
[50] *Ibid.*

Philip the Fair and his lawyers has remained much as it was then. Perhaps one reason for this is that Langlois left the teaching profession in 1913 to become director of the Archives Nationales. His administrative duties prevented him from returning to his favorite subject. But one line of attack which he had advocated was followed by French medievalists who proceeded to edit the major unpublished documents on Philip the Fair's reign. Outside of the chronicles and the records of the Parlement de Paris which had already been published, three major categories of state documents remained to be edited, those of the Treasury, the Chamber of Accounts, and the Chancery. The *Journaux du Trésor de Philippe IV le Bel* was edited by Jules Viard in 1940.[51] But the original records of the Chamber of Accounts had long since been destroyed in disastrous fires. The tremendous task of reconstituting the accounts of Philip the Fair was undertaken by Robert Fawtier and completed in 1956.[52] Professor Fawtier, more than any other French scholar, has succeeded to the unfinished work of Langlois. He represents the ideal of Langlois' tradition and that of the scientific school in that he determined to edit the documents before writing the history of Philip the Fair. What would appear to have been the easiest task was completed recently when Professor Fawtier edited a calendar of Philip's Chancery Registers.[53] The

---

[51] Jules Viard, *Les journaux du trésor de Philippe IV le Bel* (Paris, 1940).

[52] Robert Fawtier, *Comptes royaux (1285-1314)*, in Recueil des historiens de la France. Documents financiers, III (Paris, 1953-1956). Fawtier has in effect added to the work of Petit and Langlois on the accounts of Philip the Fair. He edited the accounts for four widely separate years of the medieval French kings in *Comptes du trésor (1296, 1316, 1384, 1477)*, in Recueil des historiens de la France. Documents financiers, II (Paris, 1930). Recently, M. François Maillard has added to this work in his edition of *Comptex royaux (1314-1328)*, in Recueil des historiens de la France. Documents financiers, IV, Part 1 (Paris, 1961). Part 2 is soon to appear.

[53] Robert Fawtier, *Registres du trésor des chartes. I. Règne de Philippe le Bel* in Archives Nationales: Inventaires et Documents (Paris, 1958).

time has come for a definitive interpretation and study of
Philip the Fair's reign based upon all that modern scholarship can reasonably produce in the form of published
sources. To that end, two outstanding medievalists on either
side of the Atlantic have addressed themselves: Professor
Strayer in America and Professor Fawtier in France.[54]

But Langlois had another line of attack on the age of
Philip the Fair which was best illustrated by his own brief
study of Geoffroi du Plessis. Whether or not the documents
were ever edited, Langlois seemed to say that one approach
to an understanding of the period would be specialized
studies on individual figures. He conceived the outlines of
a plan whereby, through the most painstaking and laborious
research, one might tear the veil of obscurity from the faces
of these men and give to them the character and all the
appurtenances of individuality which they undoubtedly
possessed. The number and nature of the studies envisioned
in this plan are unknown, but several books emerged from
Langlois' circle of students and friends and these provide
an idea of what he had in mind. The earliest of these was
Abel Rigault's detailed treatment of Guichard de Troyes
and the strange *procès* that entangled him in the early years
of the fourteenth century.[55] Another was Joseph Petit's
Charles de Valois, which is as good a study as we shall need
for Philip's famous brother.[56] One of the great works to come
out of Langlois' plan was Georges Lizerand's study of Clement V and his relation to Philip and the affair of the Tem-

---

[54] Professor Strayer has recently published an article on the basic
question of Philip the Fair's reign and believes that Philip was responsible for the policies of his reign. See Joseph R. Strayer, "Philip
the Fair—A 'Constitutional' King," *American Historical Review,* LXII
(1956-1957), 18-32.

[55] Abel Rigault, *Le procès de Guichard, évêque de Troyes, 1308-
1313* (Paris, 1896).

[56] Joseph Petit, *Charles de Valois, 1270-1325* (Paris, 1900). This
work was done at Langlois' suggestion and was dedicated to him.

plars.[57] An equally significant work, long in the making and
published posthumously, was Georges Digard's work on
Philip and Boniface VIII.[58]

Rigault mentioned that Langlois had other such studies
in mind, and it is interesting to speculate on their titles.[59]
High on the list would be the young and tragic queen Jeanne
de Navarre, who may have been more responsible than we
suspect for the character of Philip's reign. In the realm of
military leadership, Raoul de Clermont and Gaucher de
Châtillon would be likely subjects. Langlois did put one
of his students to work on the lawyer Guillaume de Plaisians,
but his endeavors did not result in a book.[60] And if the work
of Renan and Holtzmann had not pre-empted the field,
Langlois would surely have sent some student in pursuit of
Guillaume de Nogaret.[61] It is reasonable to suspect that
Langlois would have suggested another sort of specialized
research and writing, the treatment of groups of persons in
Philip's reign. The French episcopate would be an admirable
topic as also would be the French baronage under Philip the
Fair. But the most interesting group of all, and the most apt
subject for research, is the lawyers of the last Capetians.

The last Capetian lawyers deserve this specialized treatment for several reasons. The earlier nineteenth-century
historians assigned them a place in French history which
has never been accorded any other group. And the scientific
school with its historical agnosticism continued to regard
them as the most unusual group of men produced by Capetian France. But most of all, scholarly opinion at all times

[57] Georges Lizerand, *Clément V et Philippe le Bel* (Paris, 1910).

[58] Georges Digard, *Philippe le Bel et le Saint-Siège de 1285 à 1304*
(2 vols; Paris, 1936).

[59] Rigault, *Le procès de Guichard*, p. xi.

[60] Abel Henry, "Guillaume de Plaisians," *Le Moyen Age*, v (1892),
32-38.

[61] Ernest Renan's essay cited above, and Robert Holtzmann, *Wilhelm von Nogaret: Rat und Grossiegelbewahrer Philipps des Schönen*
(Freiburg-im-Breisgau, 1898).

has considered that, next to the king himself, the lawyers were the most powerful group in the reign of Philip the Fair and were most responsible for the character and significance of that reign. The sensible dictum of Langlois that these men can never be given human dimensions can be applied most accurately to the individual lawyer. But it is just as sensible to assume that if all of these lawyers were studied together and their origins, careers, and conduct compared, one with the other, the individual might acquire a personality where he had none before. More than this, the lawyers must be followed not only through Philip the Fair's reign but through the remaining years of the Capetian era, for many of those who served him survived him.

The evidence concerning these lawyers who were active in the reigns of the last four Capetians has never been brought together. The answers must be sought to the questions which Langlois asked: Who were these men before they came to power? How did they come to power, and what is the meaning of their behavior, their ambitions, their achievements, and their fate? It is not difficult to believe that if Charles Victor Langlois had been able to pursue his favorite historical problem to its logical end, he would have conceived of a book which encompassed the lawyers of the last Capetians.

CHAPTER ONE

Philip the Fair:
The Triumph of the Lawyers

THE first decade of the fourteenth century was represented in France by a nightmare of scandalous affairs of state, prolonged judicial ordeals based often on outrageous charges, confiscations secretly prepared and violently executed, disastrous alterations of money, and a crushing military defeat.[1] No other country in Europe was subjected to such violence at that time, and France never again witnessed a similar spectacle unless we consider the decade of the Revolution. This was the ten-year span that gave to the reign of Philip the Fair its historic character and flavor. Except for the brief dispute with the pope in 1296-1298, no celebrated events occurred in the first half of Philip's reign. By the same token, little can be said about the lawyers and ministers of the king in this earlier period; events and the men involved in them remain obscured in the shadows of insufficient evidence. On the other hand, the incidents and great affairs that came after 1300 not only marked the monarch and his age but also made the reputations of the lawyers. The historical image of Philip the Fair's lawyers is founded on what they did in the second half of their master's reign.

The affair of Boniface VIII was the outstanding event of Philip the Fair's reign.[2] It was divided into two distinct

[1] The best coverage of the period is that by Langlois in Lavisse, *Histoire de France*, III, Part 2, 119-319.

[2] The oldest and best known study of Philip's struggle with Boniface is the seventeenth-century work of Pierre Dupuy, *Histoire du différend d'entre le pape Boniface VIII et Philippe le Bel, roi de France* (1655). The most recent scholarly study is that of Digard, *Philippe le Bel et le Saint-Siège de 1285 à 1304.*

phases although a growing hostility and distrust between king and pope connected one to the other. The first phase occurred in the last years of the thirteenth century and was relatively mild and brief in its duration; the second came at the beginning of the fourteenth century and was violent with far-reaching consequences. The royal agent common to both quarrels was Pierre Flote, who probably first met and negotiated with his future antagonist when Benedetto Gaetani came to France as papal legate in 1290. Six years later, when Gaetani had become Boniface VIII, the first struggle took place over royal rights to a clerical subsidy. Boniface prohibited lay taxation of the clergy in *Clericis laicos* and Philip responded by blocking the export of gold and silver from France. But the major points of this dispute were resolved within a year as Boniface softened his stand in the face of royal opposition.

Pierre Flote's influence in the king's answer to *Clericis laicos* cannot be seen but must be suspected. He was clearly the dominant figure in the formulation and execution of Capetian policy during these years. He provoked and intimidated the pope on one occasion only to mollify him on another in order to exact more easily what his master wished. On his mission to Italy in 1297, Flote feigned sympathy with the Colonnas in order to give Boniface discomfort. But he later abandoned the Colonnas and obtained retraction of *Clericis laicos*, consent to the canonization of Louis IX, and a host of papal favors for himself and his family. In the next year he was again in Rome to arrange for Boniface's private arbitration in the Anglo-French quarrel, and he carried a third embassy to the pope in 1300. In the meantime he managed royal negotiations at Neufchâteau with the German representatives and at Montreuil-sur-Mer with the English. While Flote was the dominant figure in these developments, he had important assistance from two other Capetian lawyers. These were Gilles Aicelin, archbishop of Narbonne, and

Pierre de Mornay, bishop of Auxerre. The trio of Flote, Aicelin, and Mornay was most conspicuous in managing Philip's
affairs in the last decade of the century.[3]

Pierre Flote appeared fully engaged against the papacy
in 1301, when relations between Philip and Boniface wors-
ened. Clerical taxation had led to the first dispute; now the
king's right to try criminous clerks created the second and
more violent quarrel. A secret inquest was made by two royal
agents into the actions and statements of Bernard Saisset,
bishop of the recently created diocese of Pamiers. Saisset
was accused of predicting the ruin of the Capetian house,
of treasonable conduct during the recent war with the
English, and of libelous remarks about the French king.
Conducted to Senlis by royal guards, he was arraigned before the king and a formidable assembly of bishops, barons,
and knights. To Pierre Flote was given the task of the formal
declaration of charges, at the end of which he called for the
imprisonment of the bishop lest he flee beyond the jurisdiction of church and king. From that point, the king appealed
to Boniface to condemn canonically and to degrade the
southern bishop. But Boniface replied that Saisset could not
be condemned unless he appeared at Rome. When Philip
refused to send the accused to Rome an impasse was reached
wherein the pope, seeking punitive action, renewed the conditions of *Clericis laicos* and issued *Ausculta fili.*[4]

In the face of a papal threat to convoke a council of
French bishops at Rome that would pass judgment on him,
Philip countered with orders which led to the celebrated assembly of estates at Paris in April 1302. This was the time of
propaganda and publicity, and no man was more adept in
such maneuvers than Pierre Flote. Speaking before the as-

[3] For Flote, Aicelin, and Mornay at work in the affair of Boniface
VIII, see *ibid.*, I, *passim.*

[4] Good coverage of Bernard Saisset's trial, and its background, is
in *ibid.*, II, 49-104, and in *H.L.*, IX, 216-224, 229-231.

sembled orders, he played upon their patriotic susceptibilities, reminding them of the pope's claims that Philip was subject to him in temporalities, and that the king held his crown from the Vicar of Christ. Flote's harangue accomplished what he sought—the rallying of French opinion and support to the side of the king. The French clergy begged off from the papal convocation on grounds that the king refused to let them leave France and that the nobles and bourgeoisie were prepared to do violence to church property if they disobeyed. Finally, they prayed Boniface to revoke his injunctions. When the French embassy presented these views to the pope, Boniface delivered a scathing indictment of Flote, denounced him as diabolical and heretical, and promised that he would receive spiritual and temporal punishment. A few days later in July 1302, Pierre Flote was killed in the battle of Courtrai.

Guillaume de Nogaret came to prominence in the legal councils of the king after the death of Flote and remained the outstanding lawyer during the remainder of the reign. His hand can be seen in every one of the legal assaults Philip made against his enemies. Although he had been in the royal service for a decade, he did not enter the struggle with Boniface until 1300 when Flote dispatched him to Italy. On that occasion he gave Boniface clear warning of his future conduct when he turned the clergy's complaints of royal oppression into clerical complaints of papal oppression. After the issuance of *Unam sanctam* Nogaret formulated a new line of action and publicized it in the Louvre assembly of March 1303 when he charged Boniface with numerous crimes and called him to judgment before a future council. Guillaume de Plaisians was the companion who now came to Nogaret's aid. In the Louvre assembly of June 1303, he repeated Nogaret's demand for a council and delivered twenty-nine articles of accusation against the pope. Founded mainly on rumor, gossip, distorted remarks, and pure concoction, Plaisians' accusations were probably the most savage and vitriolic ever hurled at a bishop of Rome. He then departed for the south, where he worked busily during the summer to obtain support for Nogaret's plan from the clergy, nobility, and towns.[5] With the accumulation of public support, Nogaret pushed the affair of Boniface on to the encounter at Anagni that resulted indirectly in the death of the pope and the coming of the Avignon Papacy.[6]

But Nogaret had the capacity for more than one affair at a time. While he fought Boniface, he was engaged in some degree in the scarcely comprehensible proceedings against the Franciscan of Carcassonne, Bernard Délicieux—proceedings which went beyond his lifetime.[7] In addition to this case, he was more definitely involved in the trial of Guichard de Troyes. Before Guichard became bishop of Troyes in 1298, he had long been associated with the administration of Champagne and thereby with the dowager queen Blanche, and her daughter Jeanne, queen of Navarre and countess of Champagne and Brie. Jeanne was the wife of Philip the Fair and therefore queen of France; it was through Philip's marriage to the young heiress that the way was prepared for the eventual return of Champagne to the crown. There is a hint that Guichard and the young queen had been at cross purposes for some time. In any event, when an accused receiver of revenue in Champagne, who had been entrusted to Guichard for safe-keeping, fled his keeper, the latter was quickly accused of complicity in the escape. To confound the situation, the dowager queen, who was evidently responsible for

[5] Documents on the assemblies of 1303 and Plaisians' work in the south are in Georges Picot, *Documents relatifs aux Etats Généraux et assemblées réunis sous Philippe le Bel* (Collection de documents inédits, Paris, 1901), pp. 94-200.

[6] Robert Fawtier, "L'attentat d'Anagni," *Mélanges d'archéologie et d'histoire*, LX (1948), 153-179.

[7] B. Haureau, *Bernard Délicieux et l'Inquisition albigeoise (1300-1320)* (Paris, 1877).

the initial charges, died in 1302, and this event was followed three years later by the entirely unexpected death of Jeanne who was only thirty-two years of age. For a while, the case of Guichard hung in abeyance. Then in 1308 new and more serious charges were brought against the bishop. He was accused of the most depraved acts: of usury, murder, sodomy, and heresy, of having poisoned Blanche, of having poisoned his predecessor in the priory of Saint-Ayoul, of having planned to poison the count of Valois and the young prince Louis, and of having been responsible by sorcery for the death of Jeanne de Navarre.[8]

It is of some value at this point to mention those who accused and who gave testimony in the affair of Guichard. Simon Festu, who had been a favorite of the late queen, was formerly archdeacon of Vendôme and was rewarded for his part in the process of Guichard by being promoted to the bishopric of Meaux. Richard Leneveu was a trained lawyer and had been active in the early stages of the cases against Saisset and Délicieux. Formerly archdeacon of the Auge in Normandy, he had moved up to the southern bishopric of Béziers, and was a faithful servant of Philip the Fair. Enguerrand de Marigny had come out of the queen's household into the central government and had achieved most of his power and titles by 1307. Marigny has been indiscriminately grouped with the *légistes*. There is no reason to believe that he ever studied law or that he even knew much about it as a formal system. He was from the *petite noblesse* and had shown a remarkable talent for financial administration. During the last seven years of Philip's reign, Marigny was probably the most important man in France and certainly the most powerful in the field of governmental finance.

[8] The special study of Guichard and his trial is by Rigault, *Le procès de Guichard.* See also Guillaume Mollât, "Guichard de Troyes et les revelations de la sorcière de Bourdenay," *Le Moyen Age,* xxxi (1908), 310-316.

Others involved in the process of Guichard were Guillaume de Plaisians, who was the shadow of Nogaret, and Nogaret himself, who appears to have been after 1308 the chief administrator and manager of the prosecution.

The process of Guichard de Troyes continued until 1313, when he finally sought refuge at the papal court, from which he was assigned to a bishopric in Bosnia. Before he left France, he was cleared of the charges by the confession of Noffo Dei, an agent of the Lombard bankers and one of the first to accuse him. Aside from the inconsequential finish to the case, the affair of Guichard shows most of the outstanding lawyers at the Capetian court occupied in prosecuting the king's business. The modern historian of Guichard has even suggested that the bishop was actually the target of a group of lawyers whom he had in some way offended.[9] Like a pack of hounds they pursued him and, while they did not kill him, they destroyed all of the wealth, position, and favor which he had accumulated in a lifetime. From this point of view, the violence, excess, and conspiratorial atmosphere of the first decade of the fourteenth century is more easily comprehended.

During the summer of 1306, while the process of Guichard was temporarily suspended, orders were given to despoil the Jews. On the surface, there was nothing particularly new in this move; the Jews had been put to "ransom" many times in many countries of Europe. Their position in any country was completely tenuous since they lived, flourished, and engaged in business at the absolute pleasure of the ruler. But in 1306, they were not put to ransom; rather, their goods were confiscated from one end of the kingdom to the other. Furthermore, the plans for confiscation were well-laid and the orders to royal agents were secretly given. On June 21, a royal commission was delivered to Jean de Saint-Just,

---

[9] Rigault, *Le procès de Guichard,* p. 25.

precentor of Albi and financial expert of the king, to Guillaume de Nogaret, and to the seneschal of Toulouse, on a matter which the king had previously explained to them by word of mouth. This commission invoked obedience and cooperation from all bishops, barons, and royal officers in the *sénéchaussée* of Toulouse who would come in contact with the three commissioners. Similar letters were sent to agents in the other administrative divisions of the kingdom. Exactly one month later, all of the Jews in France were arrested and their goods confiscated. A large number of royal agents and lawyers were required to fulfill this commission; it would be useless to name those involved in this process who are of importance to our study. The name of Nogaret suffices to show that the lawyers of Philip the Fair were again occupied in one of the celebrated incidents of his reign.[10]

While the affairs of Boniface VIII, Bernard Saisset, Guichard de Troyes, and the spoliation of the Jews show the Capetian lawyers at work, one series of events which forms a salient feature of Philip the Fair's rule has left historians in the dark as to the personnel involved. Beginning in 1295, and on several occasions during the remainder of the reign, French money was overvalued on orders from the king.[11] In their own way, these alterations of money created almost as much violence and publicity as the other, more dramatic incidents of Philip's age. Such a policy resulted in an enormous amount of social and economic unrest; debtors and

---

[10] The work of Nogaret, Saint-Just, and other agents who seized Jewish goods can be found in *Mignon*, pp. 265-272. For general comment, see *H.L.*, IX, 292f.

[11] Outstanding among the studies of monetary policies under Philip the Fair is that of L. Borrelli de Serres, *Les variations monétaires sous Philippe le Bel et les sources de leur histoire* (Paris, 1902). For a short study of royal responsibility in the money alterations, see de Saulcy, "Philippe le Bel a-t-il mérité le surnom de roi faux-monnayeur," *B.E.C.*, XXXVII (1876), 145-182. For a more general and theoretical study of monetary policy in the fourteenth century, there is A. Landry's *Essai économique sur les mutations des monnaies dans l'ancienne France de Philippe le Bel à Charles VI* (Paris, 1910).

creditors were continually uncertain as to what their condition would be on the morrow. When the king in 1306 ordered
a return to "good money," serious riots broke out in Paris
and Châlons-sur-Marne. One point is clear: the king sought
to ameliorate his own financial difficulties by these manipulations. What is very unclear is whether his lawyers and
councillors anticipated private profit in suggesting or recom-
mending this line of action to him. We have no knowledge of
the role played by lawyers or other royal agents in the decisions to alter the value of money. We do not know the name
of a single person involved in the affair of the money alterations. A recent writer, for instance, has cleared Enguerrand
de Marigny of any complicity in the debasement of coin-
age.[12] On the other hand, it is reasonable to wonder if certain of the lawyers closest to the king encouraged him in this
direction because their private financial situations would
profit from such action. Be that as it may, the monetary policy of Philip the Fair has acquired historical rank equal to
that of the processes and affairs which have given the peculiar character of force and connivance to his reign.

The horrible defeat suffered by the French in 1302 at
Courtrai meant far more than the loss of a large number of
mounted warriors. The disaster was especially galling because it was wrought by Flemish burghers and footmen of
lesser status. For the French people, it was the worst defeat
since Mansourah. So far as royal government was concerned,
Courtrai meant the loss of great military and administrative
leaders, among them two marshals, the constable, and the
chancellor of France. Raoul de Clermont, seigneur of Nesles,
had been constable of France for most of Philip's reign; his
brother, Gui de Clermont, was one of the two marshals killed
at Courtrai. For his new military leaders, Philip turned to
two distinguished families of Champagne. Gaucher de Châ-

---

[12] Jean Favier, *Un conseiller de Philippe le Bel: Enguerran de Marigny, P.T.E.C.* (1956), p. 41.

tillon, seigneur of Châtillon and constable of Champagne and descended from one of the most famous and ancient of French noble families, was made constable of France. Already in his fifties, he was to play a leading role in French affairs for the next twenty-five years. Mile de Noyers has been called more accurately a Burgundian.[13] His ancestral lands lay on the border between Champagne and Burgundy. Mile de Noyers was to be one of the great royal councillors for the next half-century. When he was made marshal of France after Courtrai, the military leadership of the kingdom came again into the hands of two men closely related by kinship, for the seigneur of Noyers was the nephew of Châtillon.

This new military leadership had little opportunity to prove itself during the succeeding eight years, for the king proceeded to establish workable truces with his two most troublesome enemies, Flanders and England. At first, the humiliation of Courtrai served only to compound the vexatious problem of Flanders. Inconclusive campaigns in 1302 and 1303 were followed in the next year by a French naval victory off the Flemish coast and a disputed military victory in August at Mons-en-Pevèle. In 1305 a treaty was arranged between Philip and the new count of Flanders, Robert de Béthune. Two conditions made this an ill-founded truce: the doubtful trustworthiness of the count and the equally doubtful acquiescence of the Flemish towns. But four years later, Guillaume de Plaisians was sent with the count through Flanders to receive from each town its formal adherence to the treaty. By 1310 the Flemish border was comparatively quiet. One reason why Robert de Béthune reached an agreement with Philip was the temporary settlement of

[13] Raymond Cazelles, *La société politique et la crise de la royauté sous Philippe de Valois* (Paris, 1958), pp. 90-94, 115-132. The standard biography of Mile de Noyers is by Ernest Petit. *Les sires de Noyers. Le maréchal de Noyers. Mile X de Noyers* (Auxerre, 1874).

Anglo-French differences in 1303 wherein the English abandoned the cause of Flanders. For several years negotiations
had dragged on between Edward I and Philip, with Boniface
VIII arbitrating at one point. By the treaty of 1303, the
matter of Gascony was settled for the time being, Philip's
daughter, Isabella, was affianced to the Prince of Wales,
and an uneasy peace existed between two ancient antago-
nists.[14]

No adequate reason has ever been given for Pierre Flote's
presence on the battlefield at Courtrai. Despite the fact that
he was a noble and owed military service, he could well have
avoided the engagement. At his death, Philip was confronted
with the need of a new chancellor and a new "first lawyer of
the realm." For the moment, he chose not to combine the
two positions in one person as he had done in the case of
Flote. Nogaret acceded to the latter position. The office of
chancellor or keeper of the seal was nevertheless to be held
by lawyers throughout the period of the last Capetians, and
Etienne de Suizy and Pierre de Belleperche filled these duties during the years after the death of Flote. Suizy was
archdeacon of Bruges in the church of Tournai and became
a cardinal in 1305. Pierre de Belleperche was one of the
most illustrious of medieval French lawyers. He had spent
many years in the academic atmosphere of the law school
at Orleans. His teaching career must have extended to the
end of the thirteenth century. It is difficult to associate him
with the nefarious happenings of the age although he was
engaged during the nineties in many embassies on behalf
of the king. While Belleperche and Suizy were keepers of
the royal seal, they never became the foremost lawyers of
the king as Flote had. But the dual role played by Flote

---

[14] A succinct discussion of foreign policy during these years is that
by Langlois in Lavisse, *Histoire de France*, III, Part 2, 283-319. Comment on negotiations with the English may be found in G. P. Cuttino,
English Diplomatic Administration, 1259-1339 (Oxford, 1940),
Chap. 3.

soon devolved upon Nogaret, and that moment came in 1307 when the affair of the Templars began.

Next to the struggle with Boniface VIII, the arrest and destruction of the Templars has been the most publicized incident of Philip the Fair's reign. There were great differences and few similarities in the nature of the two events. The earlier affair was a power struggle between two authoritarians, each unwilling to yield to the other. Their charges and accusations were only incidental to the major theme, and have never been taken seriously by historians. In the case of the Templars, however, the reverse was true. Although shades of a power conflict were present in Philip's campaign to destroy the Order, the charges, accusations, and evidence have always held the center of the stage. This is as it should be, for the dispute with Boniface was a political affair whereas the other event was a legal process, and a criminal one at that. There was, however, one striking similarity in the two events; in both cases Philip gave the management of the affairs to his army of legal experts, who proceeded by chicanery, innuendo, threats, and other questionable means to bring each of the struggles to a successful conclusion. In both cases, Guillaume de Nogaret played the prime role. Finally, one must also note a similarity between the process against the Templars and the confiscation of Jewish wealth, which preceded the former by only a year. In both of these instances, the plans were carefully laid in advance, orders to execute were given in secret, and the first moves were made swiftly and unexpectedly.

For several years rumors of vice and corruption in the Templars had circulated across Europe, and in the wake of these stories had come half-formed suggestions for the reform of the Order. The rumors could never be verified but the mere fact that they existed was due in part to the conduct of the Order itself. For two hundred years the

Templars had grown in power and wealth. Originally created as permanent shock-troops for the crusading armies of western Christendom, the Order had, by the beginning of the thirteenth century, turned to other pursuits. Through the natural acquisition of land, strongholds, and liquid wealth, knights of the Temple had become bankers and investors. For several decades in France and other countries of Europe they had managed the royal treasuries, and Philip the Fair let them serve him in the additional role of money lenders and receivers of royal revenue. Common people and kings became envious and resentful of an amassed wealth that they could not even accurately estimate. Furthermore, the Order created an unfortunate image in the minds of the public by its secret practices. Its strongholds were inviolable, its rule was partly secret, its chapter assemblies were held in secret, and the installation of new members took place in secret. For a populace easily given to superstition and scandalmongering, such conduct was an invitation to suspicion of the most sinister malpractices and evildoing.[15]

Recommendations for the reform of the Templars had been entertained for some time before Philip struck his famous blow. One of the oldest suggestions provided for a fusion of the two military Orders, the Templars and the Hospitalers. The most recent proposal had come from Pierre Dubois, the Norman lawyer who had incorporated his ideas in his pamphlet on the recovery of the Holy Land.[16] Jacques

---

[15] The bibliography on the Templars is voluminous. The oldest study is that of Pierre Dupuy, *Histoire de la condamnation des Templiers* (rev. ed.; Brussels, 1713). The standard German work is by Konrad Schottmuller, *Der Untergang des Templer-Ordens* (2 vols; Berlin, 1887). The best modern account in French is by Georges Lizerand, *Clément V et Philippe le Bel*. See also E. Boutaric, *Clément V, Philippe le Bel et les Templiers* (Paris, 1874), and C.-V. Langlois, "L'affaire des Templiers," *Journal des Savants*, VI (1908), 417-435.

[16] Pierre Dubois, *The Recovery of the Holy Land*, trans. by Walther I. Brandt (New York, 1956), p. 81f.

de Molay, Grand Master of the Order, had returned to France from the East in the summer of 1307 and had lodged a protest with Clement V against the planned fusion of the two Orders. Shortly afterwards the French king obtained an interview with Clement. The talks which Philip had with the pope were inconclusive. The king informed the pontiff of various charges and accusations against the Templars. Clement hesitated as was his habit, desperately sought excuses for delay, begged off from action for reasons of health, and vaguely promised to institute an inquest upon the truth of the charges. This vague promise was twisted by Philip to suit his purpose. On September 22 at the abbey of Maubuisson, he made Guillaume de Nogaret keeper of the seal; the latter now combined in his person the powers formerly held by Pierre Flote. Three weeks later, all of the Templars in France were arrested at a given hour, and their goods were seized.[17] The charge was heresy. Philip had in effect taken unilateral action without the express compliance of the pope. On the other hand, he had the machinery at his disposal that gave to the proceedings the semblance of papal and royal sanction. Guillaume de Paris was not only the king's confessor, he was Grand Inquisitor of France and willingly gave orders to the Dominicans to cooperate with the royal agents.

The process of the Templars from October 1307 to April 1310 is a story of fear, reluctance, and vacillation on the part of Clement and of force, impatience, and compulsion on the part of Philip. Horrified at first that the king had taken such action in his name, Clement nevertheless saw the need to save face. He issued letters praising Philip for his zeal and ordered the arrest of the Templars throughout Christendom. But at the beginning of 1308, he repented of this action, took the entire matter under his personal control and sus-

[17] Lizerand, *Clément V et Philippe le Bel*, pp. 96ff.

pended the action of the Inquisition and the bishops. From this point on, Nogaret, Plaisians and the other lawyers around the king launched a war of nerves against Clement as they had against Boniface. An assembly of estates was called just as had been done in 1302, with the purpose of providing popular support for Philip's designs.

Finally in the summer of 1308, king and pope met again at Poitiers. Despite an intimidating speech by Plaisians that was filled with innuendo, Clement V won a point in having the final decision in the process committed to a general council to meet in 1310.[18] He also created a papal commission whose purpose it would be to collect evidence for presentation to the council. For the presidency of this commission, the pope chose Gilles Aicelin. Archbishop of Narbonne and a lawyer of Philip the Fair, Aicelin was again placed in a position of divided loyalties as he had been earlier in the trial of Bernard Saisset. Aicelin's commission began its sessions in Paris in November 1309, and over the course of four months, hundreds of Templars came to the chamber of inquiry in the episcopal palace and testified that the Order was innocent of the charges made against it.[19] Many others from their places of detention gave similar testimony by means of their proctors. Jacques de Molay appeared on several occasions and made eloquent defense of his Order. The hearings ran on to April 10, 1310, and no incriminating evidence was received. It seemed that the Templars might be saved after all.

On the Saturday before Palm Sunday, April 11, 1310, the papal commissioners began the audition of witnesses. The documents which have survived give only two of the depositions delivered during this phase of the process. The first was by Raoul de Presles and for several reasons deserves full translation:

[18] *Ibid.*, p. 125.
[19] *Ibid.*, p. 150f.

"Master Raoul de Presles, of the diocese of Laon, learned in law, advocate in the court of the king, and a sworn witness according to the form contained above, being present before the lords commissioners and having read the articles sent to the lords commissioners from the Apostolic Seat, was asked by the lords commissioners to tell them if he knew of anything concerning the contents of the aforesaid articles. Then under oath he spoke and gave his deposition which was written down at dictation:

"When I lived in Laon, there was a Templar by the name of Brother Gervais de Beauvais, who was rector of the house of the Templars in Laon, and with whom I had close ties of friendship. He told me on several occasions and in the presence of several persons—it was four, five or six years before the arrest of the Templars—that in his Order there was a point so astonishing and which must remain so secret, that he, Gervais, would rather have his head cut off than reveal such a secret, especially if it were discovered that the revelation had come from him. He also told me that in the General Chapter of the Templars there was a point so secret that if I, Raoul de Presles, discovered this mystery, or even if the king of France discovered it, those who presided over the Chapter would have us put to death, no matter what penalty they would incur. Brother Gervais also told me that he had a certain little book of statutes of his Order which he would willingly show to me, but that he had another more secret book which he would not show for all the world. Gervais besought me to speak on his behalf to the great officers of his Order that he might be called to the General Chapter of the Order, and he said that if he could gain promotion to the General Chapter he did not doubt that he would, in time, become the Grand Master of the Order. I did as he requested, and he gained admission to the General Chapter. His power increased and I saw the other great and powerful men of the Order give him authority just as he had predicted.

"The lords and commissioners then asked him if he knew anything concerning the other articles of inquiry. He replied that he knew nothing more except that article in which mention is made of the force and coercion used against disobedient brothers who were punished with imprisonment:

"On several occasions I heard Brother Gervais and other brothers speak of the terrors of an imprisonment such that they did not know of anything else so terrible. All that the preceptors of the Order exacted must receive execution. Those who resisted were thrown into prisons where they remained until they died.

"When asked about the names of persons who, like him, had heard the revelations of Brother Gervais, he cited Jacques de Neuilly, Nicholas Simon and Adam de Chalandry who were clerks then living in Laon.

"When asked where the conversations with Gervais had taken place, he answered that they had taken place in Laon, sometimes in the house of the Templars of Laon of which Brother Gervais was the keeper, and sometimes in his, Raoul de Presles', own house.

"When asked again about the aforesaid articles of inquiry, he replied that he neither knew nor had heard anything else before the arrest of the Templars. He was asked his age and answered that he was about forty years of age. He was then asked if he had given his deposition at the special order of someone, or for a price, or out of love or fear, or for some worldly compensation. He replied that he had not."[20]

The final acts in the drama of the Templars were played out between 1310 and 1314. Dissatisfied with the work of the papal commission, Philip ordered the archbishop of Sens to begin the sessions of his provincial council. Clement V had provided that Gilles Aicelin's commission would investigate

[20] The deposition is found in Jules Michelet, *Procès des Templiers* (Collection de documents inédits, Paris, 1841), p. 174f., and in Dupuy, *Histoire de la condamnation des Templiers*, p. 164f.

the Templars as an Order and that provincial councils would collect evidence against the Templars as individuals. But the archbishop of Sens was Philippe de Marigny, brother of the king's first minister, and the actions of his council were clearly in the best interests of the king. Convening in Paris a few weeks after Raoul de Presles' deposition, Philippe de Marigny's council quickly proceeded to condemn fifty-four Templars as lapsed heretics; they were immediately burned at the stake outside the gate of Saint-Antoine. Disheartened by this display of arbitrary will, Gilles Aicelin suspended the hearings of the papal commission, and terror once more gripped the Order. The Council of Vienne did not assemble until the autumn of 1311, and in the following spring, after Philip the Fair's arrival, the pope gave sentence on the Order in the bull *Vox in excelso*. No evidence had been rendered to put the guilt of the Templars beyond doubt, but the mere fact of the process and charges had done dishonor to the Order, which made questionable its future usefulness. The Order of the Knights Templars was therefore suppressed but not condemned.[21] What remained was the disposition of the Order's wealth and its members still in prison. Although the worldly goods were committed to the Hospitalers, Philip made certain, through various financial claims and ruses, that the vast majority of the Templars' wealth ended up in his coffers. Most of the imprisoned brothers were released to enter various occupations and callings. The two most important members, Jacques de Molay and Geoffroi de Charney, were found to be lapsed heretics by an examining board of three cardinals.[22] In March 1314, they were delivered to the secular arm and were burned at the stake

[21] Lizerand, *Clément V et Philippe le Bel*, pp. 251-271.

[22] Lizerand, "Les dépositions du grand maître Jacques de Molay au procès des Templiers, 1307-1314," *Le Moyen Age*, xxvi (1913), 81-106.

on an island in the Seine. So ended the dark night that was
the process of the Templars.

The deposition of Raoul de Presles has never received the
close attention of scholars although it is well known and even
Langlois mentioned it. Occasionally, historians have insisted
that it was the most important testimony in the process and
the cornerstone in the ultimate suppression of the Order.[23]
Others have maintained that it was utterly without significance or value. On the face of it, the deposition provided no
concrete evidence of any sort.[24] It was vaguely reminiscent
of the testimony which had been used so often by men like
Nogaret and Plaisians—guilt by inference, shrewdly directed aspersions, hearsay obviously lifted out of context—all cloaked under the legalistic objectivity of an impartial witness. It was unlike Nogaret and Plaisians in that it
lacked invective, cynicism, and malice. Perhaps Raoul de
Presles spoke the truth and simply reported what he had
heard, but this does not increase the value of his testimony.
In fact, this deposition is fairly typical of the sort of evidence
which was accumulated against the Templars. Nothing more
acceptable or substantial was produced, and Clement,
therefore, upheld the definition of legal evidence in refusing
to condemn the Order. But whether the Order was condemned or suppressed, Philip the Fair obtained what he
sought and, from this point of view, he may have considered

---

[23] Auguste Matton, "Le Collège de Laon et ses bienfaiteurs," and
Maximilien Melleville, "Raoul de Presles," both in *Bulletin de la
Société Académique de Laon*, III (1853), 240, and IV (1855), 494.
Langlois mentioned Presles' deposition in Lavisse, *Histoire de France*,
III, Part 2, 178f.

[24] Edouard Fleury, "Chapitre inédit de l'histoire locale. Procès des
Templiers," *Bulletin de la Société Académique de Laon*, XIV (1864),
108-167, maintains that Presles' testimony had no great importance
and that it was probably only a repetition of what he had already
said in an inquest at Laon in 1309. There is no evidence of the inquest
at Laon. Fleury's article is good on the personnel from Laon and
Vermandois who took part in the affair of the Templars.

Presles' testimony as immensely valuable for his own purposes.

Raoul de Presles' deposition against the Templars was
the only occasion on which that lawyer appeared in the
great state events of Philip the Fair's reign. In fact, his deposition is the only evidence that pictures him engaged in
any sort of work for the king. Viewed in this way, there is
every reason to believe that he was not an important man.
But the information that is otherwise available on his life
points in every instance to the conclusion that Raoul de Presles was one of the significant lawyers during the late years
of Philip's reign. Certainly, he acquired sufficient power,
wealth, and enemies to make him a victim of the state trials
of 1315. One other lawyer appeared more engaged than
Presles in the events that made Philip's reign memorable,
and he was Philippe de Villepreux. Unlike Presles, the evidence on Villepreux's career leaves no doubt of his importance in the Capetian monarchy.

As the affair of the Templars came to an end, further instances of violence marred Philip the Fair's reign. In 1311
the Jews, who had been despoiled of goods and property in
1306, were finally expelled from the kingdom on the charge
that they pressed their debtors, and particularly widows and
children, too severely. The event was not unique in medieval
history and a better-known expulsion of the Jews was that
by Edward I of England in 1290. Besides the Templars and
the Jews, the other powerful money group was the Italian
Lombards. Like the Templars, they had organization, far-
reaching lines of communication, and were used by the king
as royal treasurers, collectors, and bankers. Like the Jews,
they were commercial and business people *par excellence*.
As was the case with both of the former groups, the accumulated wealth of the Lombards excited and tempted the king.
When he ordered that they also be driven from the kingdom
in 1311, he justified his action by charging the Italians with

gross usury, violation of royal ordinances, and with having
adverse influence on the French monetary system. There was
also precedent for this action, for the Lombards had been
put upon by French kings more than once before. The expulsion of the Jews and the Italians did not result in permanent exile; after a few years they were permitted to return,
to build up their businesses, to accumulate wealth, and to
await the next instance of royal confiscation.[25]

Apart from these two events of 1311 and the final events
in the trial of the Templars, no further affairs and no serious
disturbances occurred until the last year of the reign. For a
brief period the kingdom was at peace. There were no groups
left to prey upon and the monarch appeared to have
achieved the complete sovereignty and absolute authority
that he is reputed to have sought. For the lawyers and ministers these were the years when they realized and enjoyed
the influence and status which were their reward. This was
their golden age and they seemed unaware of the possibility
that acquisition of excessive power might prepare the way
for their greater fall. For the king the tranquillity of the
moment was somewhat spoiled when Nogaret and Plaisians
died in 1313. He was confronted again with the choice of a
chancellor and a lawyer who would assume the leadership
in affairs that had been held for so long by Nogaret.

Pierre de Latilly was assigned to the post of chancellor, but
a new "first lawyer of the realm" did not emerge. Time had
run out, and the last few months of the reign failed to see
such a lawyer appear. If more time had remained, perhaps
Latilly would have become the true successor to Nogaret.
As it was, he already had sufficient stature to make him one
of the major lawyers of the age. He had been a prime figure
in the royal service for twenty years and, while he played
a minor role in the affair of Boniface, he contributed more

[25] For general coverage of these events, see Langlois in Lavisse,
Histoire de France, III, Part 2, 198-200, 222-230.

importantly to the process against the Templars, the confiscation of Jewish wealth, and the crushing of the Lombards. At the same time, he had accumulated a large number of ecclesiastical prebends and benefices. Almost at the moment that he was named chancellor, he also gained the bishopric of Châlons-sur-Marne and came to the height of his ecclesiastical career.[26] Pierre de Latilly was assuredly the most influential of the lawyers after the passing of Plaisians and Nogaret.

The man who capped his career with the greatest fortune and influence during these last years was Enguerrand de Marigny, knight, chamberlain of the king, and controller of the treasury, the *chambre aux deniers,* and the *chambre des comptes.* He was, in short, the finance minister of the king. If any man knew the secrets of the king and had unlimited access to the royal presence, it was Enguerrand de Marigny. He was not a lawyer, but he must be studied if only briefly because he rose and fell with the lawyers. It may even be that their success was tied to his. A recent student of Marigny has estimated his annual income in 1314 at 14,600 *l. tour.*[27] His lands were located almost completely in Normandy and comprised an area that extended from Dieppe on the coast to Gisors in the Vexin.

The height of Marigny's influence is well represented by the personal favors which he obtained from Clement V in 1312 at the Council of Vienne. In the month of April alone, approximately forty letters of papal dispensation and license were written for Enguerrand de Marigny, but none for his personal benefit. They concerned his two brothers, Jean and Robert, his brother-in-law Jean de Mons, his chaplains and his clerks of whom the most prominent was Michel de Bourdenay. His two brothers obtained license to study law for seven years and at the same time were permitted to increase

---

[26] *Clement V,* nos. 9,278, 9,301.
[27] Jean Favier in *P.T.E.C.* (1956), p. 40.

the number of their ecclesiastical prebends. Robert de Marigny became *écolatre* of Orléans and then held ecclesiastical benefices in Orléans, Chartres, Auxerre, Arras, and Cambrai. Jean de Marigny was promoted to the archdeaconry of Sens; he was already archdeacon of Pont-Audemer, precentor of Paris, provost of Saint Amat in Douai and held canonicates and prebends in eleven dioceses. A few months later he was named bishop of Beauvais.[28] A third brother, Philippe de Marigny, was archbishop of Sens. From his position of power, Enguerrand de Marigny over-indulged his nepotism, flaunted his influence over king and pope, and was oblivious to the dangers inherent in such conduct.

During the last year of his reign, Philip the Fair had good reason to feel that the tide was running against him. He was severely shaken in the early months of 1314 when two of his daughters-in-law were discovered to be adulterous. They were imprisoned and their lovers were mutilated and burned.[29] Never had such a scandalous affair broken within the royal house. While still reeling from the shock of this event, Philip suffered the loss of Clement V, a reluctant but indispensable agent. But worse was to come. The Flemish question was ever present and after two abortive campaigns in 1312 and 1313, the decision was made to send a third feudal levy against Flanders in 1314. The clergy, the nobility and the bourgeoisie agreed with little enthusiasm to a new subsidy in August. The feeling was widespread that the earlier taxes had been wasted with no tangible results.

Philip departed for Flanders while the tax was in process of being collected. But this campaign was no more decisive than the others; after a few skirmishes Marigny arranged a

---

[28] For some of the papal favors which Marigny obtained in April for his relatives and friends, see *Clement V*, nos. 7,748, 7,783-84, 7,790-91, 7,794, 7,798, 7,802-05, 7,840.

[29] The story is briefly recounted in Chroniques de Saint-Denis, *H.F.*, xx, 691 and Jean de Saint-Victor, *H.F.*, xxi, 658, and in several other chronicles.

peace and the army returned to France. The first point of discontent arose from the new subsidy; the second from the failure of the campaign. This infuriated the nobles in particular, who felt that they could have overrun Flanders if Marigny had not stopped them. But their anger became uncontrollable when, after the return of the army, the king's agents continued to collect the tax. In the early days of October the discontent changed to revolt when the nobility of Artois, Picardy, Normandy, Champagne, and Burgundy began to form leagues against the king. Their complaints were directed specifically against the tax and the king's agents. More generally they wanted a relaxation of all restrictions placed on them, and a return to the generous customs of Saint Louis. We shall not pursue the history of this feudal reaction. Scholars who have studied the subject have likened it to the revolt of the English barons in 1215.[30] It was a dangerous affair which darkened the last days of the king and was not completely quelled for three years. Most importantly, it formed the immediate background to the tragic events of the succeeding year.

Philip was absorbed during the last month of his reign in devising expedients to meet the feudal revolt. His first thought was to use force, but as the leagues joined in federation he resorted to more conciliatory action. He ordered the tax collection to cease and arranged conferences with several of the rebel groups to hear their complaints. Death overtook him before he could make further moves. In his last hours at Fontainebleau his brothers and sons gathered to hear his instructions. He exhorted Louis his eldest son to respect the

[30] The standard studies of the baronial revolt are those of André Artonne, *Le mouvement de 1314 et les chartes provinciales de 1315* (Bibliothèque de la Faculté des Lettres de l'Université de Paris, Paris, 1912), and Charles Dufayard, "La réaction féodale sous les fils de Philippe le Bel," *Revue Historique*, LIV (1894), 241-272. Other comment is in Petit, *Charles de Valois*, pp. 155-161, and Lehugeur, *Histoire de Philippe le Long, roi de France, passim*. The matter of the earlier campaigns and the subsidies can also be found in these works.

Roman church, to love his people, to govern his kingdom as
had Saint Louis, to heed the advice of his uncles, and not to
imitate his father in his example of avarice. At the end
Marigny besought the king to intercede for him with the
heir to the throne. This Philip would not do. He advised
Louis not to molest Marigny in his property and goods if
it were proved that he had been a faithful servant. If the
contrary were shown, Louis was to use his own judgment in
dealing with the chamberlain.[31] So far as we know, Pierre de
Latilly was the only lawyer present when the king died on
November 29. Among his executors was Philippe de Villepreux. The twenty-five-year-old prince, who had been
knighted only the year before, became the new king of
France as Louis X.

[31] Charles Baudon de Mony, "La mort et les funérailles de Philippe
le Bel," *B.E.C.*, lviii, (1897), 8.

CHAPTER TWO

Louis X Hutin:
The Ordeal of the Lawyers

WHAT happened in the month after Philip's death cannot be determined because of an almost total lack of evidence. The chronicles are not helpful because the events which they record are not precisely dated. Guillaume Baldrich, an agent of the king of Majorca, was in Paris when the king died. On December 7 he sent a report to his superior in Majorca relating the circumstances of Philip's death, the events of his last moments, and the condition of the government at the time of the report. Since many of the statements in his letter were verified by later events, it seems that Baldrich had access to reliable sources of information. For its candor and accuracy, the Baldrich letter is the most unusual source of information for developments just after the king's death. Toward the end of the report he wrote:

"It does not seem expedient that our lord the king (of Majorca) should send ambassadors to France until after the coronation of the lord Louis. It is said that his coronation will take place soon at Reims where his predecessors were accustomed to receive their crowns. And it is presumed and hoped that the new king will reform his council and will cleanse the house of France of evil men—if there were any—according to the written instructions left him, as it is said, by his father.

"I have since heard that the lord king will not be crowned before the Feast of Epiphany and it is possible that the coronation will take place even later. Therefore, the matter of the ambassadors should be attended to accordingly. I wish your lordship to know that the lord king of France has not yet provided himself with a council or a chancellor so far as is known. It is believed that he will do this soon and that he will hold a meeting of the council in the following week. It is said for a certainty that the lord king has accepted as chamberlains, *hostiarios armorum,* and secretary the same persons whom his father had. It is doubted that the lord Enguerrand (de Marigny) has been accepted as chamberlain because of what I have written above."[1]

The Baldrich letter provides crucial information on two government officials—Marigny and Latilly—and hints at the possible course of future events. The chamberlains referred to in the letter were Hugues de Bouville, Mathieu de Trie, and Pierre de Chambly. The secretary was probably Pierre Barrière or Jean Maillard. The letter also informs us that the king had not chosen a chancellor. In the last Chancery Register of Philip the Fair's reign there is a note which briefly records that the king's seal was given to Etienne de Mornay on January 1, 1315.[2] Historians have assumed that Pierre de Latilly was dismissed as chancellor on that date. The Baldrich letter clearly implies that Latilly had left the Chancery or had been stripped of his authority within the week after Philip's death. Furthermore, there is the reference to the "evil men" in the royal house who, it was hoped, would be removed. The concept of "evil men" was a popular one with chroniclers during Philip's reign.[3] These men were presumably identified by the events of the year 1315, and there can be little doubt that Enguerrand de Marigny was a member of the group.

One can say in a general way that the prosecution of royal agents in 1315 was probably caused by the revolt of the

---

[1] Baudon de Mony in *B.E.C.,* LVIII (1897), 10-14.
[2] A.N., JJ. 50, fol. 66 v.
[3] The idea was best presented in the rhymed chronicle of Geoffroi de Paris.

nobles and was used partly to assuage baronial anger.[4] But the truth of this statement cannot be proved in any particular case save that of Marigny, and even then other factors were at work. Marigny had enemies on two fronts. He had incurred the wrath of the entire baronial faction by his conduct in the Flemish campaign of 1314. The nobles felt that he had made fools of them when he settled for peace without military victory, and there were some who felt that his conduct bordered on treason. Furthermore, they had grown antagonistic to him because of his influence over the king. Marigny personified all that they thought evil and hateful in Philip's government. And when they began to form leagues in October 1314, their movement was directed as much against Marigny as against the king. But Marigny had a more violent enemy in the king's brother, Charles de Valois, who resented and hated Marigny for personal reasons. For ten years, Marigny had exerted more influence and power in Philip's government than had Valois. Valois felt that Marigny had robbed him of his rightful role in the management of the kingdom, and the baronial revolt was a handy tool to use against his personal enemy. The antagonism of the barons and of Valois toward Marigny is well known. What has never been emphasized is the role which Philip the Fair played in Marigny's downfall.

The process which Louis X and Valois used to destroy Marigny originated under Philip the Fair. Historians have usually believed that Philip never turned against his servants and that he always defended them against criticism. But the baronial revolt which the king faced in his last days was a new and frightening development. In October or early November Philip began to question Marigny's financial administration; this action was undoubtedly a device to help reduce baronial anger and discontent. The evidence says that

[4] This is the view generally taken by Dufayard, *Revue Historique*, LIV (1894), 256, and by Artonne, *Le mouvement de 1314*, p. 31f.

Marigny asked Philip to examine his accounts so as to satisfy himself on the question of Marigny's financial operations.
The count of Saint-Pol, the count of Evreux, and Pierre de
Latilly were named to a commission to audit Marigny's accounts for the treasuries of the Louvre, the Temple, and the
chambre aux deniers. Only five terms of the treasury were
examined before the king died.[5] The Baldrich report of
Philip's death-bed scene gives supporting evidence to the
view that Marigny was in trouble with the king before the
latter's death. His plea that Philip intercede for him can only
mean that he feared the worst. And Philip's refusal to save
him points to the king's distrust of the man to whom he had
given so much power. Marigny's fate hinged on the outcome
of the audit, and the king, in his dying moments, was willing
to let him stand or fall on that point.

The subsequent process of Enguerrand de Marigny was
played out in three stages. Louis X formed a new commission
to continue the audit his father had ordered. Among the
members of this new group were the king's younger brother,
his two uncles, Miles de Noyers, Gaucher de Châtillon, the
new chancellor Etienne de Mornay, and Jean de Marigny,
bishop of Beauvais.[6] The finance minister remained under
house arrest while this commission pursued its work. In late
January Louis heard the final report on the examination and
completely absolved and cleared Marigny of any malfeasance or responsibility for the treasuries.[7] But Valois would
not be robbed of his prey and now pushed other charges on
Marigny's conduct outside of the treasuries.

[5] The information on this audit is found in A.N., JJ. 50, no. 115.
This document was edited with comment by Léon Lacabane, "Dis-
sertations sur l'histoire de France au quatorzième siècle," *B.E.C.*, III
(1841-1842), 1-16.
    [6] A.N., JJ. 50, no. 115.
    [7] *Ibid.* That Marigny was kept under house arrest during this time
is made clear in the Baldrich letter [Baudon de Mony, *B.E.C.*, LVIII
(1897), 8].

On March 15, 1315, at Vincennes, Jean d'Asnières, prosecuting for Valois and the king, delivered forty-one accusations against Enguerrand de Marigny.[8] A remarkable aspect of these charges was their concern with financial matters. When Valois exchanged Gaillefontaine for Marigny's Champrond in 1310, the latter had the count's lands appraised at 800 *l.* of annual income when they were actually worth 1,200 *l.* When Philip the Fair gave land to Marigny, his chamberlain had a real value of 800 *l.* appraised at 200 *l.*, and thereby made tremendous increases in his private wealth. He had bought estates from Béraud de Mercoeur, constable of Champagne, and had never paid the full purchase price. When he built his own church at Ecouis in Normandy, he had 4,000 stones taken from the royal quarry at Vernon and transported at royal expense. He was asked again about unaccounted sums of money and was accused of possible collusion with the Flemish in 1314. So ran the charges. Marigny neither denied nor confessed his guilt and Valois had to settle for his banishment to Cyprus.

The third and final stage of Marigny's trial came when Valois, still unhappy over this light sentence, accused his enemy of plotting, in prison, to poison him and the count of Saint-Pol. Marigny's wife and sister-in-law were implicated. On such a matter, we cannot even speak of evidence. Marigny was condemned to die and the other two parties were imprisoned. On April 30, 1315, Marigny was hanged on

[8] The most complete account of Marigny's trial is that in J. Viard, *Les Grandes Chroniques de France*, viii (Paris, 1934), 305-316. Another good account of the charges can be found in Chroniques de Saint-Denis, *H.F.*, xx, 694. See also Clément, *Trois drames historiques*, pp. 95-99. For Marigny's role in French policy toward Flanders, see Favier, "Enguerran de Marigny et la Flandre," *Revue du Nord*, xxxix (1957), 5-26, and Godefroy-Ménilglaise, "Lettre d'Enguerrand de Marigny, ministre de Philippe le Bel, à Simon de Pise, chapelain du cardinal Napoléon des Ursins, au sujet des affaires de Flandre," *Bulletin de la société de l'histoire de France* (1868), pp. 121-125.

the gallows of Montfaucon.[9] Louis X was faithful to his father's instructions. Because his accounts were proved sound, Marigny was not molested in goods or property. But his father also wished him to heed his uncles' advice, and in doing this Louis had to let Marigny die.

Enguerrand de Marigny is the best known of Philip the Fair's officials who fell from power after the king's death. Although he was not a lawyer his case must be the starting point in any discussion of the trials which followed in Louis X's reign. Marigny's trial involved the three basic factors which worked against Philip's servants. These were the baronial revolt, the last-minute doubts of Philip about his officials, and the personal hostility of Valois and perhaps others toward these officials. Each of these factors has been seen to have played a part in Marigny's fall. What cannot be demonstrated is the part they played in the trials of other royal agents at this time. It is clear that several agents were dismissed because they were directly linked to Marigny's financial administration. Michel de Bourdenay was not only a master of accounts and in charge of the *chambre aux deniers;* he was also Marigny's creature and had gained his ecclesiastical preferments and worldly wealth through Marigny's personal intervention. How Bourdenay came to know the royal chamberlain and how he won his confidence are unknown. Neither do we know the charges against him. He was probably removed from office with Marigny. Pierre Remi had control of the *chambre aux deniers* by April 1315, and Bourdenay's lands had been confiscated by May.[10] Others who fell with Bourdenay were Guillaume Dubois, Pierre d'Orgemont, Geoffroi de Briançon, and Nicole le Loquetier. Dubois and Briançon were royal treasurers and d'Orge-

[9] Viard, *Les Grandes Chroniques de France*, VIII, 315.

[10] See A. N., JJ. 52, no. 49 for Pierre Remi. For the confiscation of Bourdenay's lands, A.N., JJ. 52, no. 200. For Bourdenay's advancement through Marigny's intervention, see *Clement V*, no. 5,841.

mont was connected in a financial capacity with the fairs of Champagne.[11] Nicole le Loquetier was manager of the king's building program in Paris; his immediate superior was Marigny. There is no evidence on the trials of any of these men, but their careers had a common denominator: they were all engaged in financial administration and their fall was tied to that of Marigny.

The trial of Pierre de Latilly is more difficult to reconstruct than Marigny's process. He was dismissed from the Chancery just after Philip's death, but we know nothing of his whereabouts during the first six months of 1315. Marigny's enemies can be identified to a certain extent. Nothing of the sort can be done for Latilly although there is reason to believe that he was implicated in the malversations of Marigny and presumably had the same enemies. The official documents which contained the charges against him have not survived and we must rely on the chroniclers for this information. The chroniclers all agree that Pierre de Latilly, bishop of Châlons and former chancellor of France, was accused of having murdered his predecessor in the bishopric of Châlons and of having played a part in the death of Philip the Fair.[12]

The persons who made these charges and the evidence

[11] For mention of these men and their trials, see Artonne, *Le mouvement de 1314*, pp. 31-42. Guillaume Dubois can be seen as treasurer in A.N., JJ. 49, nos. 181, 218. He seemed not to be in prison in August 1315 (A.N., JJ. 52, no. 231). Geoffroi de Briançon also owed his rise to Marigny who obtained papal privileges for him as early as 1309 (*Clement V*, no. 4,539, and also nos. 5,419, 9,599, 9,604, in which he was called treasurer). For Pierre d'Orgemont, see Léon Mirot, *Une grande famille parlementaire aux XIVe et XVe siècles. Les d'Orgemont* (Paris, 1913), pp. 4-6, and A.N., JJ. 48, no. 216. Mention of the seizure of d'Orgemont's goods is in *Mignon*, p. 360.

[12] Chroniques de Saint Denis, H.F., xx, 696; Contin. de Nangis, H.F., xx, 613; Viard, *Les Grandes Chroniques de France*, viii, 316. Dufayard, *Revue Historique*, liv (1894), 256, maintained that the trials of Presles and Latilly were only the prelude to the trial of Marigny. In fact, Marigny was dead before the trials of Presles and Latilly began.

for them are unknown. Perhaps the chroniclers simply reported the rumors which circulated among the populace. We
would have every reason to regard these accusations as ridic-
ulous and incredible if we did not know that Marigny was
sent to his death on charges of having plotted to poison
Valois and the count of Saint-Pol. Therefore, in the case of
Latilly as in that of Marigny, witchcraft and sorcery became
part of a legal process. But the chronicles which report these
charges say little or nothing of Latilly's trial. For this we
must rely on one royal letter, several episcopal letters, two
important papal letters, and occasional financial reports. The
scarcity of evidence is made worse by the fact that the papal
throne was vacant during the first year of Latilly's trial.

Because Pierre de Latilly was a bishop he was tried by
ecclesiastical justice in the court of his immediate superior,
Robert de Courtenay, archbishop of Reims. But this fact did
not preclude Louis X from taking an active interest in the
case. The king was in fact the most interested party throughout the early stages of the process. He wrote personally and
repeatedly to the bishops exhorting them to attend Latilly's
trial. What we take to be the first of these letters was written
in July 1315. The following example was addressed to the
Bishop of Laon:

"Louis by the grace of God king of France and of Navarre,
to his beloved and faithful G[azo] bishop of Laon, greeting
and love. Since our beloved and faithful archbishop of Reims
has declared that according to Holy Canons a certain number of bishops is necessary for the examination of certain
crimes of which Pierre, bishop of Châlons, stands accused
by him, and since this affair is known to touch our person
in several ways, we strictly require and command, enjoining
by the tenor of these present letters, that you under debt of
the fealty by which you are bound to us, be personally
present at Senlis on the sixth day of August according to the
requirement of the said archbishop, which day has been as-

signed by the said archbishop to the said bishop of Châlons for answering to the articles of the said crimes. And take care that on account of your absence the examination of the aforesaid business be not delayed. Dated at Paris, 10 July 1315."[13]

According to the evidence, which is often obscure and difficult to date, the trial of Pierre de Latilly proceeded in the following manner. Robert de Courtenay's provincial council which was to meet in Senlis on August 6 either did not convene or did not accomplish its business, for a second session took place in the same city in October. One of the prelates at that meeting was Raoul Rousselet, bishop of St. Malo, and a king's clerk of long standing. He seems to have had his expenses paid by the king.[14] From Senlis the council was adjourned to meet in Paris. We know nothing about the Paris session beyond the fact that Pons d'Aumelas, a southern lawyer who had been associated with Plaisians and Nogaret, was paid *pro facto episcopi Cathalaunensis, tenendo audienciam Parisius extra parlamentum*.[15] This hearing, which occurred outside of the Parlement, is reminiscent of the manner in which the king's lawyers, in earlier years, took part in the trial of Guichard de Troyes. A further meeting, set for Senlis in May 1316, failed because of insufficient attendance, and a fifth session was called for July.[16] Throughout these proceedings, which were supposedly in the hands of Courtenay and the French bishops, the agents of the king were clearly at work. Pierre Bertrand, archdeacon of the

[13] The letter from Louis X to Gazo can be found in J. D. Mansi *Sacrorum Conciliorum nova et amplissima collectio* (31 vols; Florence and Venice, 1759-1798), xxv, col. 560; Dom Luc d'Achery, *Spicilegium* (new ed.; Paris, 1723), iii, 707; and in B.N., Collection Moreau, Vol. 222, fol. 18.

[14] Evidence of the first meeting of August 6 comes from Louis' letter to Gazo. For Rousselet at the October meeting, see *Mignon*, p. 361.

[15] *Ibid.*, p. 364.

[16] Mansi, *Sacrorum Conciliorum*, xxv, col. 561.

Bourbonnais, was at the May session and about the same
time another king's clerk and notary, master Raoul de Jouy,
was sent to Toulouse on business which concerned Latilly's
trial.[17] Either the king or someone who influenced him was
deeply interested in prompting and pushing the bishops to
a decision.

The outstanding characteristics of Latilly's process were
the continuous delays and postponements and the frantic
intervention of the crown. Both conditions had also been
present in Guichard de Troyes' case, and both pointed clearly
to the absence of legal evidence and the presence of grudge
and malicious design. But a third factor was at work in
Latilly's case; this was the behavior of the bishops. It is a
curious fact that only two letters which we have from bishops
involved in the process express a total lack of interest. Milo
de Chailly, bishop of Orléans, begged off from the trial at
the very beginning, claiming that he was ill and that he had
too many cases to hear in his own bishopric.[18] To say that
the letter written in 1316 by Gilles Aicelin expressed a lack
of interest is perhaps inaccurate. If there was one prelate
whom Louis X wanted to participate in Latilly's trial, it was
Gilles Aicelin, archbishop of Rouen. He was a man who had
retained through the years tremendous respect and prestige.
He had been the president of the papal commission before
which Raoul de Presles gave his deposition in 1310, and
he conducted himself at that time with fairness and objectivity, adjourning the hearings in disgust when Philip the
Fair became impatient over results. Despite the fact that
he had been a reluctant and unhelpful agent of Philip the
Fair, Aicelin had constantly owned access to the king's inner
chambers and was informed on most of the deliberations

---

[17] *Mignon*, pp. 360, 363.
[18] The only copy of Milo de Chailly's letter is in B.N., Collection
Moreau, Vol. 222, fol. 17 v.

which had taken place in Louis' council since December 1314.

The king had written many letters to the archbishop beseeching him to attend the sessions of Courtenay's provincial council and had received only refusals. In the spring of 1316 Aicelin refused again and in his letter gave reasons as well as he could. The tone of this letter was reproachful, antagonistic and even sarcastic. But its most important aspect was its terrible and disarming revelation, and for this we must quote it in part:

"On this day, the Thursday after the feast of Pentecost, I received the letters of your royal serenity in which you require me, as formerly in other letters you have required me, to be present at Senlis on the Monday after the feast of St. Mary Magdalene for the trial of the bishop of Châlons. Indeed, O dearest lord, you know that on the days assigned for this business I have not been able to be present for secret reasons which are not to be published in letters and which I have explained secretly in your presence and in the presence of your council at Vincennes . . . nor can I [take part in this trial] in any way on account of these reasons unless I wish to be an evil man and a prevaricator and to act against my conscience and honor."[19]

[19] The letter of Gilles Aicelin was published in Dom Luc d'Achery, *Spicilegium*, III, col. 708. A manuscript copy is in B.N., Collection Moreau, Vol. 222, fol. 19 v. As important as this letter is, only two historians have commented on it. Léopold Delisle, "Gilles Aicelin," *Histoire littéraire de la France*, XXXII, 501, felt that Aicelin believed that he would be a bad man for joining in a case against Pierre de Latilly, who was an old friend, and that this was his reason for abstaining from the trial. There is no evidence to show that Aicelin was a friend of Latilly, and the sense of the letter and especially Aicelin's use of the word *praevaricator* points in an entirely different direction from that of Delisle's explanation. The abbé Pêcheur in his "Notice sur Pierre de Latilly, chancelier de France et évêque de Châlons," *Bull. Soc. Arch. Soissons*, 2nd ser., I (1867), 225, simply noted that Aicelin was not present for secret causes.

The key word in this passage is *praevaricator,* a sham accuser, a faithless advocate guilty of collusion, one who perverts the truth. Gilles Aicelin's letter was the letter of a man who had wrestled a long time with his soul. His admission gave the lie to the charges against Latilly. More than that, his remarks can be read as an indictment of the entire atmosphere of conspiracy and collusion which so often pervaded the court circles of the last Capetian kings. On the general subject of the celebrated trials and processes which took place under and after Philip the Fair, of the cases against Bernard Saisset, Guichard, Bernard Délicieux, the Templars, Marigny, Latilly, and others, the letter of Gilles Aicelin must be regarded as one of the most important documents although it tears the fraudulent façade from only one of these events.

Whether or not the other bishops were aware of the awful secret that Aicelin knew, their conduct was similar to his. The king was confronted with a group of reluctant bishops who either were uninterested in the case or dared not participate. Lack of cooperation on their part was the major reason why the case dragged on. At one point Robert de Courtenay invited twenty-one bishops and five archbishops to Senlis in the hope that the necessary number of twelve would come.[20] It seems that he was unsuccessful. Furthermore, of the twenty-six prelates invited, only two—those of Clermont and Mende—were from the south. Most of the bishoprics concerned were north of the Loire. To study these prelates as a group of men is useless for no generalizations or rules can be derived. The vast majority of them were, of course, nobles. Simon Festu was still bishop of Meaux. If he was true to his earlier form, he took an active part against Latilly for that is the role which he had played in the trial of Guichard de Troyes. The bishop of St. Brieuc was Alain

---

[20] Mansi, *Sacrorum Conciliorum,* xxv, col. 561; Dom Luc d'Achery, *Spicilegium,* III, 707-708; B.N., Collection Moreau, Vol. 222, fol. 17.

de Lambale, who had formerly been treasurer of Châlons and knew Pierre de Latilly well. But we do not know how he behaved during these mysterious events.

After Louis X died suddenly in July 1316, the trial continued in its desultory fashion until the new pope, John XXII, took it out of the hands of Courtenay and committed it to the bishops of Cambrai, Amiens, Mende, and Arras. The pope referred to Latilly's crimes as "those enormous, abominable and villainous deeds which are accursed."[21] These bishops were instructed to proceed with the trial, to send to the Holy See the record of the process, and to hold Latilly in custody with all diligence. A year and a half later, in March 1318, these bishops had made no progress, and John XXII ordered the archbishop of Bourges and the bishops of Laon, Amiens, and Mende to remit the process of Latilly to the Apostolic Seat.[22] This is the last document that we have on the trial of Pierre de Latilly.

Pierre de Latilly was one of only two lawyers caught up in the trials of 1315; the other lawyer was Raoul de Presles. Aside from his deposition against the Templars, there is no evidence that pictures him at work for the king between 1310 and 1315. The mere fact of his involvement in 1315 points to the acquisition of power and influence. But Raoul de Presles had amassed more than power and influence; in the previous five years he had accumulated extensive landed wealth in the valley of the Aisne, and his property played a prominent role in his trial. He was in trouble in June 1315, when his seigneury of Lizy was confiscated and given to Pierre de Machau, chamberlain of Louis X.[23] Other favorites

---

[21] *Jean XXII*, no. 1,457: "propter enormia et detestabilia scelera et facinora execranda . . . ."

[22] *Ibid.*, no. 6,665.

[23] A.N., JJ. 52, no. 114. Raoul and his wife were presumably forced, during the summer of 1315, to sign documents which renounced their claim on all properties at Lizy, which were given to Pierre de Machau (*Livre Rouge*, nos. 882-884).

of the young king or of his uncles also benefited from Presles' forfeiture. Jean Rousselet and his wife were given the lawyer's holdings in Presles and Vailly. Rousselet was a former clerk of the count of Evreux, uncle of the king.[24] Clair Bridoul, a native of Crépy-en-Valois, was *châtelain* of Senlis and evidently owed his reward to the count of Valois. He was given the château and *châtellenie* of Neuilly-Saint-Front.[25] Other lands of Presles were granted to another chamberlain of Louis X, Philippe de Saint Martin, who married Pierre de Machau's daughter.[26]

There is far less evidence on Raoul de Presles' trial than on those of Marigny or Latilly. The charges are again found only in the chronicles, which tell us that Presles was implicated with Pierre de Latilly in the death of Philip the Fair.[27] Since we know the truth of Latilly's case, thanks to Gilles Aicelin, we can reasonably say that the accusation against Presles was also fraudulent. But the truth was of little comfort to Presles, who was stripped of his wealth and put in prison on Mont-Sainte-Geneviève, where he remained throughout the summer months of 1315. Unlike Latilly, he did not come under ecclesiastical jurisdiction but was forced to submit to all the rigors of a secular process. Depositions were presumably delivered against him, he underwent long and arduous legal examination, and was subjected to torture. But the lawyer, who was familiar with such procedure, knew his only hope of salvation lay in silence. No confession could

---

[24] A.N., JJ. 53, nos. 285, 309; JJ. 59, no. 108. Rousselet was called the clerk of Louis d'Evreux when goods of Bourdenay were given to him (A.N., JJ. 52, no. 200). He had held prebends as recently as 1313 (*Clement V*, nos. 7,379, 9,038), although he was married when he received the confiscated properties of Presles and Bourdenay.

[25] A.N., JJ. 53, no. 14.

[26] *Ibid.*

[27] Chroniques de Saint-Denis, *H.F.*, xx, 696; Contin. de Nangis, *H.F.*, xx, 613.

be wrung from him, and by September Raoul de Presles' trial had reached an impasse.[28]

The mission of Philippe de Villepreux and Michel Mauconduit in the summer of 1315 was in marked contrast to the somber procession of events which entangled Latilly and Presles. On July 3 at Paris, someone—lawyers or notaries—struck off one of the most famous royal letters ever to issue from the medieval French Chancery. Declaring that "all men are by nature free," the king promised that the actual condition of Frenchmen would henceforth agree with the meaning of their name and that they would indeed be free.[29] It is possible that Villepreux and Mauconduit were the authors of the letter; both men were trained lawyers and familiar with the Roman natural law doctrine. In any event these two legists were given a royal commission to go throughout Vermandois and to grant freedom to all royal serfs in that *bailliage*.[30] One important condition was attached to his grand gesture; the serfs were to give sufficient financial compensation for their newly gained freedom. This move was no innovation on Louis X's part. The freeing of serfs had been a part of Capetian fiscal policy for almost two centuries but only under Philip the Fair was the practice broadened to include entire administrative districts.[31] Louis X in 1315 was motivated by need of money for another Flemish campaign. It is ironic that the royal council had determined on another military offensive since the last three

---

[28] Viard, *Les Grandes Chroniques de France*, VIII, 316. The chronicler's account of his imprisonment and torture is corroborated by A.N., JJ. 53, no. 43.

[29] *Ordonnances des Roys de France de la troisième race* (23 vols; Paris, 1733-1847), I, 583.

[30] At least two commissions were sent out at this time, one to the *bailliage* of Senlis, and the other (Mauconduit and Villepreux) to Vermandois. See also A.N., JJ. 53, no. 22, and Marc Bloch, *Rois et serfs* (Paris, 1920), pp. 132-172.

[31] *Ibid.*, pp. 40-70.

had failed and the third one had led to the baronial revolt of 1314.

The weather should have been enough to warn the king away from his Flemish venture. The summer of 1315 was the most unusual in decades, and it seemed as if the elements had suited themselves to the mood and nature of the dreary proceedings in the kingdom of France.[32] The rains began in April and continued incessantly across the summer months. Wheat molded and rotted in the fields, and the vineyards yielded bitter grapes. A bad harvest gave impetus to an inflation that had been long in progress. Undaunted by these developments Louis took the *oriflamme* at Saint Denis in late July. Delaying his military plans for the moment, he hastened to Troyes, where he married Clemence of Hungary, and then moved on to Reims, where he was crowned on August 3. Immediately after his coronation he resumed his march toward Flanders and was encamped at Arras on September 1.[33] But there was no engagement with the Flemish. Moving north from Arras, the French skirted Lille and settled near the village of Bondues, where they finally realized that the real enemy was the weather. The fields of Flanders were a sea of mud, and the army was scarcely able to save its animals and baggage. More important for our purpose than the rain and mud and the ill-fated Flemish campaign was the pitiful little band of people who followed the king across the plain of northern France pleading for the life of Raoul de Presles. Like the Flemish campaign it-

[32] Contin. de Nangis, *H.F.*, xx, 614; Chroniques de Saint-Denis, *H.F.*, xx, 697f.; Viard, *Les Grandes Chroniques de France*, viii, 321. All of the chronicles were agreed on the matter of the weather in 1315. See also H. van Werveke, "La famine de l'an 1316 en Flandre et dans les régions voisines," *Revue du Nord*, xli (1959), 5, and Henry S. Lucas, "The Great European Famine of 1315, 1316 and 1317," *Speculum*, v (1930), 343-377.

[33] A.N., JJ. 52, no. 232. This is a letter ordered by the king at Arras and dated September 1. It is the last letter in the Chancery Registers of Louis X, since the Register JJ. 53 has disappeared.

self, the trial of Raoul de Presles came to an end in the tents at Bondues.

The document which was drawn up in the tents at Bondues in September 1315 is the only source of information on the acquittal of Raoul de Presles. It reveals that Presles' wife, his brothers, and his friends had followed the French army across France pleading their case at various points. While we know that Jeanne de Chastel was Presles' wife, the document does not say who were his brothers or friends. Furthermore, his relatives and friends did not gain personal audience with the king but negotiated through the mediation of Gaucher de Châtillon and Béraud de Mercoeur, constable of Champagne. Finally, and what was most curious, the document of acquittal was not a royal letter but rather a letter drawn up with royal authority by Châtillon and Mercoeur and sealed with their seals.[34] The question naturally arises as to why the constables of France and Champagne played the role of mediators in this strange process between the king and the friends of Raoul de Presles. No adequate reason can be given for Béraud de Mercoeur's participation in this affair. As constable of Champagne he could have been well acquainted with Presles, but there are no known instances in which he was ever associated with the lawyer. In seeking out Gaucher de Châtillon, Jeanne de Chastel and the brothers and friends of Raoul de Presles could have had only one purpose in mind: to use as intercessor the man who knew Presles well and was possibly his great friend and benefactor and who, at the same time, had tremendous influence with the king. What cannot be explained is why the king, having decided to free Presles, asked Châtillon and Mercoeur to make out the letter in their names and to seal it with their seals. "And for certain and secret reasons

---

[34] A.N., JJ. 53, no. 43. This is a *vidimus* of Philip V in February, 1317 of Châtillon's letter. Another confirmation is in A.N., JJ. 53, no. 110.

our lord the king commanded us that we deliver to the said master Raoul [de Presles] these letters pendent and open, sealed with our seals in witness of the truth until the said pronouncement is made in his palace at Paris."[35] Louis X promised that when he returned to Paris he would reissue this letter under his great seal. Why he did not do this in the tents at Bondues remains a mystery.

Louis' decision to free Presles was explained in Châtillon's letter. "Considering the state of the war in which he was engaged, wishing to examine and address his conscience, and considering the good and agreeable services which the said master Raoul had rendered in times past to his dear father and to him, and which he hoped that he would continue to render in times to come," the king went on to say that he had received the report of those who, by his special order, had examined Raoul in prison on the charges for which he had been placed in prison and that no truth or malefaction had been found either by Presles' confession or by inquest, presumption, or repute.[36] It seemed therefore that "the said master Raoul had suffered much pain, grief and damage of body and of property to which it was fit that remedy be given." By deliberation of several of his Great Council, the king re-established Raoul de Presles in "his honor, his estate, his good repute and in all of his movable and non-movable goods." So ran the explanation that Louis gave for dropping the case against Presles. He admitted that there was error in the case, and that nothing had been found against the lawyer. At Vincennes in December 1315, the king issued letters to the *baillis* of Vermandois, Vitry, and Meaux, to the provost of Paris, and to all of his other officers

[35] A.N., JJ. 53, no. 43. One possible reason is that the king did not have the great seal with him, and his chancellor, Etienne de Mornay, apparently did not go on the Flemish campaign. But the king did have some seal for he issued letters during the campaign. Furthermore, Châtillon's seal was not more important than any of the royal seals.
[36] *Ibid.*

that the property and goods of master Raoul de Presles be restored to him.[37]

But there was another reason behind the king's decision to free Raoul de Presles, a reason that was glossed over and barely mentioned in the letter written at Bondues. When Jeanne de Chastel came to the tents at Bondues she was prepared to make a bargain for her husband's freedom and the king was prepared to accept it. Châtillon's letter mentioned that after many exchanges of messages between Louis and the party of Presles, the king felt that their "responses sufficed and that he held himself well paid." This hint became broader when, in the same letter, the constable remarked that Louis, in freeing Presles, considered the state of the war in which he was engaged. But the meaning behind these vague references became clear only when Raoul de Presles in December 1315 sold his house at Vailly "out of necessity to pay what he owed to our lord the king as well as to others." Even in so desperate a situation, the lawyer arranged that the property would never stray far from his family, and made the sale to his nephew, Robert de Presles, canon of Laon. The price was 2,000 *l.* of *petits tour.*[38] In 1317, still hard pressed to meet his debts, Presles took the more drastic step of selling his wife's property of Monglas, and gave to her in compensation what remained of his lands at Vailly. He did not actually sell Monglas but seems to have used it as surety for a loan, and expressed the hope that he would later redeem it.[39] There can be little doubt that Raoul de Presles paid the king a large indemnity as part of the price for his freedom.

[37] The letter of December 1315 ordering restoration is attached to Philip's *vidimus* of the acquittal letters (*ibid.*).

[38] A.N., JJ. 56, no. 205. Once again, this letter is a *vidimus* by Philip V in March 1317. The original letter was probably registered in JJ. 53, one of Louis' Chancery Registers which has disappeared.

[39] A.N., JJ. 56, no. 294. Presles made homage for Montglas only a year earlier (Longnon, I, 429).

For five years after he was released from prison, Raoul de Presles was engaged in legal suits to recover his confiscated properties. In November 1316, Philip V intervened and established a commission of five persons to investigate the conflicting claims of Presles on the one hand, and of Philippe de Saint-Martin, Pierre de Machau, Clair Bridoul, and Jean Rousselet on the other, concerning the lawyer's landed estates. In this letter of commission, the king asserted that his late brother had ordered in his will that Presles' property be restored to him and "*quod foresfactura sua emendetur.*" The interpretation given to this phrase is that Louis X died a repentant king and felt that his behavior toward Presles had amounted to forfeiture.[40] But what had been done could not so easily be undone. Raoul de Presles was put to tremendous expense in litigating his claims on his former lands. In the early part of 1317, a fierce legal argument occurred between Presles and Jean Rousselet on the nature of the former's crime and on whether he had been proved innocent or not.[41] At the same time, Philip V had Gaucher de Châtillon's letter of Bondues read publicly in the Parlement de Paris.[42] As late as 1319, Raoul was still involved in establishing his title to lands around the village of Presles.

In the end he regained everything—Lizy, Presles, Vailly, all of his holdings in the valley of the Aisne, and his lands

[40] A.N., JJ. 53, no. 14. The commission was composed of Raoul Rousselet, bishop of Saint-Malo, Pierre Bertrand, Brother Imbert (a Dominican), and Guillaume de Harcourt.

[41] The legal debate between Rousselet and Presles is recorded in the same letter that set up the commission of inquiry (*ibid.*). Presles seems to have argued his own case and pleaded to the point that the goods and property of anyone who has been accused of *lèse-majesté* or charged with a capital crime ought not to be alienated or assigned until the accused has been convicted and condemned for the said crime. Since he had not been convicted, Louis X had illegally assigned his properties to Rousselet and the others.

[42] A.N., JJ. 53, no. 110. The reading in the Parlement occurred in March 1317, and the contents of Châtillon's letter and of Louis' letter of December 1315 were incorporated in an *arrêt* of the Parlement.

scattered elsewhere. And in so doing, Raoul de Presles manifested a characteristic that is helpful to the historian in re-
constructing his life and career. Presles had a fierce impulse
to record and register everything that pertained to himself
and thereby to safeguard his rights, his wealth, land, and
status. He exhibited this impulse more than any other person in the royal service except perhaps Philippe de Villepreux. It drove him repeatedly to the royal Chancery, where
he had every personal charter and document transcribed
in the Chancery Register and reconfirmed by the king. He
felt that in this way his acquisitions and rights would be safe
against all future questions and debate. This desire to put
in writing and to record and register was the hallmark of
the lawyer's mind. It gives us more insight into his character
and personality than any other facet of his behavior. In
1310 and 1311 he had been careful to see that the charters
which recorded the accumulation of his empire were each
inserted in the Chancery Registers so that a double record
existed. And in 1320, when he had completed his struggle
to recover his empire, he went again to the Chancery and
had the earlier charters of grant and donation recopied, reconfirmed by Philip V, and reinserted in the contemporary
Chancery Register.[43] This drive to record and register will
ultimately provide us with the key to his origins if not to his
rise to power.

Raoul de Presles was the first of Philip's agents to be acquitted. There is no evidence to indicate when Pierre de
Latilly was released and restored to his bishopric. The last
document on his trial came from John XXII in 1318, when
the pope ordered the process to be sent to Avignon. He was
presumably free by 1320 and reinstated at Châlons. The children of Enguerrand de Marigny were restored to "good
repute" in 1317.[44] At the same time his remains were cut

---

[43] A.N., JJ. 59, nos. 535, 592. The keeper of the Chancery Registers,
Pierre d'Etampes, had the extracts made for Presles.
[44] A.N., JJ. 53, no. 226.

down from the gallows of Montfaucon and given Christian burial. But his wife was not released from prison until 1325.[45] Michel de Bourdenay, like Marigny, did not live to regain his wealth. He was dead by 1317 when his heirs and executors sued to recover his lands.[46] We do not know if he was hanged or if he succumbed to the torture which Presles survived or if he died a natural death. Guillaume Dubois, Nicole le Loquetier, and Pierre d'Orgement were presumably freed; the first two were in the royal service in later years.

No historian has ever explained satisfactorily the fall of Philip the Fair's agents in 1315, and it is doubtful that an explanation, supported by adequate evidence, can be found. To get as close as possible to the truth, we must return to Marigny's trial and to the initial idea behind his trial. One terrible fact confronted Louis X and his retinue when they assumed the government of France in late 1314. The treasury was empty. Successors to thrones have often been faced with this predicament, but the situation in France was especially perplexing. The astonishment and, indeed, the rage of the young king and his uncles may well be excused when one considers the extraordinary sources of revenue that had been made accessible to Philip the Fair. Aside from the normal income from the royal domain, the wealth of the Jews, the Lombards, and the Templars had poured into the king's coffers. Moreover, Philip had received repeated aids and subsidies from the clergy, the nobles, and the towns. He had sold freedom to the serfs and he had overvalued the currency. Where had it all gone? The question had occurred to Philip before he died, and he had ordered an investigation of Marigny's accounts. From the moment that Marigny's financial administration was put in question, all those con-

[45] A.N., JJ. 64, no. 212. For the burial of Marigny, see Viard, *Les Grandes Chroniques de France*, VIII, 337.
[46] A.N., JJ. 53, nos. 285, 309.

nected with royal finance were in danger. Of the numerous charges levelled against Marigny in 1315, the vast majority were financial in nature. And this happened after his accounts had been audited and approved. The bone of contention was not a matter of financial records but of what had never been put on record and what could not be proved or explained by records.

The trials of 1315 dealt, therefore, with financial intangibles. There were all sorts of reasons for believing that Philip's servants were guilty of graft, corruption, fraud, and misappropriation of royal funds. But there was no evidence. What could the prosecution do in these circumstances? Those who prosecuted in 1315 did what Philip the Fair's lawyers had done against Guichard, Saisset, and the Templars. They fabricated evidence, tried to arrange false depositions, and used other forms of chicanery. And fearful that this would not suffice, they altered the charges and accused Marigny of trying to kill Valois, Latilly of the death of his predecessor, and both Latilly and Presles of having a part in the death of Philip the Fair. In making the crimes more heinous, the prosecutors hoped to secure some punishment for a financial malfeasance that could not be proved. This view acquires more support when we consider the victims as a group. Marigny controlled the entire financial apparatus, Bourdenay managed the wardrobe or *chambre aux deniers,* and Dubois and Briançon were treasurers. Latilly was chancellor and Presles was the king's chief advocate. All except Presles were heads of governmental departments and four or more were directly involved in finance. There was no coincidence here; too many of these persons were connected with guardianship of royal funds. Even Latilly as chancellor exercised financial functions.

There is little hope of twentieth-century historians' discovering evidence of financial malfeasance that could not be found by prosecutors in 1315. The evidence that exists is extremely oblique, inconclusive, and obscure, but it is worthy of notice. Marigny's conduct in finance was sufficiently exposed by d'Asnières at Vincennes and needs no further comment. We must also dismiss Dubois and Briançon because there is no information on them. Michel de Bourdenay presents a more interesting prospect. In 1323 several persons presented old bills of debt to the treasury, and these debts concerned Philip the Fair's *chambre aux deniers* when it was managed by Bourdenay. The debts involved jewels, clothing, and even subsidies that amounted in one case to 2000 *l. par.*, in another to 1677 *l. par.*, and in another to 758 *l. par.* In almost every instance Bourdenay had apparently failed to order payment. At one point, an obligation of 339 *l. par.* could not be found among Bourdenay's accounts but was ultimately found in the accounts of one of the treasurers. On another occasion, it was found that Bourdenay had never accounted for a debt of 223 *l. par.*[47] Bourdenay was guilty of ragged bookkeeping, and there is good reason to suspect that he was guilty of more than that.

The case of Nicole le Loquetier further supports the theory of financial intangibles. During the last ten years of Philip the Fair's reign, Enguerrand de Marigny supervised the rebuilding and expansion of the royal palace in the Cité. One of his chief subordinates was Loquetier, who attended to the appraisal of houses that had to be destroyed to make way for the new structure. Those who prosecuted him in 1315 had good reason to suspect that he had more than once catered to personal friends or otherwise engaged in profit-taking in the business of constantly appraising and compensating for the properties taken. One of Loquetier's accounts covered the period from 1310 to 1315 at which point he

---

[47] *Journ. Charles IV*, nos. 2,401, 2,492, 2,528, 2,910. For some of his earlier accounts, see Fawtier, *Comptes royaux*, Part 2, pp. 540, 547, 549, 757. Bourdenay had a heavy financial responsibility during the last seven years of Philip the Fair's reign.

must have been arrested. This account was not audited until 1317, and concerned more than 27,000 *l.* that had passed through Loquetier's hands to private persons. The record is unclear as to whether or not the account was satisfactorily settled.[48]

The accounts of Pierre de Latilly came under scrutiny in 1323, long after he had left the Chancery. It was discovered that he had never received wages or expenses during the twenty months that he held the Great Seal of Philip the Fair. But neither had he rendered account of the revenues of the seal for his term of office. Latilly acquitted the king of all that was owed him for his wages and expenses, and at the same time returned to the treasury the revenues he had received while chancellor.[49] Other items relating to Latilly enhance this view of laxness in accounting. One in particular concerns the revenues taken by the king from the bishopric of Châlons before Latilly was confirmed as the new bishop. The revenues amounted to 1514 *l.*; the collectors said that they had paid Latilly 1000 *l.* of this sum in return for a loan made by Latilly to the king. But there was no record of the loan, and the Chamber of Accounts ordered that the cause of the loan be known or that Latilly be made to return the money.[50] In the cases of both Bourdenay and Latilly there were grounds for suspicion of misappropriation of royal funds, or of failure to account. This suspicion is reinforced by the possibility that both men may have been acquitted of accountability during the last year of Philip the Fair's reign. Royal agents were strictly required to render account of all funds which passed through their hands, but the king occasionally acquitted a favorite of this responsibility. This rare conces-

[48] *Mignon,* pp. 273, 274.
[49] *Journ. Charles IV,* nos. 6,329, 6,330. There is a definite hint there of an indemnity on Latilly's part.
[50] *Mignon,* p. 54. This matter was uncovered in 1313 shortly after Latilly became bishop.

sion was also a liability, for the recipient always knew that a later king might call the acquittal in question.

Pierre de Latilly and Raoul de Presles were the only two lawyers caught up in the trials of 1315. While Latilly had been immersed in financial responsibility throughout his career, there is no evidence that Raoul de Presles was ever involved in the handling of royal funds. Of all those arrested in 1315 he was the only one not overtly involved in financial administration. One may conjecture that the reasons for his trial must be related to the reasons for the trials of the financial officials. But Presles' property holdings and financial behavior will be discussed at another place. The cases of Marigny, Bourdenay, and Loquetier are simply instances to support the view that financial intangibles were behind the trials of 1315. All of the evidence points to the conclusion that Pierre de Latilly and Raoul de Presles had so conducted themselves in financial dealings with Philip the Fair and in the handling of royal funds that they fell under the same blow that struck down Marigny and ruined Bourdenay and the treasurers.

CHAPTER THREE

The Southern Lawyers

PIERRE FLOTE and Guillaume de Nogaret are the two lawyers most familiar to students of Philip the Fair's reign because these two men directed and managed the most celebrated affair of that reign, the struggle with Boniface VIII. Nogaret acquired the added notoriety of having played the major role in the destruction of the Templars. In addition to Flote and Nogaret, three other southern lawyers acquired prominence and influence under Philip the Fair. These three men were Gilles Aicelin, Guillaume de Plaisians, and Pons d'Aumelas, and together with Flote and Nogaret they comprise a group of five lawyers who came from the south of France. Flote, Nogaret, and Plaisians have always been used to typify the legists of Philip the Fair. All five lawyers have been the subjects of brief or lengthy studies and little that is new can be said about them. But they have never been compared as a group with respect to their family origins and background, their training, and their behavior in the king's service. Through such a study their characters and personalities may take on new meaning, and their roles in Capetian government may be assessed more accurately.

The publicity given by historians to Pierre Flote is out of proportion to the information we have on his life and career. Père Anselme, leaning heavily on François Duchesne's work, could say only that his father was N. Flote and that he had a sister and a brother, Géraud Flote, who was *bailli* of Macon.[1] This could be the same Géraud Flote who was seneschal of Quercy and Périgord in 1300 and *châtelain* of Tournon a year later.[2] Because of his seign-

---

[1] Père Anselme, *Histoire généalogique*, VI, 275.
[2] A.N., JJ. 38, no. 10; *Journ. Philippe IV*, no. 5,316. Léopold Delisle

eury of Ravel, Pierre Flote has been regarded traditionally as a native of Auvergne. But in view of Digard's research, it appears that Flote was a member of the great Dauphiné family whose fiefs were located around La Roche des Arnauds near Gap.[3] This places his family origins east of the Rhone and distant from Auvergne. There can be no doubt of his nobility, and, if he was of the cadet branch of his family, he probably had to go far afield to accumulate his own landed holdings. He was seigneur of Ravel in 1294; whether he received the fief through inheritance or as a gift from Philip the Fair is unknown.[4] For almost a decade before Pierre Flote became a lawyer of Philip the Fair, he worked in the service of Humbert I, dauphin of Vienne. From 1283 to 1291, various charters picture him as the legal aid and representative of the dauphin, and this fact points to an important connection with the powerful La Tour du Pin family of which Humbert was a member.[5] It is not surprising that Philip the Fair, who was vitally interested in Lyon and the Dauphiné, should have taken Flote into his service.

The career of Pierre Flote spanned little more than a decade. What did he do during these ten years that gained him reputation and notoriety in the eyes of historians? His position in the Parlement de Paris took him into all corners of the realm on the king's legal business. He appeared at the parlement of Toulouse in 1291.[6] In 1293 he was at Agen negotiating the differences over Gascony between Edward I and Philip the Fair.[7] In that same year Jeanne de Navarre named him as her proctor, along with Gilles Aicelin, to go to

---

made no mention of kinship between Pierre and Géraud Flote (*H.F.*, xxiv, Part 1, pp. 175, 215).

[3] Digard, *Philippe le Bel et le Saint-Siège*, i, 111, note 3.
[4] *Comptes royaux*, Part 2, p. 43.
[5] Digard, *Philippe le Bel et le Saint-Siège*, i, 111, note 2.
[6] *H.L.*, ix, 154; B.N., Collection Moreau, Vol. 212, fol. 100-103.
[7] *Olim*, ii, 13, 19, 21; B.N., Collection Moreau, Vol. 212, fol. 111.

Auvergne and make her homage for the county of Bigorre to the church of Le Puy.[8] In 1295 he was again dispatched to Auvergne to settle a dispute between the bishop and abbot of Clermont.[9] While some of these missions were important, they were not enough to make him famous. His significant contributions to Philip the Fair's reign began in 1296, when he undertook to advise the king on the growing problem of royal taxation of the French Church. For the next six years Flote was occupied mainly in the struggle between Philip the Fair and Boniface VIII. But apart from his embassies to Rome, Flote appeared as the central figure in only two incidents. In 1301 he delivered the prosecution's case against Bernard Saisset at Senlis, and in 1302 he was the key speaker before the assembly of estates in Paris.[10] A few weeks after the Paris meeting Flote was killed at Courtrai and therefore had no part in the climax of the struggle with Boniface. His fame is based upon the two events of Saisset's prosecution and the Paris assembly. But in a larger sense Flote may be considered as the author and director of the king's papal policy from 1296 until his death. Because of this role Flote has been depicted by French historians as perhaps the first Gallican lawyer and one of the great figures of Philip the Fair's reign.[11]

The seigneury of Ravel and the lands of Pierre Flote lay

[8] *H.L.*, ix, 171.   [9] *Olim*, ii, 386.

[10] *Ibid.*, p. 397, shows Flote at work in the business of taxation. For his part in the affair of Saisset and the meeting of the estates, see *H.L.*, ix, 219-221, 230-231, and Langlois in Lavisse, *Histoire de France*, iii, Part 2, 142-146.

[11] As a lawyer and chancellor, Flote engaged in routine administrative business, helping in the work of the Norman Exchequer and undertaking embassies. The king gave him the unusually large annual salary of 500 *l. tour.* to which was added 200 *l. tour.* from the royal revenue of Vienne (*Journ. Philippe IV*, nos. 1,903, 3,748). For his work in the Exchequer and other financial affairs, see *ibid.*, nos. 1,389, 1,786, 2,393, 3,315, and for his diplomatic missions, nos. 1,263, 2,423, 2,670, 2,959, 3,103, 4,622, 5,195. Additional and interesting glimpses of Flote at work may be found in *Comptes royaux*, Part 1, pp. 382, 392, and Part 2, pp. 43, 400.

fifteen miles to the east of Clermont in the countryside between the Allier and the Dore. A scant three miles south of Ravel lay the ancestral lands of the Aicelin family in and around Billom. The assertion of Père Anselme that Gilles Aicelin was Pierre Flote's nephew finds substantiation in the proximity of the two seigneuries.[12] Furthermore, the nephew was associated with his uncle throughout the latter's career. In 1293 Aicelin was named by Jeanne de Navarre to accompany Flote in rendering homage to the church of Le Puy. In 1298, when Boniface permitted Flote to name two persons to the office of *tabellion*, Gilles Aicelin was given authority to confer the office upon the two nominees. In the same year the uncle, the nephew, and the count of Saint-Pol obtained a prebend in Reims for the son of the count of Auvergne.[13] Copies of the papal favors given to Artaud Flote were sent to Gilles Aicelin.[14] When Pierre Flote was sent on the royal embassy to Lorraine in 1299, Aicelin accompanied him, and two years later the nephew went with his uncle on royal business to Flanders.[15] The two men most prominent in the affair of Bernard Saisset were Flote and Aicelin. The uncle prosecuted the case and the nephew sought to make the trial legitimate and to safeguard the rights of Saisset as an ecclesiastic.

The prominence of the Aicelin family is uncontested, for it was one of the most distinguished houses in Auvergne during the thirteenth and fourteenth centuries. Whether its power was based on land or on marriage alliances and influence is a question that cannot be answered. Gilles' generation was notable for the contacts it enjoyed in the Church and the papacy. Most prominent among his brothers was Hugues Aicelin, who became cardinal bishop of Ostia and

[12] Père Anselme, *Histoire généalogique*, vi, 301.
[13] *Boniface VIII*, nos. 2,679, 2,681, for the matters of the tabellion and the prebend.
[14] *Ibid.*, nos. 2,673, 2,732, 2,857, 3,664.
[15] *Journ. Philippe IV*, nos. 2,423, 5,195.

had the complete confidence of Nicholas IV and Boniface VIII. Through Hugues' intervention two of his brothers and a nephew moved up rapidly in the service of the Church. Jean Aicelin became secular abbot of Bourges and Clermont, held prebends in the family church of Billom and in three other churches in the diocese of Clermont, and, moreover, obtained prebends in Beauvais, Le Puy, and Narbonne.[16] Guillaume Aicelin was the brother who inherited his father's lands and continued the family line. He gave to the crown its great fourteenth-century servant, Gilles Aicelin de Montaigu. Albert was another of Guillaume's sons who profited from his uncle Hugues' position and acquired prebends in Langres, Chartres, Rouen, Narbonne, and in several churches of Clermont, including his family church of Billom. He accomplished this despite the fact that he was under age and deficient in orders.[17] Viewed in this manner, it appears that the Flote family took the profit when Pierre Flote's sister married Gilles Aicelin's father. Furthermore, Pierre Flote was not only the uncle of Gilles but also of the cardinal, and may have owed far more to his nephews than they to him.

The cardinal used his influence most effectively in favor of his third brother, Gilles, whom he brought into the service of Nicholas IV and thereby paved the way for his further promotion. Born about 1250, Gilles Aicelin's advancement was not precocious for at the age of thirty-five he held only the provostship of Clermont.[18] But Nicholas IV took a deep interest in the cardinal's nephew, made him a papal chaplain, and was largely responsible for the success of his ecclesiastical career. Perhaps Gilles Aicelin's late advance-

---

[16] *Boniface VIII*, nos. 295, 2,018.

[17] *Ibid.*, nos. 300, 2,019. He was identified as the son of Guillaume Aicelin, lord of Montaigu, and the nephew of the cardinal in no. 2,005. In 1296 Albert was given permission to study civil law for five years (no. 1,318). For Guillaume Aicelin in the service of the king, see *Comptes royaux*, Part 1, p. 420.

[18] *Nicholas IV*, no. 1,005.

ment was due to long years spent in the university. His biographer, quoting the Continuator of Nangis, suspected that he was a lawyer.[19] This fact is confirmed by Nicholas' letter of 1289 in which he addressed Gilles as "professor of civil law."[20] After he became a papal chaplain he moved forward rapidly in the Church and by 1289 held the provostship and archdeaconry of Clermont, three priories in Clermont, pensions in various monasteries, and prebends in Bayeux, Rouen, Le Puy, and Billom.[21] In 1290 Nicholas IV named him archbishop of Narbonne.[22]

While Gilles Aicelin advanced in his ecclesiastical career through the patronage of Hugues Aicelin and Nicholas IV, he probably owed much in the way of influence to the family of La Tour du Pin. Two members of this family held the bishopric of Clermont in the early part of Aicelin's life. One of them was Guy de la Tour du Pin; as early as 1274 Aicelin served the bishop as legal counsellor at Lyon in an arbitration between the archbishop of Lyon and the chapter of Romans.[23] As the family came to hold the bishopric of Clermont across several years they also came to know the Aicelin family, whose members held various posts in the church at Clermont and in the diocese. This acquaintance with the house of La Tour du Pin also gives the Aicelin family an additional link with Pierre Flote, who was in the service of Humbert I by 1283.

For twenty years Gilles Aicelin held the archiepiscopal see of Narbonne. Yet he was rarely ever resident in his city and spent most of his time in Paris, where he became one of the foremost lawyers and councillors of Philip the Fair. He had entered the king's service by 1288, when he was used as a royal ambassador to the papal court.[24] Throughout his career,

---

[19] Delisle, *Histoire littéraire de la France*, xxxii, 496; *H.F.*, xx, 602.
[20] *Nicholas IV*, no. 980.   [21] *Ibid.*
[22] *Ibid.*, nos. 3,709, 4,963.
[23] Digard, *Philippe le Bel et le Saint-Siège*, i, 56f.
[24] *Nicholas IV*, no. 1,005.

one of his most important functions was that of ambassador and treaty maker, and he served in almost all of the missions at the end of the century. Within the space of three years he made two trips to Rome, was present in Lorraine for negotiations with the emperor, at Montreuil-sur-Mer for the Anglo-French talks, and in Flanders in 1301.[25] In every instance he worked in company with Pierre Flote, Pierre de Mornay, or Pierre de Belleperche, all top negotiators and lawyers of the Capetian king. If he held a post in any particular department of government it was the Parlement de Paris, although the records depict him only on few occasions in this capacity. The most crucial point in his career as a royal agent came in 1301 when he played a leading role in the case of Bernard Saisset.

Gilles Aicelin had just returned from Rome in the late summer of 1301 when he learned that the bishop of Pamiers had been arrested and was proceeding under armed guard to Senlis for his hearing on charges of treason. As bishop of Pamiers, Saisset was his suffragan, and Aicelin had to play the dual role of an archbishop and metropolitan of Saisset and of a loyal servant of the crown. From the outset Aicelin took a vigorous part in Saisset's process, pleading not for his innocence or against the charges but for order and regularity in the trial and treatment of the bishop. On the one hand he insisted that Saisset must be sent to Rome to face the pontiff. On the other hand he remonstrated with the king that Saisset must not be kept under armed guard, that he had rights of privacy which must be respected, and

[25] *Journ. Philippe IV*, nos. 1,272, 2,664, 3,105, 4,993, 5,674. Perhaps the best view of Aicelin's work in the Parlement comes from the ordinance just after 1307 when he was named as one of two prelates sitting in the Parlement. With the bishop of Rennes, the counts of Dreux and Boulogne, he had under him most of the personnel of the Parlement, among whom were Nogaret as chancellor, Latilly, Philippe de Villepreux, the constable of France, and Plaisians. See Langlois, *Textes relatifs à l'histoire du Parlement depuis les origines jusqu'en 1314* (Paris, 1888), p. 178.

that royal agents were disobeying the king in this matter. In the end, he won his point but not before he had incurred the hostility of Philip the Fair. Philip's suspicions of Aicelin grew as the archbishop seemed intent on thwarting the designs of the king. Finally Philip called Aicelin to his council and asked why he was so fervent in support of Saisset and so opposed to the interests of the crown. Aicelin replied that fear of God, fear of displeasing the pope, and fear of sinning against his suffragan was the sole motive for his actions. Aside from this he admitted that his first duty was to the king.[26]

The archbishop was put to the test again within the year when he had to make the decision of submitting to Boniface or of remaining loyal to Philip. Boniface was furious at Philip's conduct in Saisset's trial and announced that a council of French prelates would be convened at Rome in November 1302. His clear purpose was to sit in judgment on Philip, and he even hinted at dethronement. Philip's answer was the Paris assembly of April in which he forbade French prelates to leave the kingdom on pain of forfeiture. It cannot be said that Aicelin cultivated any devotion to the pope as a person. Boniface was not a man to inspire love. Furthermore, he had earlier blocked Aicelin's plan of reaching an agreement with the obstreperous *vicomte* of Narbonne.[27] Aicelin called a provincial council at Nîmes to debate the issue of going to Rome, but the results of this council are unknown.[28] We do know that Gilles Aicelin did not go to Rome and that he was not only present at the council of Nîmes in the summer of 1303 but also gave some assistance to Guillaume de Plaisians in the assembly held at Montpel-

[26] The story of Aicelin's conduct in the trial of Saisset is told in *H.L.*, IX, 216-223.

[27] *Boniface VIII*, no. 3,666; *Olim*, III, 312; *H.L.*, IX, 209, 214, 215, 237.

[28] *Ibid.*, p. 238f.

lier.[29] Even at this point, while Aicelin supported the appeal to a future council, it is doubtful that he approved of the tactics used by Nogaret at Anagni. In any event, Aicelin took his stand beside his monarch and remained there during the remainder of the struggle with Boniface.

Gilles Aicelin stands out from the entire group of Capetian lawyers as the man who opposed and took issue with his royal master. Even more remarkable is the fact that he was not penalized for his independence. He continued as one of Philip's close advisers and constantly assisted in the affairs of state. There was no profusion of gifts for Aicelin but then the king rarely offered grants to prelates in the way that he offered them to men like Nogaret and Villepreux. The only direct gift to Aicelin for which we have evidence was a grant of undetermined income on the royal holdings at Puy-Guillaume in Auvergne.[30] As a private person, the archbishop accumulated landed revenues with his own resources, and these included a rent on the salt of Carcassonne amounting to 250 *l.* of *bons petits tour.*, and an income on the *prévoté* of Monton in Auvergne by reason of a debt which the count of Joigny owed him.[31] He also had income from many of his ancestral lands, but the most interesting disclosure of his landed wealth came in 1310. Sometime before 1300, Jean Aicelin had acquired Châteldon and the châteaux of Le Breuil and Pierremont from the count of Dreux. When Jean died, the lands passed to the archbishop and to his nephew, the younger Gilles. They were held in fief of the king's uncle, Robert, count of Clermont and seigneur of Bourbon. Philip charged the archbishop and his nephew that since these lands lay on the borders of the realm near Lyon they were

[29] *Comptes royaux*, Part 1, pp. 672, 675f., gives clear evidence of the convocation of prelates at Nîmes, and of the "parlement of Montpellier" at which Plaisians and Aicelin were present.

[30] *Livre Rouge*, no. 344.

[31] *Ibid.*, nos. 416, 537, 539; A.N., JJ. 37, nos. 74, 75; JJ. 38, nos. 154, 155; JJ. 40, nos. 144, 181; JJ. 42A, no. 46; JJ. 48, no. 115.

never to be alienated from the French crown and were always to be held in fief of the lord of Bourbon.[32] Perhaps this was one reason why the king could not afford to make an enemy of the archbishop. The Aicelin family was important because it held large estates in a frontier region of the kingdom.

Another reason for Aicelin's independence was the respect which he commanded from the king. He was a trained lawyer from a noble family whose judgment and service were highly valued by the French king. After his objective stand in the Saisset affair it seemed that he surrendered to Philip in the struggle with Boniface. But this was not the last time that Aicelin played a leading part in crucial events. In the summer of 1308, when Philip and his lawyers confronted Clement V at Poitiers, Aicelin was conspicuous by the address he delivered to the pope. He seemed utterly convinced of the heresy of the Templars, urged Clement to take action, and reminded him that because the Arian heresy was not stamped out at its inception it swept almost the entire world.[33] This speech places Aicelin in a peculiar light. He was subsequently made president of the papal commission before which Raoul de Presles delivered his deposition. Whatever hopes Philip had of collaboration from Aicelin in this position were disappointed. The archbishop evidently expected to find honest and convincing proof of the Templars' guilt, and when it did not come he acted as though he were unconscious of the king's ultimate aims. His behavior was as impartial and independent as it had been in Saisset's case. Still the king did not dispense with him and even let him carry the great seal for a brief period. Aicelin's greatest moment came in 1316 when Louis X urged him to help prosecute Pierre de Latilly. He had in the meantime exchanged the see of Narbonne for that of Rouen. We have

---

[32] A.N., JJ. 41, no. 194; JJ. 42B, no. 193; JJ. 44, no. 170.
[33] Lizerand, *Clément V et Philippe IV le Bel*, p. 125.

noted his reply to Louis X in which he laid bare the fraudulent substance of Louis' scheme, and provided us with one of the most important documents of the early fourteenth century.

After some twenty-seven years of constant service, Aicelin faded from the public view in 1316 and died two years later. Perhaps he lost favor when he refused Louis X's request to help in the prosecution of Pierre de Latilly. It is more probable that due to approaching age he gradually withdrew from governmental activities. In 1314 he drew up his will and provided the outlines of a college which was to be founded at Paris after his death.[34] Gilles Aicelin and Raoul de Presles were the only two lawyers of the last Capetians who founded colleges, and Aicelin's institution, known as the Collège de Montaigu, was destined to become one of the most famous institutions of medieval and early modern France. The Collège de Montaigu played an important role in laying the intellectual foundations of the Protestant Reformation and, two hundred years after its founder's death, helped to produce such widely divergent personalities as Erasmus, John Calvin, and Ignatius Loyola.

As a lawyer and a royal agent, Gilles Aicelin represented the forces of moderation under the last Capetian kings. Despite Langlois' despair of ever determining the roles or personalities of the lawyers, Aicelin displayed his attitude clearly on four important occasions and left little doubt about his political stance. If the king had put the management of affairs completely in Aicelin's hands, the Templars would have survived and there would have been no trials in 1315. Saisset would have been arraigned but his process would have been an ecclesiastical one. Through these three events, we can discern the essential ingredient which made Aicelin's character as a lawyer; it was his tremendous concern for evidence, justice, and due process. His behavior in the mat-

[34] Delisle, *Histoire littéraire de la France*, XXXII, 500.

ter of Boniface is more difficult to explain. He clearly did not accept Boniface's extreme claims, and we may believe his sincerity when he supported the appeal to a future council. This was due process and was in keeping with his character. Throughout his career, the archbishop was besieged by the inner struggle between what his king desired and what his conscience demanded. In heeding his conscience, Aicelin exerted a restraining influence, however unsuccessful, on royal policy. Because he was a moderate in an age which did not speak to moderation, Gilles Aicelin offers a striking contrast to the general character of Capetian lawyers.

Guillaume de Nogaret has been studied more closely than any other lawyer of the last Capetians. In fact, one may confidently say that as much or more has been written about Nogaret than about his king. He has found his way into every work that deals with Boniface VIII, Philip the Fair, or the Templars. Extensive remarks can be found in Dupuy and the *Histoire de Languedoc,* and special studies have been made by Ernest Renan, Robert Holtzmann, and Louis Thomas.[35] There is good reason to believe that little or nothing new will be found on Guillaume de Nogaret. Every nefarious scheme which was executed between 1303 and 1312 has been laid directly or indirectly at his door. He was certainly responsible for the incident at Anagni and for the grand assault against the Templars, and he probably sponsored the confiscation of Jewish wealth and the expulsion of the Lombards. His work for Philip the Fair is particularly well known and there is no need for further comment here.

[35] The studies of Renan and Holtzmann have been cited in Chapter One. A biographical sketch can be found in *H.L.,* x, 53-59. The best study made of Nogaret as a private individual and landed seigneur was that by Louis Thomas, "La vie privée de Guillaume de Nogaret," *Annales du Midi,* xvi (1904), 161-198. Among other materials Thomas sifted carefully the archives of the château of Marsillargues and was able to reconstruct a detailed picture of Nogaret's landed acquisitions.

For the purposes of this study, it is necessary to examine certain other, little known aspects of his life and career so that he may be compared to the other lawyers of the last Capetians.

Nogaret's birthplace was the village of Saint Félix-de-Caraman near Toulouse, but the lawyer never accumulated lands in that area. He first appeared in 1287 as a witness to a charter in which the king of Majorca confirmed the privileges of Montpellier.[36] He was then a doctor of laws and spent the next few years as a professor in the law school at Montpellier. During this time he acted frequently as a legal counselor for the king of Majorca and for neighboring townsmen and feudal lords. In 1291 he took the first step toward the status of a landed seigneur when he acquired part of Tamarlet from the seigneur of Lunel. Two years later he bought the remainder of Tamarlet and styled himself "seigneur of Tamarlet."[37] Between 1292 and 1295, Nogaret entered the royal service. He played a large part in the legal arrangements whereby the bishop of Maguelonne ceded his part of Montpellier to Philip the Fair, and in 1294 was *juge-mage* of the *sénéchaussée* of Beaucaire. He entered the Parlement de Paris in the following year and in 1296 was given a royal commission with sweeping powers to reform the administration in Champagne.[38] By 1299 he had received letters of nobility from Philip.[39]

Nothing is known of Nogaret's parents or of their status. Perhaps they had been middle-class for several generations. Perhaps they had only recently come out of humbler origins. At some moment in his youth Nogaret tentatively decided upon the clerical life and presumably took first tonsure for he was termed a clerk in his early years and bore that title

[36] *Ibid.*, p. 163.
[37] *Ibid.*, pp. 168-170.
[38] *Olim*, II, 408; A.N., J. 206, no. 1; *Comptes royaux*, Part 1, p. 154.
[39] *H.L.*, x, 55.

until he was ennobled.[40] Unlike several other notaries and lawyers—Raoul de Presles for instance—Nogaret never used the title of clerk in his later career. The patronage behind his introduction to the royal service is difficult to determine, but as a well-known professor of law whose legal services were sought by the king of Majorca, the city of Montpellier, and various other parties, Nogaret had no problems of patronage. And having shown his ability as a lawyer and judge in the royal administration of Beaucaire, it was only natural that the king should bring him into the central government.

Nogaret succeeded in amassing enormous landed wealth and most of it came to him through royal patronage. He made no further acquisitions after Tamarlet until 1304 when Philip, seeking to reward him for his role in the defeat of Boniface, gave him two grants of 300 *l.* and 500 *l.* of landed rents to be assessed in the neighborhood of Tamarlet. The larger part of these grants was assessed on Marsillargues and the seigneury of Calvisson at the moment that royal money was devalued in 1304. Nogaret saw that the appraisal was made in good money and realized a tremendous profit. One other curious fact emerged from this matter. After extensive appraisals, the sum total of rents still did not amount to 800 *l.*, and the royal agents had to go back into the field to make additional assessments. This occurred so often that one is led to suspect that Nogaret acquired far more than the king intended. At the beginning of 1306, over 200 *l.* still remained to be assessed and Nogaret's lands extended almost to the banks of the Rhone. In the end, his estates reached from Sommières to Nîmes and from Nîmes to the Mediterranean.[41] Louis Thomas estimated that the area of

[40] Holtzmann, *Wilhelm von Nogaret,* p. 12, discusses Nogaret's early clerical status. In 1296, in the commission for the reformation of Champagne, he was called "clerk" (*Olim*, ɪɪ, 408; A.N., J. 206, no. 1). He was called "master" in 1298 (*Olim*, ɪɪ, 423), which implied clerical status, but was a knight in 1299 (*Livre Rouge,* no. 136).

[41] For Nogaret's career as a landed seigneur, I have relied on

his lands was about 400 square miles and that his seigneury was probably the largest in lower Languedoc. He had jurisdiction over 10,475 inhabitants living in some forty or fifty villages.[42]

As a landed seigneur, Nogaret's behavior toward his neighbors and dependents was similar to his conduct in the affairs of state. After the acquisition of Tamarlet, he cultivated the river bottom lands of the Vidourle which by custom should have remained in pasture for the people of Marsillargues. He cleared additional land, built roads and dams, all to the grief of his neighbors. They constantly lodged complaints against Nogaret's refusal to recognize their customary rights. But each time that Philip ordered an inquest into the differences, royal agents made judgment in favor of Nogaret. The people of Lunel complained in 1313 that Nogaret's conduct as a seigneur had caused them 10,000 *l.* of damages. At one point he consented to give 500 *l.* of indemnity to the inhabitants of Marsillargues for cultivating the river bottom lands. Other complaints were lodged by the abbey of Psalmodi and the monks of Franquevaux. Persons at Nîmes asserted that he had set up new customs for his barony of Manduel and was collecting as much as 100 *l.* of new revenue. Three hundred families were forced to move away from Lunel because Nogaret usurped their rights of pasture. The complaints continued during his life and after his death, and rectification was not made in some instances until 1327.[43] Nogaret's policy was one of crushing seigneurial aggression toward those who were his neighbors or else

Thomas in *Annales du Midi,* xvi (1904), 161-198. Renan gave some attention to his estates, but Holtzmann scarcely mentioned his landed acquisitions.

[42] Louis Thomas, "La population du Bas-Languedoc à la fin du XIIIe siècle et au commencement du XIVe," *Annales du Midi,* xx (1908), 469-487.

[43] Thomas, *Annales du Midi,* xvi, (1904), 161-198.

had come under his jurisdiction in the vast landed estates that he accumulated in Languedoc.

Guillaume de Plaisians worked more closely with Nogaret than any other person between 1303 and the end of Philip's reign. His birthplace was the hilltop village of Plaisians located in the Dauphiné near Vaison-la-Romaine and two or three miles north of the celebrated Mont Ventoux. His biographer has presumed that he studied law at Montpellier, probably as a student of Nogaret, but there is no information on him until the beginning of the fourteenth century. Before joining the royal government he gave legal counsel to Humbert I, dauphin of Vienne, who in turn rewarded him with letters of nobility and the château of Vinzobres in the valley of the Aygues. In 1301 Plaisians held Nogaret's former position of *juge-mage* at Beaucaire and two years later came to Paris, where he was associated with Nogaret in the work against Boniface.[44]

After Nogaret and Flote, Guillaume de Plaisians is the best known of Philip the Fair's lawyers. This publicity is due to his constant embroilment in the great affairs of the reign. Throughout his career he served as royal commissioner, ambassador, and treaty-maker, and constantly assisted Nogaret. His debut consisted of the violent harangue against Boniface delivered to the Louvre assembly of 1303. He testified in the trial of Guichard de Troyes and was as fully involved in the trial of the Templars as were Nogaret and Aicelin. His speech before Clement V at Poitiers in 1308 was reminiscent of his 1303 address, and he let Clement know that he would be less than a good Christian if he refused to prosecute the Templars.[45] The over-all value of Plaisians to Philip the Fair

----

[44] The only published notice on Plaisians is that by Abel Henry, "Guillaume de Plaisians," *Le Moyen Age*, v (1892), 32-38, in which Henry proved, among other things, that Plaisians was a native of the Dauphiné and not of Languedoc as Renan had supposed. Brief biographical comment can also be found in *H.L.*, x, 59.

[45] Lizerand, *Clément V et Philippe IV le Bel*, p. 125.

can best be gauged by studying the incredibly long list of items, published by Langlois, which shows the quantity and variety of administrative business that passed through his and Nogaret's hands.[46] This portrait of an important lawyer scrutinizing the significant and insignificant business of the king is somewhat enlarged by a remark of Philip when he gave to Plaisians an annual salary of 500 *l. tour.* in 1307: "He will have no wages when the court is in France or the neighborhood. But he will receive expenses when he is, by royal order, in distant regions such as Toulouse, Lyon, Poitiers, Boulogne, etc."[47] While many of his relatives remained in the region of the Dauphiné and upper Provence, Plaisians became a neighbor of Nogaret and acquired extensive estates at Vézénobres, Ferrairoles, and Boucoiran in lower Languedoc, presumably through royal gift."[48]

While no proof exists of a connection between Flote and Aicelin on the one hand and Nogaret on the other, there can be little doubt that Nogaret and Plaisians were acquainted with Pons d'Aumelas at Montpellier. The career of d'Aumelas illustrates the Capetian lawyer who served long years in provincial administration before joining the central government in Paris. He first appeared in 1287 as *jurisperitus* when he was associated with Nogaret as witness to a recognition given by the king of Majorca to the townsmen of Montpellier.[49] He had studied in various law schools and probably studied under Nogaret at Montpellier.[50] For over a decade,

[46] Langlois, "Les papiers de Guillaume de Nogaret et de Guillaume de Plaisians au Trésor des Chartes," *Notices et extraits des manuscrits de la Bibliothèque Nationale et autres bibliothèques,* XXXIX (1909), Part 1, pp. 211-254.

[47] *Livre Rouge,* no. 831.

[48] *Clement V,* no. 7,927; Henry, *Le Moyen Age,* V (1892), 37f.

[49] Langlois, "Pons d'Aumelas," *B.E.C.,* LII (1891), 674.

[50] *Ibid.,* 675. The information comes from a letter of 1292 addressed by the bishop of Maguelonne to the professors of law at Montpellier, among whom was Nogaret. The bishop remarked on d'Aumelas' studies

Pons d'Aumelas confined his activities to the region between Montpellier and Beaucaire. On many occasions he seemed to act as legal counselor to the city of Montpellier; on other occasions he was engaged in specific work for either the bishop of Maguelonne or Philip the Fair. His legal business carried him to Beaucaire, where he dealt with Plaisians, who was then *juge-mage*. He undoubtedly had a thriving law practice during these years and there is a great possibility that he was also professor of law at the University of Montpellier in the last decade of the century.

By 1305 Pons d'Aumelas was definitely in the service of Philip the Fair as *juge-mage* of the *sénéchaussée* of Rouergue, a post which he held for about four years. One would logically assume that he obtained this position through the recommendations of Nogaret and Plaisians. But such an assumption is contradicted by the apparent failure of the same two men to secure for d'Aumelas a position at Paris; in fact d'Aumelas did not come to Paris until after the death of Nogaret and Plaisians. There is also the possibility that he had a patron in the bishop of Maguelonne, for a person with the same surname, perhaps a relative, was a sacristan at Maguelonne. Two incidents in the career of d'Aumelas show how a Capetian lawyer used patrons as intercessors with the king and also how certain officials could hinder that lawyer's rise to more important positions. In 1308 Bérenger de Frédol, a cardinal priest and celebrated canon lawyer, wrote to Philip the Fair on behalf of d'Aumelas. He reminded the king that d'Aumelas had worked faithfully and assiduously in the royal service but had never received a fitting reward. He asked the king to give to d'Aumelas a better office and one

---

elsewhere and insisted that, in spite of recent changes in doctoral examinations at Montpellier, the doctorate held by d'Aumelas would remain valid. The letter is also found in M. Fournier, *Statuts et privilèges des universités françaises, depuis leur foundation jusqu'en 1789* (4 vols.; Paris, 1890-1894), II, no. 905.

more suited to his merits and ability.[51] This intercession still did not bring d'Aumelas to Paris, but it may have moved him to the office of *juge-mage* in Toulouse. There, however, the seneschal of Toulouse refused to assign certain business to d'Aumelas because he maintained that the lawyer was a long-time friend and servant of the count of Armagnac, who in turn was one of Philip the Fair's chief enemies in the south.[52] Information of this nature, showing the influence used for and against a lawyer, is unavailable on the other lawyers of Philip the Fair.

From the moment that Pons d'Aumelas came to the Parlement de Paris in 1313, his career became singularly uninteresting except for the evidence that portrays him at work in the trial of Pierre de Latilly. Later assignments were of a routine nature, and he disappeared from view in the reign of Charles IV.[53] He probably came from the region of Aumelas in the vicinity of Montpellier but his social status cannot be determined until 1308 when he was called a knight. He married a noble widow in 1317 and acquired some property in Languedoc.[54] His life story is valuable only because he represents the type of lawyer who struggled to get to Paris and succeeded only late in his career. Dozens of other Capetian lawyers never succeeded and remained in provincial administration throughout their lives. In fact, the Capetian lawyer who came to the central government from provincial administration was a rarity despite the examples of Nogaret and Plaisians.

The southern lawyers deserve some further comment with respect to their origins and rise. Flote, Aicelin, and Plaisians

---

[51] The letter is reproduced in Langlois, *B.E.C.*, LII (1891), 260. It is also found in Etienne Baluze, *Vitae paparum Avenionensium* (2 vols.; Paris, 1693), II, col. 116.

[52] Langlois, *B.E.C.*, LII (1891), 261. As late as 1310, he was still *juge-mage* of Toulouse and Albi (A.N., JJ. 47, no. 114).

[53] For notices of d'Aumelas at work after he came to Paris, see *Olim*, III, 908, 923, 924, 1,293.

[54] Langlois, *B.E.C.*, LII (1891), 262f.

had in common a connection with the family of La Tour du Pin. Aicelin served one of the family's bishops and Flote and Plaisians were in the employ of Humbert de la Tour. Flote and Aicelin were themselves highly placed nobles and had little difficulty in gaining access to Capetian government. Plaisians came from middle-class origins or even from a lower station; his legal ability and the patronage of the dauphin must have been crucial in his rise to importance. The value of all three men to Philip the Fair was greatly enhanced by their knowledge of the frontier region along the Rhone and by their connections with the ruling families in that district. Philip the Fair was always sensitive to the eastern frontier, from Avignon to the northeastern corner of Champagne. While Flote, Aicelin, and Plaisians came from the southeast, the origins of Pons d'Aumelas and Guillaume de Nogaret lay in the southwest. The patronage behind d'Aumelas has already been noticed; Nogaret remains a problem. The most famous of Philip the Fair's lawyers, he seemed to be a man without friends. His origins have remained obscure and his rise to power can best be explained by his position and connections in the law school at Montpellier. But the frontier was also in question at Montpellier, and a lawyer who understood the situation there and was acquainted with the important people in the region would be valuable to the king.

Nogaret and d'Aumelas are the only two lawyers who can be definitely associated with the law school at Montpellier. Circumstantial evidence also links Plaisians with Montpellier, and tradition has it that Flote and Aicelin studied there. But there is no evidence whatever that places these two nobles at Montpellier. Although it was the most reputable of French law schools in the late thirteenth century, one should not send all of Philip the Fair's lawyers to it. Recent research has shown that, contrary to earlier opinion, there were many places in France where one could study law.[55] One of the most likely places in the Rhone valley was Lyon, and Flote and Aicelin could easily have received their training there. In addition to the better known centers at Montpellier, Toulouse, and Orléans, other cities where legal training may have been available were Bourges, Nevers, Clermont, Angers, Poitiers, and Laon. The study of law could be pursued formally or informally, and men who had greater or lesser training in the discipline seemed to be everywhere in the late thirteenth century. Furthermore, as in the case of d'Aumelas and as will be shown for Philippe de Villepreux, law students, like other students, frequently studied at many schools. It is often fruitless to trace a lawyer to his center of training; even the popes in their numerous grants of non-residence to prospective law students usually failed to mention the intended place of study.

[55] See Digard's comments in *Philippe le Bel et le Saint-Siège*, I, 57, note 3, and in "La papauté et l'étude du droit romain au XIIIe siècle," *B.E.C.*, LI (1890), 381-419.

CHAPTER FOUR

The Northern Lawyers

THE most distinguished of the northern lawyers who served Philip the Fair was Pierre de Belleperche. Most of his life and career belonged to the thirteenth century and, due to lack of information, a large body of tradition that cannot be verified has grown up about him. His family came from the valley of the Allier north of Moulins, and he may be called a native of the Bourbonnais. He was born about 1230, probably of nobility, and studied law at Orléans and perhaps also at Bologna and Toulouse. What cannot be disputed is the fact that he taught at Orléans in the period between 1280 and 1295 where he undoubtedly knew the bishop Pierre de Mornay, who took a great interest in the development of the law school. Belleperche was one of the few lawyers of the last Capetians who wrote formal law tracts and commentaries. At the same time he pursued an ecclesiastical career and finally entered the employ of Philip the Fair about 1296.[1]

As a royal agent, the career of Belleperche, like that of Flote, spanned only ten years. It is difficult to understand why Belleperche, after a lifetime of academic work and writing, wished to enter the battleground of Capetian government. For his part, Philip always seemed willing to add

---

[1] Several short articles have been written on Belleperche as a professor and lawyer. See Méplain, "Notice sur la législation civile et les jurisconsultes du Bourbonnais," *Bulletin de la société d'émulation de l'Allier*, III (1853-1854), 124-155, 234-245, and François Perot, "Esquisse biographique sur Pierre de Belleperche," *Bulletin de la société archéologique et historique de l'Orléannais*, VII (1878-1882), 510-514. Léopold Delisle furnished a note on Belleperche as a professor at Orléans (*ibid.*, p. 363). Some little biographical information can also be found in A.N., JJ. 44, no. 108; JJ. 45, no. 158; *Livre Rouge*, nos. 487, 547, in which executors founded a chapel in Belleperche's home at Villeneuve-sur-Allier.

another reputable professor of law to his entourage, and must have been pleased when he secured the services of Belleperche. As a councillor of the king Belleperche became immersed in a variety of administrative and ambassadorial assignments, performing the same sort of tasks required of Flote, Nogaret, and Plaisians. In one year alone he helped with the Exchequer business at Rouen, made a trip to Arras, advised the king at Saint Germain-en-Laye, attended royal cases at Troyes, and went on an embassy to England. When not on the road, he was occupied in the work of the Parlement in Paris. For an unspecified period toward the end of his career, he performed the duties of chancellor. In 1306 he was made bishop of Auxerre and died two years later. It is impossible to assess Belleperche's role in Capetian government.[2] He counseled the king during his difficulties with Boniface and was a member of the group that included Pierre de Mornay, Flote, and Aicelin, and which was closest to Philip the Fair at the turn of the century.

The information available on Pierre Dubois has been carefully mined by a host of scholars which has resulted in an unusually large bibliography. As is the case with Nogaret, there is little hope that any new items will be uncovered on Dubois. Yet we know as little about him as we know about Pierre de Belleperche, although we can follow the latter to some extent in his governmental career. If this Norman lawyer who was king's advocate in the *bailliage* of Coutances had never written a pamphlet his name would be as meaningless today as those of dozens of lawyers who served throughout their lives in remote provincial posts. Yet, because he did write, he has achieved a fame equal to that of Flote and Nogaret. After general studies at Paris and training in law, probably

---

[2] On the day-to-day work performed by Belleperche as a royal councillor, see *Journ. Philippe IV*, nos. 974, 2,383, 2,805, 2,941, 3,737, 4,629, and for revenues of the great seal when he was chancellor, no. 5,973. For work in the Parlement, see *Olim*, II, 423; III, 126.

at Orléans, Dubois returned to his native Normandy and remained there for most of his life. He left Normandy only for brief periods when, for example, he represented Coutances in the Paris assembly of 1302 and in the Tours assembly of 1308. The archival material on his life and career is almost nonexistent. What we know of him comes from his writings, and we may place his practice as a lawyer between 1295 and 1314, within the reign of Philip the Fair. He knew the influential Richard Leneveu, who helped in the case against Saisset, but Dubois' friends could not or would not aid him in realizing his greatest ambition, that of being brought to Paris where he could work beside Flote, Nogaret, and the others. He therefore fell victim to the fate which Pons d'Aumelas barely escaped. It is even uncertain whether his pamphlets had any influence on the course of Capetian politics, and he must stand as an unusual example of the Capetian lawyer who remained in a provincial office. Thwarted in his eager desire to serve his king as a man of action, he resorted to authorship and thereby gained for himself a historical recognition which he would not otherwise have won.[3]

There would be little justification for mentioning Simon de Bucy if he had not been a close friend of Raoul de Presles and if he had not given to the crown a son who became one of the influential and controversial lawyers of the mid-fourteenth century. He serves moreover to illustrate the type of man who we know was a trained lawyer but whose influ-

[3] The most recent biographical note on Dubois is the introduction to Walther I. Brandt's translation and edition of Pierre Dubois' *The Recovery of the Holy Land* (New York, 1956), pp. 3-10. The only mention of Dubois in the Chancery Registers is in A.N., JJ. 38, no. 228, in which he is called royal advocate in the *bailliage* of Coutances (1307). The only full length studies are those by Ernest Renan, "Pierre Dubois, légiste," *Histoire Littéraire de la France*, xxvi, 471-536, and Ernest Zeck, *Der Publizist Pierre Dubois* (Berlin, 1911). The most recent study of Dubois' ideas is by Mario Delle Piane, *Vecchio e nuovo nelle idee politiche di Pietro Dubois* (Florence, 1959).

ence and contribution we cannot assess. He must be distinguished from Simon Matiffas de Bucy, who was bishop of Paris from 1290 to 1304. The bishop's testament mentioned a sister, Ada de Bucy, and a nephew and niece, but no other person with the name of Simon.[4] The bishop came from nobility but we are almost sure that the lawyer was not noble. Yet, both the bishop and the lawyer came from the village of Bucy-le-Long, situated just east of Soissons and some ten miles west of Presles. In 1303, a master Simon de Bucy was clerk of the bishop of Cambrai and the document in which he was so named dealt with rents in the diocese of Soissons.[5] This could well be the lawyer. His biographer maintained that after the death of his wife, Jeanne de Luat, Bucy entered the clergy and became a canon of Pontoise, which he exchanged in 1310 for a canonicate in Châlons.[6]

As a canon of Châlons he undoubtedly knew Pierre de Latilly, who was then archdeacon of Châlons and who had earlier been a canon of Soissons. Bucy's friendship with Raoul de Presles is attested by a transaction of 1313 when he acquired from Presles 24 *l.* of rent on Condé, which he used to endow a chaplaincy in his house at Bucy. At that moment he was called "king's clerk and proctor," and the bishop of Soissons, in authorizing the chapel, referred to him as canon of Châlons.[7] Simon de Bucy's role in Philip the Fair's government can scarcely be determined due to the few items available. As a royal proctor he was engaged in handling

[4] Archives départementales de l'Aisne, G. 253, fol. 136 v.-137. He was archdeacon of Reims before coming to the bishopric of Paris (B.N., Collection Moreau, Vol. 209, fol. 76-77v.). His tomb stands today on the south side of the choir in Notre Dame de Paris.

[5] B.N., Collection Moreau, Vol. 217, fol. 190 r.-v.

[6] Félix Brun, "Note sur les Simon de Bucy et le vieux château de Bucy-le-Long," *Bull. Soc. Arch. Soissons,* xiv (1907), 359-405. The exchange by which he acquired a canonry in Châlons is noted in Archives départementales de la Marne, G. 458, no. 4.

[7] Archives départementales de l'Aisne, G. 253, fol. 131, 132 v.-133; A.N., JJ. 48, no. 186.

inquests and prosecuting for the king. In July 1315 he was instrumental in settling differences between the bishop of Paris and a religious house in Pontoise, on which occasion he was entitled "professor of laws and proctor of the king."[8] Nothing is known of his legal training but he furnishes evidence that Philip the Fair used formally trained lawyers to do work which had not the importance of that assigned to Nogaret and Plaisians. Simon de Bucy was not implicated in the troubles of 1315 that brought his friends Latilly and Presles to grief. He probably died before 1320. He is important mainly because he represents the Capetian lawyer whose children served in more conspicuous positions under later French kings.

The history of Pierre de Latilly is the history of his career under Philip the Fair. There is no information on his origins and rise, but his work for Philip is fully documented across twenty-five years to the beginning of his trial in 1315. He came from the village of Latilly, which lies north of the Marne between Château-Thierry and Soissons. Nothing is known of his family or relatives, and we are unable to say whether he was noble or of some lower station.[9] He appeared for the first time on royal business in 1290, when he was given a commission to collect fines for noble lands acquired

---

[8] A.N., JJ. 52, no. 214. For other duties which he performed, see Boutaric, no. 3908; *Olim*, III, 675; and *Mignon*, p. 359, in which he went into Brittany in 1314 collecting the sudsidy for the Flemish campaign. Some faint reference to his university background is found in the bishop of Soisson's letter which confirmed his chapel in Bucy and which spoke of Simon as "Deum habens pre oculis piis ductus consiliis dignisque studiis excitatus . . ." (Archives départementales de l'Aisne, G. 253, fol. 131-132 v.).

[9] A.N., JJ. 64, no. 187, is a letter in which, at the request of Pierre de Latilly, Charles IV freed Philippe, son of Henri Richard de Latilly, so that he might receive tonsure and become a clerk. Whether these were relatives of the bishop or simply someone he knew in his native village cannot be determined. In 1265 a Raoul de Latilly was rector of the parish church of Latilly, and founded a chaplaincy there. There is, again, no way of knowing if he was an ancestor of Pierre de Latilly (A.N., L. 742, no. 112).

by ecclesiastics and non-nobles in the *bailliages* of Senlis and Gisors.[10] This work kept him busy for three or four years; for part of this commission he was associated with no less a lawyer than Philippe de Beaumanoir, who was then *bailli* of Senlis.[11] At this moment Latilly was already a member of the Parlement de Paris.

Next to his trial in 1315-1317, the most publicized incident in Pierre de Latilly's career was his behavior on the royal commission which he and Raoul de Breuilli carried into Languedoc in 1297. The king was in urgent need of money for war with the English, and Latilly had the dual assignment of not only collecting the money but also of seeing that it was transferred for use by the army in Gascony. Latilly's methods of collection and his harassment of the population gave rise to such violent repercussions that the king was obliged to send a second commission into Languedoc to investigate the complaints of the villagers and townsmen. A large portion of these grievances are still on record; from them and the recently published accounts of Philip the Fair one can reconstruct the story of Latilly's commission. The picture that emerges presents not only a good example of a royal tax commission but also lets us see one of the better known Capetian lawyers at work in the field.[12]

The ostensible purpose of Latilly's commission was to col-

[10] There is a note in the Archives départementales du Loiret, D. 668, fol. 12 v., which shows Latilly at work on this commission in 1290. Most of the evidence on this commission comes from the years 1292-1293. Good reports of his collections on this assignment are in Archives départementales de l'Eure, G. 92, no. 1, and G. 122, fol. 133-134. Other notices of Latilly on this commission are in B.N., Collection Moreau, Vol. 211, fol. 210-211; Vol. 212, fol. 55 r.-v., 61-62 v.; *Mignon*, pp. 179, 231, 232.

[11] For his work with Beaumanoir, see B.N., Collection Moreau, Vol. 212, fol. 62 r.-v.; Vol. 217, fol. 250 r.-v.

[12] The story of Latilly's commission is reconstructed by Langlois in "Les doléances des communautés du Toulousain contre Pierre de Latilli and Raoul de Breuilli, 1297-1298," *Revue Historique*, xcv (1907), 23-53.

lect various servile dues from southern villages, dues that were ordinarily classified under the title of *casalages*. But Latilly's operations went far beyond this, and inhabitants over a large area were arrested for injuries to royal officials, for sacrilege and heresy, private appropriation of royal rights, fraud against the king, default in justice, default in military service, use of prohibited monies, non-noble acquisition of noble lands, and other charges. It seemed that Latilly was bent on sweeping clean the entire countryside and gathering up every small and great offender from whom a few shillings or pounds could be extracted by way of fine. Perhaps no grievances would have come if he had confined his oppression to individuals. In the end, however, whole communities were caught up in the net that his delegated agents spread through the region around Toulouse. Throughout the process of collection Latilly and Breuilli remained in Toulouse, where offenders and representatives of communities were brought for final composition and payment. The terrorizing of the population took place, therefore, at two levels, in the villages where the serjeants and other agents behaved in the most arbitrary fashion and in Toulouse where delegates from the communities were forced by Latilly and Breuilli to agree to their demands.

The case of the village of Laurac illustrates the methods of Latilly.[13] To Laurac Latilly dispatched a notary with about two dozen serjeants who seized pledges from among the inhabitants, including clothing and bedding. Many were expelled from their homes, their doors were locked and the keys later ransomed for a small price. Calling the leaders of the community together, the notary stated his business and forced several among them to go to Toulouse to negotiate their fine with Latilly and Breuilli. Once in Toulouse the representatives of Laurac did not face Latilly but negotiated with still another notary who put their fine at 3,000 *l. tour.*

[13] *Ibid.*, pp. 29-36.

and cautioned that, if not agreed upon there, it would be 3,500 *l.* on the morrow and would continue to increase for every delay. While certain of the leaders returned to Laurac to obtain agreement on the price, the others were held virtually as prisoners in Toulouse. Their spirit and will to resist were finally broken by the terrorism and intimidation of Latilly's agents and they agreed to pay. The sum of money was collected not as individual dues or fines but in the name of the corporation and community of Laurac. Viewed in this manner, we may say that an entire village was put to ransom. To call it wholesale extortion would be scarcely an exaggeration.

Langlois, who studied carefully the *doléances* of the villages determined that about nine communities complained of similar treatment. Sometimes the representatives dealt directly with Latilly and Breuilli; at other times the two commissioners did not appear in the proceedings. But their directing hands appeared behind it all, and they never showed any reluctance to accept the responsibility. That the procedure in every case was similar if not identical shows a centralized organization. The people of Fanjeaux were informed by Latilly that their fine was 30,000 *l.*, and that they could get off for 15,000 *l.* if they agreed immediately. The deputation of Villemur was told that they were dutiable for 6,000 *l.*, but 4,000 *l.* would be acceptable. Although the people of Cintegabelle produced a royal charter acquitting them of servile dues, they were made to pay 5,000 *l.* Nor did the violence end when the communities agreed to pay; for the actual payment the serjeants returned to the villages and lodged with the inhabitants while the money was collected. Those who did not pay saw their cattle, horses, and sheep driven away by the agents.[14]

The accounts of Latilly and Breuilli list 125 villages and

14 *Ibid.*, pp. 41-45.

towns that paid various fines.[15] The extant *doléances* come from only nine communities. It is reasonable to assume, however, that many more than nine were terrorized in the manner related above. So oppressive was the atmosphere created by Latilly and his agents that some towns could not find proctors or advocates willing to present their complaints to the king or to the Parlement de Paris.[16] Those that did protest made such an impression on the king that he ordered an investigation. Latilly was recalled from Languedoc in the early part of 1298. The witnesses for the defense and the defendants themselves rarely denied the charges. On the contrary, they insisted that their actions were justified and—most revealing of all—that it was the custom to do things in that fashion. It has been said that the ordinance of 1299 abolishing serfdom in the *sénéchaussée* of Toulouse was a royal move to assuage the anger of the southerners.[17]

From 1290 to the end of his career everything that Pierre de Latilly did points to his importance in the reign of Philip the Fair. He was given another rough assignment in 1301 when he was sent to Senlis to seize usurious Lombards.[18] He appeared late in the struggle with Boniface VIII; in the summer of 1303, while Guillaume de Plaisians was securing support for Nogaret's plan along the Mediterranean coast, Latilly and Richard Leneveu were sent to Toulouse and upper Languedoc for the same purpose. It is almost incredible that the king chose Latilly for this mission to the south where the hatred created by his behavior in 1297 had scarcely subsided. He was also engaged in the confiscation of Jewish wealth from the beginning to the end of that affair.

---

[15] *Comptes royaux*, Part 1, pp. 525-535; Part 2, pp. 657-660.

[16] Langlois in *Revue Historique*, xcv (1907), 40f.

[17] *Ibid.*, p. 51f. Additional comment on Latilly's mission of 1297 is in Boutaric, *La France sous Philippe le Bel*, p. 158.

[18] *Journ. Philippe IV*, no. 5587. For other brief comment on his career, see the abbé Pêcheur in *Bull. Soc. Arch. Soissons*, 2nd ser., i (1867), 218-229.

With Gilles Aicelin he helped to revise and modify the royal order of 1310 that dealt with the confiscated Jewish wealth and he probably had something to do with their ultimate expulsion.[19] In the affair of the Templars he operated most often in company with Plaisians and made several trips to the papal court. He carried commissions into every corner of the realm, negotiated with Henry VII of Germany, and was used on three embassies to England.[20] With more than twenty years of such experience behind him, he was in 1313 the logical choice for the post of chancellor.

Latilly's acquisition of private wealth was not as impressive as that of Nogaret or of some other lawyers. He was paid wages for his work in the Parlement and there was a curiously isolated gift from the king in 1292.[21] But the king did not heap gifts upon him. In the autumn of 1311 the abbey of Saint Médard of Soissons sold to Latilly the village and lands of Epieds for the price of 1,470 *l.* of *bons petits tour.* In fact, the abbey had already received and spent the money and simply transferred the land to him in payment of a previously incurred debt. At the same time, Saint Médard contracted with Latilly for his legal services during his lifetime regardless of any offices that the archdeacon might obtain.[22] This incident proves that Latilly was engaged in private law practice despite his constant involvement in royal business. Latilly made another and smaller acquisition in 1313 when he purchased from Thomas de Cernay for 200 *l.* the land of Amblény west of Soissons.[23] His most obvious financial

[19] *Olim,* II, 507.

[20] *Journ. Philippe IV,* nos. 699, 4864, 5801, 4870. Latilly was one of the few Capetian lawyers for whom there are documents in English archives concerning his embassies. See *Cal. Close Rolls, 1296-1302,* p. 445; *Treaty Rolls, 1234-1325,* ed. Pierre Chaplais, no. 500; and the unpublished letter in Ancient Correspondence, Vol. 36, no. 134 (Public Record Office, London).

[21] *Comptes royaux,* Part 1, p. 346.   [22] A.N., JJ. 46, no. 152.

[23] A.N., JJ. 49, no. 43; B.N., Collection Moreau, Vol. 220, fol. 7-9 v.; Vol. 221, fol. 50-53 v.; Archives départementales de l'Aisne, G. 253, fol. 29-30.

success came in the field of ecclesiastical preferments. He had obtained the treasurership of Angers at an early date, and throughout the following years accumulated prebends, canonicates, and two archdeaconries. In April 1312, Pierre de Latilly was named bishop of Cahors.[24] This was doubtless one of the many papal favors showered upon royal clerks during the closing months of the Council of Vienne. For several reasons Latilly did not want this southern bishopric. He was a native of northern France and had most of his interests and duties there. He also had enemies in the south. More than this, he had his eyes on the bishopric of Châlons, which he was in a good position to receive and which would make him a peer of the realm. In any event, he refused the nomination to Cahors and a year later received the bishopric of Châlons-sur-Marne.

The most striking characteristic of Pierre de Latilly's career was his involvement in the king's tax business. To say that he was a mere tax collector would be a gross misstatement of his importance. He rarely if ever collected taxes. Like most of the royal commissioners and lawyers, he was the administrator who determined methods and procedures and saw that the machinery moved. Wherever he went he had at his command a small army of lesser officials who were usually attached to the *sénéchaussée* or *bailliage* in which he was working. These men did the actual work as shown by the mission of 1297-1298. Because of his constant work in fiscal matters, we may say that Latilly played a large—perhaps the most important—role in formulating Philip the Fair's fiscal policy. Most of the evidence points to the conclusion that the major figures in the Parlement who were sent out

---

[24] *Clement V*, nos. 7,827, 9,044, 9,278. He had received a canonry at Châlons in 1305 and was made archdeacon in 1307. For these and his other prebends, see *Ibid.*, nos. 557, 1,661, 2,848. Although he was excused from making residence in the archdeaconry of Châlons, he kept a house in that city. See Archives départementales de la Marne, G. 475, no. 2.

to execute royal policy were usually the men who had made the policy. Convincing proof of this theory exists in the careers of Nogaret and Plaisians, and especially in the work of Philippe de Villepreux.

In brief, Pierre de Latilly was one of the four or five men who were the work horses of Philip the Fair's regime, and his career was turbulent and perilous. From the beginning of his service to Philip he was subjected to a crushing financial liability. In his first commission on new acquisitions of noble land, he handled large sums of money and was held fully accountable. In two accounts rendered during this commission he delivered to the Treasury some 4,000 *l. tour.* and this was not all that was collected from that assignment. But the responsibility that he bore at that moment was insignificant when compared to the sums that he handled during the mission of 1297-1298. Something like 70,000 *l. tour.* passed through his hands over a period of two years.[25] And we can only guess at the liability which he incurred during the collection of confiscated Jewish wealth. This sort of accountability signified Philip's confidence in Latilly, but it also carried the seeds of suspicion that could blossom at a later date. More than this, the lawyer made enemies by his conduct in these fiscal matters. He brooked no interference where the king's financial interests were concerned, and he became one of the most hated royal agents. This reputation grew and followed Latilly until the king found it necessary to defend him. When Plaisians and Latilly were sent to Clement about 1309, Philip sent a letter ahead asking the pope not to give ear to the malicious reports made against these two by their enemies.[26] Because of his constant responsibility in money matters and because of the hatred that he created, it is not surprising that Pierre de Latilly came to grief in 1315.

[25] *Journ. Philippe IV*, nos. 559, 2266, 3128.
[26] A.N., JJ. 42A, no. 67.

Of Philip the Fair's lawyers, Pierre de Latilly fell most completely from view after his trial. There is no evidence that he ever returned to the government after he was arrested, and we may say that his career of twenty-five years ended in December 1314. He was re-established in his bishopric about 1319 and spent the next decade attending to affairs in Châlons. Perhaps he did not wish to come back to the royal service; perhaps Philip V and Charles IV would not have him. As a peer of the realm, he was present at the coronation of Charles IV and there was the incident when he asked the king to free a serf in his native village of Latilly.[27] Otherwise he spent his last years administering his bishopric, settling jurisdictional disputes, and purchasing new holdings.[28] It seems that he acquired these lands as a private person and not as a bishop. He had his episcopal house at Paris and may have been a frequent visitor there, but his influence and work in government ended with the death of Philip the Fair.[29] He lived to see the end of the Capetian dynasty and died on March 15, 1328.

There were many cases of relatives serving in the government of the last Capetians. Fathers and sons, uncles and nephews, brothers and inlaws, some established service dynasties and others did not. So far as lawyers were concerned, the most interesting of these family groups under the last Capetians was the noble Mornay family, whose ancestral lands lay between Bourges and Nevers. We have to deal

---

[27] A.N., JJ. 64, no. 187.

[28] Most of the information on Latilly after he was acquitted comes from the ecclesiastical documents at Châlons. In point of time, they present a picture of him administering his bishopric between 1320 and 1326. See Archives départementales de la Marne, G. 171; G. 198; G. 200; G. 250; G. 406, no. 12; G. 484, no. 4. Among these documents is a register (G. 10) which appears to be Latilly's own cartulary as bishop. These sources show the bishop acquiring land, consecrating churches, litigating with his chapter, and making gifts.

[29] Archives départementales de la Marne, G. 199, in which the Hôtel de Châlons at Paris is mentioned in connection with Pierre de Latilly.

here with an uncle and three nephews. The uncle was Pierre de Mornay, who became bishop of Orléans in 1288 and later transferred to the bishopric of Auxerre. Learned in civil and canon law he appeared as a king's clerk at the beginning of Philip's reign and served him loyally until his death in 1306. Pierre de Mornay participated, like Flote, Aicelin, and Belleperche, in some of the most important diplomatic negotiations at the turn of the century. He assisted in the peace talks of 1295 between France and Aragon and was present at Montreuil-sur-Mer in 1299. With Aicelin he exercised a restraining influence on Philip in Saisset's case but sided with his king in the ultimate break with Boniface. His role in the development of the law school at Orléans is hinted at but never elaborated. With his university background and love of learning it is clear that it was he who steered his three nephews into an academic and ecclesiastical life.[30]

We presume that these three nephews were brothers, and the most important was Etienne de Mornay, who replaced Pierre de Latilly and served as chancellor during the brief reign of Louis X. Historians know that he was Charles de Valois' protégé, having been the count's own chancellor, and Valois was responsible for his entry into Capetian government after the death of Philip the Fair.[31] We also know that he reappeared after 1320 as an officer in the Chamber of Accounts and that he died in 1332. His career before he came to Valois' service and his fate after he was removed from the Chancery in 1316 have never been noticed. In 1302 Boniface VIII gave Etienne de Mornay permission to

[30] F. Guessard, "Pierre de Mornay," *B.E.C.*, v (1843-1844), 153-170; B.N., Collection Moreau, Vol. 211, fol. 170; *Boniface VIII*, nos. 202, 904 (for transfer to Auxerre), 1130, 2940, 4823, and no. 4013 in which the pope asked for his advice in the matter of adding another doctor of civil law to the faculty at Orléans.

[31] There is little information in the short study of Guessard, "Etienne de Mornay, chancelier de France sous Louis Hutin," *B.E.C.*, v (1843-1844), 373-396. See also Joseph Petit, *Charles de Valois*, p. 252f., which is taken from Guessard's article.

study civil law for seven years while nonresident in his ecclesiastical prebends.[32] He was then a canon of Auxerre
where his uncle was bishop. There is little doubt that he
studied law at Orléans for he was a professor of law there in
1306 when he and Michel Mauconduit besought Clement V
to give privileges to the university.[33] The date of his entry
into Valois' service is uncertain but he probably came to it
through his uncle who had served in 1295 as the count's
proctor.[34]

Philip V brought his own chancellor to the government in
the summer of 1316 and Etienne de Mornay returned to his
role as counselor of Charles de Valois. At the same time, he
resumed his academic career, for John XXII gave him a five-
year study permit in September 1316.[35] Study permits were
used for either study or teaching, and Mornay most certainly
used his for the latter purpose. Several Capetian lawyers
came to government from the academic profession, but
Etienne de Mornay was the only one who definitely continued his teaching career while engaged in state affairs.
His study permit was renewed in 1320, 1324, and 1328.[36] And
when he returned to the central government under Charles
IV, he remained in the service of Valois and was named
in 1328 as a counselor of the count's second son.[37] Ecclesiastic, university professor, counselor to Valois, and civil servant to Charles IV, Etienne de Mornay pursued four careers
in the last decade of his life. He was unsuccessful in his bid
for the bishopric of Auxerre in 1330 and died two years later.

Everything about the Mornay family in the early four-

---

[32] *Boniface VIII*, no. 4824. In an undated letter of Clement V, he
was called *legum professor* and given a canonry in Laon. The date of
the letter must have been 1306 (*Clement V*, no. 990).

[33] *Ibid.*, no. 359.

[34] *Boniface VIII*, no. 216.

[35] *Jean XXII*, nos. 945, 947-948.

[36] *Ibid.*, nos. 10,808, 19,062, 40,923. He was dean of St. Martin
of Tours during his later years.

[37] *Ibid.*, no. 43,106.

teenth century smacked of books, learning, and academic achievement. Despite his service in the house of Valois, Etienne de Mornay was a perennial academician. His brothers were struck from the same mold. When the younger Pierre de Mornay left the Franciscans in 1310 to enter the Benedictine Order, he received special permission from Clement V to keep the books that had been given to him by his friends.[38] In 1322 John XXII ordered the chancellor of Paris to confer on Pierre *magistralem honorem et licentiam docendi.* He never entered governmental service but became abbot of the Benedictine house of Saint Laumer in Blois and was a doctor of theology when he died in 1336.[39] The third brother, Philippe de Mornay, was a lawyer and had a long and quiet career in the government of the last Capetians, serving from 1292 until 1318 when he returned to university duties. When he died in 1327 he left to his nephew, a second Etienne de Mornay, his books of civil and canon law on condition that Etienne remain in clerical orders.[40] But the younger Etienne did not choose to follow his uncles. He returned to secular life, inherited his father's seigneury and was still living in 1357.[41]

[38] *Clement V,* no. 5,350.

[39] *Jean XXII,* no 15,708; A.N., L. 881, nos. 42, 43.

[40] On Philippe de Mornay's career, see *Boniface VIII,* no. 4,822; *Jean XXII,* nos. 6,712, 16,314, 18,299; *Mignon,* pp. 201, 235, 346; *Olim,* III, 1,053, 1,055, 1,185. His will is in A.N., L. 881, no. 42.

[41] A.N., L. 881, no. 12.

CHAPTER FIVE

Philippe de Villepreux

IN THE index to the recently published calendar of Philip the Fair's Chancery Registers, the name of Philippe de Villepreux occurs more often than any other except that of Maillard, king's secretary and notary. While the frequency with which a name occurs says nothing about the importance of a person, it is in the case of Villepreux an indication of his role in the government of Philip the Fair. Philippe de Villepreux stands apart from the other lawyers of the last Capetians in that he had an unusual connection with the king; his rise to power and wealth depended as much on this connection as on his natural talent for law and administration. He was a man of driving energy and robust health for he spent most of his career traveling on royal business, mainly in Normandy but also in other parts of the realm. At the same time he had a permanent part in the Parlement de Paris and enjoyed liberal access to the royal household. Like many of Philip's lawyers, Villepreux accumulated landed estates that made him a great seigneur although he never carried the title of seigneur. In addition to his landed rents he received the revenues from a host of ecclesiastical offices that came to him by royal intervention. Despite his prominence and power, Villepreux has never found his biographer.[1]

The basic problem of Philippe de Villepreux's career concerns his origins, identity, and relation to Philip the Fair.

[1] Villepreux received some attention in the thesis of Marie Elizabeth Carreau, *Les commissaires royaux aux amortissements et aux nouveaux acquêts sous les Capetiens, 1275-1328*, P.T.E.C. (1953), pp. 19-22. Lehugeur, *Philippe V le Long: Le mécanisme du gouvernement*, p. 81f., recognized Villepreux as a *rouage essentiel* in Philip's government. But many of Lehugeur's remarks on Villepreux's life are inaccurate. See also the notice in André Guillois, *Recherches sur les maîtres des requêtes de l'Hôtel* (Paris, 1909), pp. 219-221.

The king sponsored him at baptism and gave him his name. He was, therefore, Philip's godson and because of this relationship the king showed a personal interest in Villepreux's career and advancement. But there is something far more astonishing in Villepreux's origins than the fact that he was the king's godson. His proper Latin name was *Philippus de Villa Petrosa* but his contemporaries and the scribes in the royal Chancery most often called him *Philippus Conversus* or *Philippe le Convers*. Is it possible that we are dealing with a converted Jew? All of the evidence points to this conclusion. Medieval kings ordinarily patronized and encouraged the conversion of Jews, and Villepreux's popular name and the king's sponsorship of his baptism reinforce the belief that he was a converted Jew. This basic fact in Villepreux's life gives added significance and interest to his entire career, both in the king's service and in the Church.[2]

The native village of Philip the Fair's godson was Villepreux, located on the southern border of the Forest of Marly and just to the west of Versailles. To the north of Marly were the important royal château of Saint Germain-en-Laye and the vast forest that surrounded it. Perhaps Villepreux came to know his royal patron through relatives who served in some manner in the household organization at Saint Germain-en-Laye.[3] The recently published accounts of Philip the

[2] Without giving his source, Lehugeur, *Philippe V le Long: le mécanisme du gouvernement,* p. 81, asserted that Villepreux was the son of a *portier* in Philip III's household. He must have noticed the two references for 1286 and 1290 in Langlois, *Textes relatifs à l'histoire du parlement,* p. 129, in which a Philippot le Convers is named as *portier* in the Parlement. One cannot determine whether these items refer to Villepreux's father, to himself, or to some entirely different person. Langlois had no doubt that Villepreux was a converted Jew (*Livre Rouge,* p. 149, note 1).

[3] No relation exists between Philippe and Jean de Villepreux who was a household knight and *maître d'Hôtel* of Philip the Fair. Both men came from the same locale and their paths undoubtedly crossed many times in the royal household. Jean de Villepreux married Jeanne de l'Isle (*Clement V,* no. 7,675). See also A.N., JJ. 46, nos. 31, 108, and H. Lemoine, "Notes historiques sur Villepreux," *Revue de l'his-*

Fair contain large sections devoted to stipends and pensions that were paid to serjeants, keepers, cooks, barbers, other household servants, and their children. And scattered among these payments to household servants are numerous references to converts who also received payments that clearly constituted a part of household expenditures. For 1299 and again for 1305, stipends were registered for "Philippotus Conversus, filiolus regis."[4] Although Villepreux was well engaged in his career by 1299, he probably continued to receive a convert's pension through the royal household. Other converts whom we will later identify as his brothers and sister were also pensioned in the same block of accounts. The personal relationship between the king and his godson speaks of a household connection although it cannot be explained. So far as can be determined, the two men were about the same age, and Philip, while still a boy in his father's house, may have come to know this child of a household servant. There can be little doubt that the two knew each other before 1285, and therefore knew each other as children.

Apart from being the king's godson, Philippe de Villepreux holds another distinction among the lawyers of Philip the Fair. He appeared at an earlier date than any of the others although he was not actively engaged in governmental business at the moment. In 1285 the king was already supporting his godson with an annual stipend of 25 *l.*, with continuance until Villepreux received an ecclesiastical living.[5] Royal sponsorship of Villepreux was further emphasized when, in the same year, the king gave 40 *l.* to "master Philippe le Convers, godson of the king, to buy books of law."[6] The

toire de Versailles et de Seine-et-Oise (1931), pp. 66-86, 131-153, for comment on the history of the village.

[4] *Comptes royaux*, Part 1, pp. 34, 176.

[5] H. d'Arbois de Jubainville, *Histoire des ducs et des comtes de Champagne*, II, Appendix, p. lxxxii; Longnon, III, 31.

[6] *Ibid.*, p. 33; Jubainville, *Histoire des ducs et des comtes de Champagne*, II, Appendix, p. lxxxv.

revenue and the grant came out of the issues of Champagne, but there is no indication of where the young clerk was studying law. The logical place was Orléans, in which case he probably knew as professors such men as Pierre de Belleperche and perhaps Michel Mauconduit. By his own admission, which he made late in life, Villepreux studied at several universities and his entire education was paid for by Philip the Fair. When he came to the king's service he brought with him superb academic training, probably as good as any lawyer possessed in the late thirteenth century.

Villepreux made his debut in governmental administration in 1293 when he appeared in the Parlement de Paris. He was at that time associated with Pierre de Latilly.[7] By 1298 Villepreux had acquired a permanent position as a master in the Parlement, and his name was listed with those of Aicelin, Belleperche, and Nogaret as members of the court.[8] His education was presumably completed, and he was well equipped by his legal training to sit with the masters in the royal law courts, to make inquests, to hear *requêtes,* and to issue *arrêts.* He received payments for his robes, and he received wages for attending Parlement.[9] But most of the evidence on Villepreux concerns his work in the field. During his early years in the king's service, he was sent to collect revenues from bishoprics and to collect military subsidies and various taxes in Reims and Châlons and parts of Normandy. He was even used on an embassy to Germany in 1300.[10] The work which he did during his early career was, therefore, as varied and unspecialized as that performed by other lawyers such as Flote, Nogaret, and Belleperche. In 1300 his period of

[7] Boutaric, no. 2,857, in which Nicholas de Chartres gave to Villepreux the reports of several inquests.

[8] For his early work in the Parlement with Belleperche, Nogaret, and Aicelin, see *Olim,* II, 423.

[9] *Journ. Philippe IV,* nos. 694, 2,466.

[10] *Ibid.,* nos. 690, 3,118, 3,671, 4,103; *Mignon,* pp. 67, 151, 153, 180; Fawtier, *Comptes du Trésor,* no. 299; *Comptes royaux,* Part 2, pp. 399-401, 402-403.

specialization lay ahead of him, and the field in which he came to specialize brought him an abundance of wealth and royal favor. The second half of Philip the Fair's reign was the period in which Philippe de Villepreux reached administrative maturity and made his greatest contribution to the government of the realm. We shall never know why the king's godson came to be a specialist in the field of forest law and administration. Perhaps, while sitting in the Parlement during his early years, he showed such a talent for cases involving forest law that those above him or the king himself came increasingly to assign him to that sort of work.

There is, however, a better reason for Villepreux's specialization in forest affairs. Medieval kings considered no form of landed wealth more valuable than the royal forests. An all-important source of timber and game, these forests also yielded tremendous revenue by way of usage and rights. More than this, the king had a special attachment to his forests that amounted most often to jealous guardianship. No laws were made more abundant and detailed nor broken more frequently than those of the royal forests, and no violations were punished more earnestly than those of forest law. In the case of England, a king had been brought to his knees partly as a result of his forest administration, and Englishmen had enjoyed for a hundred years the rights and guarantees of a Forest Charter. That same king had lost in 1204 the prized duchy of Normandy to a French monarch who promptly made it his royal domain, and Normandy thenceforth occupied a particular place in the affections of French kings.[11] In proportion to the size of the duchy, the forest acreage of Normandy was probably greater than that of any other section of crown lands. Philip the Fair, who was constantly preoccupied with fiscal affairs, had to be assured

[11] J. R. Strayer, *The Administration of Normandy under Saint Louis* (Cambridge, Mass., 1932), Chapter 6 on the administration of the forests.

that the person who watched over his domanial forests in Normandy was absolutely loyal to him and would prosecute and protect his forest rights with the utmost diligence and interest. The task, therefore, took on the aspects of a very personal assignment, and Philip chose a lawyer who was bound to him as godson to sponsor, a man whom he had known from childhood and whom he had educated.

The office that Villepreux occupied from about 1300 was that of forest inquisitor. Through royal commissions he inspected and supervised an army of forest administrators and usually held authority over the masters of forests and even over *baillis* and seneschals on occasion. When he went into the forests of Normandy he was usually associated with a *bailli* or more often with Jean le Veneur and Geoffroi Danois. Both of these men carried the title of "master of the forests" or "master of the forests of Normandy."[12] In 1308 when Villepreux took a commission to the forests of Languedoc, he worked with Guillaume de Saint Marcel, "master of waters and forests."[13] The lawyer never carried any of these titles but was repeatedly named "inquisitor for the king's forests."[14] He was engaged in this capacity almost continuously from 1300 to 1314, and usually in the forests of Normandy. But he also operated in the forests of Champagne, the Ile-de-France, Poitou, and Languedoc. His methods were similar to those of Latilly and others who did not hesitate to terrorize their victims. He used the informer as well as the casual witness, and, if reticence or fear of reprisal hampered him in securing his evidence openly, he gathered it in secret.[15] He arrested and condemned malefactors whether they were officials or private persons, and reported to the

---

[12] A.N., JJ. 38, no. 35; JJ. 48, no. 92; JJ. 49, no. 200.

[13] A.N., JJ. 42A, no. 26; JJ. 49, no. 69.

[14] A.N., JJ. 37, no. 90; JJ. 45, no. 120; JJ. 50, no. 36; JJ. 53, no. 190.

[15] A revealing glimpse of Villepreux at work can be found in some of his accounts in *Comptes royaux*, Part 2, pp. 559-561. Other accounts showing his supervision of forests are in *Mignon*, pp. 285, 357, 359.

king on every instance of abuse, graft, and corruption that
he uncovered in forest administration.[16] During this period
no other man was assigned to such work; Villepreux managed it alone.

The best example of the authority conferred on Villepreux can be found in the sweeping commission of 1308 that
took him into Languedoc. He was charged with the reformation of royal forests and forest serjeants, officers, and *châte-
lains* in the *sénéchaussées* of Toulouse, Carcassonne, Sain-
tonge, Poitou, Périgord, and Beaucaire. He was given power
to create or change royal agents, to modify their wages, and
to hold inquests wherever necessary. Seneschals were ordered to obey him and to put their facilities at his disposal.[17]
This assignment kept him and his companion, Guillaume de
Saint Marcel, busy for about six months. In the early spring
of 1309 the two issued a reorganization scheme for the forests of Languedoc, named two new officers as masters of the
royal forests of five *sénéchaussées,* and stipulated their salaries.[18] All of this was approved by the king. As late as 1312
Villepreux was ordering letters out of Chancery that confirmed the actions taken by his appointees in the south.[19]

More important than his office or commissions were the
results of Villepreux's work. As forest inquisitor he made in
a concrete way a greater and more lasting contribution to
royal government than did Flote, Nogaret, or Plaisians.
Through fifteen years of constant traveling, Villepreux came
to know every forest in Normandy, its boundaries, its financial yield, royal rights, customs, laws, and the personnel
who administered it. His knowledge of the other royal forests
was almost as great. In the end he became the judge of all
matters pertaining to the forests. He amended this custom,
re-established and corrected that one, made new laws where

[16] A.N., JJ. 38, nos. 35, 36, 38.   [17] A.N., JJ. 42A, no. 26.
[18] A.N., JJ. 48, no. 133.
[19] A.N., JJ. 48, no. 160; *Mignon,* p. 287.

none existed, and settled, one after the other, conflicting claims on usage and rights between the king and bishops and nobles. When he returned to Paris after each commission he ordered letters dealing with the problems that he had encountered. The letters that he ordered out of Chancery were not in the same category with those that were ordered by the king, or the chancellor, or other men in their capacity as members of the king's council. If one looks closely at the Chancery Registers, one will see that the great majority of letters ordered by Villepreux dealt with forest affairs.[20]

The career of Philippe de Villepreux offers the most convincing proof for the theory that those lawyers of Philip the Fair who executed royal policy were usually the ones who made the policy. From a careful examination of the letters ordered out of Chancery by Villepreux and which concerned forest matters, and from an equally careful study of his work in the field, one receives the distinct impression that this man was both the author and executor of royal forest policy. In his case, the theory worked both ways. Having written a commission for the examination of forest business, Villepreux then went out and executed the commission as forest inquisitor. With the knowledge of conditions that he had acquired firsthand in the field, he returned to Paris, made his report, and proceeded to formulate corrective legislation. Once again, the 1308 commission to Languedoc serves best to illustrate this point. Villepreux must be regarded in large part as the author of that commission which gave him such broad authority, and for four years after the commission Villepreux followed up on the various appointments and orders that he had made during and after that

[20] Of some seventy recorded letters ordered out of Chancery by Villepreux between 1300-1314, more than half were concerned with the creation and revision of forest law and administration. For examples, see A.N., JJ. 45, no. 120; JJ. 47, nos. 53, 89; JJ. 48, nos. 26, 67, 89, 92, 104, 132, 133, 136, 158, 160; JJ. 49, no. 200. See also Petit, *Essai de restitution*, p. 92f.

assignment. At the end of Philip the Fair's reign, the forest law and administration of France was what Philippe de Villepreux had made it in the course of fifteen years. It was his personal monument, and no other lawyer, clerk, or agent of the last Capetian kings could claim a monument of similar dimensions or importance.

Philip the Fair liberally rewarded Villepreux for his intense devotion to the royal service and enabled him to accumulate large landed holdings in Normandy. In the end, his landed wealth probably did not compare favorably to that of Marigny or Nogaret, but it certainly rivaled that of other lawyers. He began modestly enough when he acquired in 1308 the fief of Duréçu near Cherbourg, which gave him an annual income of about 28 *l.*; to this was added 20 *l. par.* In 1310 he received the fief of Le Mouchel near Etrépagny; this fief was capitalized at 464 *l. par.*, which meant an income of about 58 *l. par.* Most of the lands in Normandy were capitalized at a rate of eight to one over their annually produced revenue. In the same year he added to his holdings the manor of Corny and Longuemare situated north of Les Andelys, which added 189 *l. par.* to his income. This was not a gift and he paid the king when one of his houses in Paris, appraised at 1,000 *l.*, was appropriated for the vast building program that Marigny had underway on the royal palace.[21]

Throughout these exchanges and acquisitions, Villepreux's method of operation became clear. He was constantly engaged in acquiring small money rents that were payable from the royal treasury; he then transferred these money rents to the king in exchange for landed rents. But the total of these small rents amounted to a large figure, and Villepreux was enabled to continue the amassing of estates. When

[21] These acquisitions and exchanges may be found in A.N., JJ. 40, no. 52; JJ. 45, no. 164; JJ. 45, nos. 147, 169, 170; *Livre Rouge*, no. 509.

it seemed that he had surrendered all of his money rents to the king, he would purchase new rents from some noble or other person who needed cash. At one time, he owned money rents on the Châtelet, the *prévotés* of Paris, Orléans, Vernon, the *vicomté* of Pont-de-l'Arche, the Norman Excheq-uer, and the royal treasury. Sometimes the purchase price of these money rents came to 800 *l.* or 1,000 *l.*, which meant that Villepreux had steady access to a cash income which he used to multiply his wealth.[22] On the face of the matter, there was no question of financial manipulations; Villepreux enjoyed a large money income from his ecclesiastical bene-fices.

Philippe de Villepreux never accumulated large estates in or around his native village. But he finally settled on a par-ticular locale in which he wished to construct a landed em-pire, and then directed all of his transactions to that end. That time came in 1311, at the very moment that Raoul de Presles was piecing together his estates in the valley of the Aisne. After the Seine passes Les Andelys, it makes a sharp swing to the south and then again to the north as it continues toward Rouen. On this northward swing, the Seine comes close to the Eure and flows parallel to it before the two rivers merge at Pont-de-l'Arche. The fertile farmland between the two rivers forms a fluvial peninsula about eight miles in length and two in width. It was this land that Philippe de Villepreux chose to make his own. The first step in its ac-quisition occurred when Philip the Fair gave him the manor and lands of Léry in exchange for Corny, La Marette, and *Monte Petrosa*, which the king wished to give to the Domini-cans at Poissy. Appended to Léry were rents on the villages of Les Damps and Poses and on the mills near Léry and on

---

[22] For Villepreux's purchases and exchanges of money rents, see A.N., JJ. 45, no. 126; JJ. 47, nos. 3, 33; JJ. 46, nos. 52, 163, 191; JJ. 47, nos. 93, 94; *Livre Rouge*, nos. 556, 571, 613; B.N., Collection Moreau, Vol. 221, fol. 12, 15 v., 18-21.

Vernon. The total was estimated at 329 *l.* 5*s.* 4*d.* of annual income, which exceeded the value of Corny and its appendages. The king remitted the excess to his godson. All that Villepreux acquired during the next three years was directed toward the increase of his fief of Léry. He gained control of the villages of Vaudreuil, Tournedos, Porte-Joie, Le Vauvray, and Incarville, sometimes by private purchase, sometimes in exchanges with the king. When Philip the Fair died in 1314, Philippe de Villepreux held all of the land between the Eure and the Seine and, moreover, enjoyed income from lands scattered throughout Normandy.[23] His landed rents and money rents must have amounted to about 2,000 *l.* at that time, and these did not include his ecclesiastical benefices.

From the moment that Villepreux began his education he also decided to pursue an ecclesiastical career. University education and clerical status went hand in hand north of the Alps although innumerable clerks left clerical status after obtaining their education. The stipend which the king gave to his godson in 1285 was intended to support him until he was provided with an ecclesiastical living. At what point he obtained his first prebend is unknown, but he was a canon of Tournai by 1300 and continued to advance in his clerical career. In 1308 Clement V confirmed his appointment as treasurer of St. Etienne of Troyes, but he surrendered this office a year later in order to keep the archdeaconry of Brie. At that time he held canonicates and prebends in Paris, Noyons, Tournai, Meaux, and Troyes. Within a few years he obtained the archdeaconry of Eu in Normandy and on one occasion was called archdeacon of Pont-Audemer. The last benefice which he obtained was the treasurership of

[23] For the manner in which he pieced together his holdings between the Seine and the Eure, see A.N., JJ. 46, nos. 5, 163, 191; JJ. 48, nos. 94, 140, 143; JJ. 49, nos. 66, 127, 143, 167, 202; JJ. 50, nos. 76, 82, 90; *Livre Rouge*, no. 570; B.N., Collection Moreau, Vol. 221, fol. 69 r.-v.

Reims in 1318.[24] All of these offices and prebends came to
him through royal intervention. He never made residence
in any of them for, as a king's clerk, he was permitted to
receive his ecclesiastical income without making residence.
It is impossible to estimate the total of his ecclesiastical income; it was large and he apparently used it to purchase
money rents which he surrendered to the king in return for
landed rents at Léry and elsewhere.

Philippe de Villepreux was not the only member of his
family who benefited from royal patronage. The evidence on
his brothers and sister supports the view that he was one of
several children who grew up as converts in the royal household. The royal accounts of 1299 and 1305 mention stipends
paid to Thomas and Isabelle, brother and sister of the lawyer, and to Jean de Villepreux, who was his nephew.[25]
Thomas was an assistant to his brother at the turn of the
century, then became provost of Pontoise and eventually
rose to be *vicomte* of Rouen.[26] Louis de Villepreux was another brother who was *vicomte* of Bayeux before he became
bailli of the Cotentin, one of the highest offices in Normandy.
He may have been the same person who acquired in 1320
the serjeantry of the *plaid de l'épée* of Valognes.[27]

One of Philippe's nephews, Simon de Villepreux, pursued
a clerical career, became a canon of Péronne, and held lands
at Léry that were undoubtedly given to him by his uncle.[28]

---

[24] *Clement V*, nos. 3,681, 3,832; A.N., JJ. 53, no. 331; JJ. 56, no.
263.

[25] *Comptes royaux*, Part 1, pp. 32, 173, 176, 179.

[26] *Journ. Philippe IV*, nos. 3,118, 3,211, 3,765; A.N., JJ. 54B, no.
36; *Comptes royaux*, Part 1, p. 230.

[27] On Louis de Villepreux, see Léopold Delisle, "Mémoire sur les
baillis du Cotentin," *Mémoires de la société des antiquaires de Nor-
mandie*, XIX (1851), 61-119, and the same author in *H.F.*, XXIV, Part
1, pp. 153-154. Delisle believed that the *bailli* was dead by 1317, and
that the person mentioned in 1320 was another of Philippe's brothers
with the name of Louis. See also A.N., JJ. 59, no. 476, and *Comptes
royaux*, Part 1, p. 320.

[28] A.N., JJ. 56, no. 480; *Jean XXII*, nos. 6,553, 12,948.

Jean de Villepreux was another nephew, son of Louis, and received as a royal gift the serjeantry of the *plaid de l'épée* of Bayeux.[29] Philippe's sister, Isabelle, married a non-noble *gruyère* of Champagne by the name of Jean de Jouy.[30] The lawyer was undoubtedly responsible for the patronage received by his relatives. It is an interesting fact that most of Villepreux's relatives held their offices in Normandy and that Normandy was the main theatre of the lawyer's career. The Villepreux family represented an increasingly common phenomenon in French government, that of several members of a non-noble family serving the king in important posts. No tradition of royal service was founded in this instance for we cannot trace the careers of Philippe's nephews.

Villepreux's career as a forest inquisitor came to an end with Philip the Fair's death. The great task of revising and remaking forest administration had been completed, and the lawyer may have asked for less strenuous duties. He was untouched by the trials of 1315 and was busy during that summer selling freedom to the serfs of Vermandois. Under Philip V his position in the council increased in importance, and he was present in the deliberations of that body more often than any other non-noble *conseiller*.[31] He also developed an attachment to the household of Philip's queen, Jeanne de Bourgogne, which cannot be explained. He served for a brief period as her chancellor. The strangest incident in his relationship with the queen was the transfer to her in 1318 of his manor and fief of Léry. This has mistakenly been called a gift, but the king gave Villepreux compensation in the fief of Le Mesnil-Ozenne and neighboring lands which were located on the southern border of Normandy near

---

[29] A.N., JJ. 59, no. 514.

[30] A.N., JJ. 56, no. 580. His brother-in-law collected from him when he was *gruyère* of Bassigny in 1305 (*Comptes royaux*, Part 1, p. 320).

[31] Lehugeur, *Philippe V le Long; le mécanisme du gouvernement*, p. 31.

Avranches almost within sight of Mont-Saint-Michel.[32] Despite the compensation one must wonder why Villepreux surrendered a rich and well-situated seigneury which he had so laboriously pieced together.

The career of Philippe de Villepreux was on the surface a smooth and continuously successful one. He escaped the troubles of 1315 and seemed incapable of arousing the king's wrath. Perhaps this was due to his unique relation as godson to Philip the Fair, a relation which Philip's sons respected. Perhaps it was due to Villepreux's indisputable loyalty and devotion to royal business. In this respect, he fits the picture usually painted of the Capetian lawyers. But these lawyers had alarming lapses of loyalty where financial acquisitions were concerned, and Villepreux was no exception. Furthermore, the king's godson was not immune to the corrupting influence that came from constant accumulation of power and success, and he was finally persuaded to violate the express will of his royal master. In 1318, Philippe was ordered by the king to remove his nephew, Jean de Villepreux, from the enfeoffed serjeantry of the *plaid de l'épée* of Bayeux. Jean had forfeited the serjeantry for "reasonable and evident causes," and the king permitted Philippe to replace his nephew with whomever he pleased. Villepreux, in defiance of the king's order, continued to let his nephew occupy the serjeantry and the situation was not fully revealed until Charles IV came to the throne and finally removed the nephew.[33]

Discrepancies in Villepreux's financial dealings with the king were also uncovered during the reign of the last Capetian, and the most interesting one concerned the transfer of Léry to Philip V's queen, which occurred in 1318. Six years

[32] *Ibid.*, p. 82. The documents on the surrender of Léry and the acquisition of Mesnil-Ozenne are found in A.N., JJ. 53, nos. 77, 331; JJ. 56, nos. 35, 174, 390, 397, 463, 481; *Livre Rouge*, nos. 1,077-79, 1,081.
[33] A.N., JJ. 59, no. 514; JJ. 61, no. 323; JJ. 64, no. 73.

later in 1324, agents in the Chamber of Accounts discovered
that Villepreux had received duplicate compensation for his
surrender of the fief. At the time of transfer, royal agents
had appraised the manor at 197 *l.* of income, which meant
a capitalized value of 1,576 *l.* Philip V had given to Villepreux the fief of Le Mesnil-Ozenne and other lands in compensation. But the lawyer had also managed to exact a cash
indemnity of 2,200 *l.* from Philip V, and had kept the affair
quiet for six years. When the error was discovered, Villepreux
was condemned to return the cash indemnity. But because
of his service to the king's brothers and father, Charles IV
acquitted him of the debt.[34] At the end of his career, short-
ages amounting to over 1,000 *l.* were discovered in some of
his old accounts, but there is no notice of any action taken
against his estate.[35] Financial malfeasance that could not
be proved against Raoul de Presles and Pierre de Latilly
was proved against Philippe de Villepreux. But the king's
godson went without punishment.

The last Capetian kings were unusually benevolent toward
Philippe de Villepreux and were even willing to close their
eyes when his use of royal funds was less than honest or
when he deliberately disobeyed a royal command. Other
royal agents were not so fortunate. The reason for this liberal
treatment must be found in Villepreux's relation to Philip
the Fair. Toward the end of Philip V's reign, Villepreux
decided to found a house for the poor in his native village
and asked for royal approval to transfer landed rents to this
purpose. The royal letters contain some comment on the
beneficence of his godfather. These remarks constitute a

[34] The appraisal of Léry at 197 *l.* is in A.N., JJ. 56, no. 481. For
notices of compensation, see A.N., JJ. 56, nos. 96, 174. At one point,
the king ceded 700 *l. tour.* of rent to Villepreux for Léry, and 130 *l.* at
another time. Other rents totalling over 300 *l. tour.* were assigned
on different occasions (*Livre Rouge*, nos. 1077-79, 1081). For the dis-
covery of the matter and Villepreux's acquittal, see A.N., JJ. 62, no.
273.

[35] *Mignon*, p. 285f.

biographical note such as we do not have from any other Capetian lawyer:

"Master Philippe le Convers, treasurer of Reims, our clerk and councillor, has remembered in all humility the immense clemency and great goodness which was mercifully accorded him by our dearest lord and father who received him from the baptismal font, named him with his name, and saw that he received gentle training. After he came to boyhood, our father caused him to be educated in the knowledge of letters in various universities, always providing him with the necessities of books, clothing and sustenance. After he returned from the university, our father conferred many benefices on him and elevated him with great and various offices, and we, inheriting the character of our dearest lord and father, have used the prerogatives of special benevolence in increasing his benefices and offices."[36]

Philippe de Villepreux had a longer career than any Capetian lawyer and, if we count him as a royal agent from the moment that he appeared as a law student in 1285, his documented activities cover almost exactly the era of the last Capetians, or a period of some forty-two years. Villepreux is the best example of the Capetian lawyer who enjoyed continuous influence and authority under Philip and his three sons. So far as the evidence is concerned, he was never engaged in the great affairs of Philip's reign. His power actually increased under Philip V and his influence on policy-making between 1316 and 1322 must be considered as greater than that of any other lawyer. He appears to have been less active in the reign of Charles IV, and he died

[36] A.N., JJ. 59, no. 339. The matter of the poorhouse in Villepreux came up again in A.N., JJ. 60, no. 186, and Philippe referred to "la ville de Villepereur, ou ie fu nez." He also repeated the reference to Philip the Fair as his godfather, "qui de sains fons de bautesme me leva." As early as 1309, Villepreux had obtained papal permission to found a chapel in the church in his native village (*Clement V*, no. 3,796).

before the end of the Capetian era, probably in January
1327. His executors were at work on his will by the middle
of that year.[37] No Capetian lawyer came closer to knowing
and understanding the enigmatic personality of Philip the
Fair than did Villepreux. Since he had grown up with the
king, the king had a deep personal interest in Villepreux that
he did not have in Flote, Nogaret, or Plaisians. Because of
his relation to the king and because of his contribution to
royal administration, Philippe de Villepreux occupied a
unique position among the lawyers of the last Capetians.

[37] A.N., JJ. 64, nos. 516, 518. Notice of his death occurs in papal
letters as early as February 1327 (*Jean XXII*, nos. 28,021 bis., 28,332-
28,334, 29,166, 40,402, 44,572).

CHAPTER SIX

The Seigneur of Lizy

THE only instance of Raoul de Presles' participation in the great events of Philip the Fair's reign was his deposition against the Templars on April 11, 1310. He was the only royal agent to play such a role in that process. His second appearance in affairs of state occurred in 1315 when he was arrested and tried on the ostensible charge of *lèse-majesté*. The chronicles assert that he was implicated with Pierre de Latilly in the death of Philip the Fair. At that moment, the vast landed estates that Presles had accumulated were confiscated and distributed to members and servants of the royal house. Apart from these events, there is no direct evidence that portrays his role in the government of Philip the Fair. His prominence in the somber events of 1315 points to his importance and influence. But the mere study of his trial and acquittal leaves him a man of mystery with respect to his life and career.

Presles' deposition provides a good introduction to his earlier life and activity. He said in effect that he was born about 1270, which made him a close contemporary of the king and of Guillaume de Nogaret. During the first years of the century he lived at Laon and was presumably engaged in the practice of law. His acquaintance and conversations with Brother Gervais in Laon fell between 1301-1303. Far from being a casual friend, he was close to Gervais and had undoubtedly known the Templar for several years. Furthermore, Presles was the influential partner in this friendship, for Gervais asked him to speak on his behalf to the higher officers of the General Chapter. Presles not only represented Gervais to his superiors in the Order but also procured his friend's promotion to the General Chapter, and Gervais went on to accumulate power and authority. There can be no doubt about Raoul de Presles' influence with highly placed persons in Paris and Laon, even as early as 1304 or 1305. He was already a man of considerable professional and social status, and the Commander of the Temple in Laon was one of the lesser persons who admired and respected Presles' influence. One other point must be noted which was not in the deposition. Gervais was not only the Commander of the Temple in Laon; he was also the royal receiver of revenue in the *bailliage* of Vermandois, a position that was often filled elsewhere in the kingdom by brothers of the Order.[1] During his residence in Laon, Presles had moved within a circle of royal agents.

His deposition is neither the earliest nor the most striking document in the life of Raoul de Presles, and it raises more questions than it answers. Who was he and where had he come from? At what point had he transferred his residence from Laon to Paris? It was after 1303 for that is the latest date mentioned in the testimony. Was he, as a lawyer, in the service of the king? Although he was called simply "advocate in the court of the king," we know from other sources that he was a royal clerk at this time. It is possible that he had been king's advocate in the *bailliage* of Vermandois and his career as such parallels that of Nogaret, Plaisians, and d'Aumelas, who first served the king in Languedoc before being summoned to Paris. Finally, because there is an obvious veil of mystery around this man, we must ask if Raoul de Presles received compensation for his testimony against the Templars. This had been a noticeable, although routine, point of interrogation at the end of his deposition, and he flatly denied any reward. To investigate fully such a question, it will be necessary to examine carefully the landed acquisitions and financial transactions of Raoul de Presles during this period.

The earliest recorded grant of revenue for Raoul de Pres-

---

[1] A.N., JJ. 44, no. 23.

les places him in the service of Philip's eldest son, Louis, king of Navarre and count palatine of Champagne and Brie. For some time Raoul had received an annual income of 40 *l. par.* on the *prévoté* of Epernay, which was an administrative center of Champagne located on the Marne halfway between Châlons and Château-Thierry. He was undoubtedly one of the lawyers of the young Louis, and an annual revenue of 40 *l. par.* was an appreciable salary. In August 1308, Presles requested that the burden of this revenue be transferred from Epernay to the commune of Cys and Presles, whence he might amortize it for the purpose of founding two chapels in the parish church of Presles, one for Notre Dame and one for Saint Nicholas. Louis acceded to this request since the commune of Cys and Presles owed him an annual rent of 100 *l. par.*, and he added the proviso that the income might be received from his *prévoté* of Oulchy-le-Château in the event the commune was unable to pay. A few months later, Louis increased the stipend with an additional 20 *l. par.*, which Presles would receive from the commune and which he could also use to further endow the two chapels.[2] In this summer, Raoul de Presles began to accumulate revenues on the countryside in and around his native village of Presles in the valley of the Aisne. But these are the only grants of revenue recorded for him before his deposition against the Templars.

After Raoul de Presles' testimony eight months passed before he received another grant of rents. In the summer of 1310, Philip the Fair made with the abbey of Corbie an exchange of rents that formed the background to Presles' next acquisition. Among the extended holdings of the abbey, there was a "house" or *prévoté* called Courdemaine located in the town of Vailly, three miles west of the village of Presles. In exchange for the rights which Philip had on the commune

---

[2] Both grants are in A.N., JJ. 41, no. 21; JJ. 42B, no. 21. See also Longnon, II, 518; *Livre Rouge*, nos. 560, 561.

of Corbie, the abbey transferred to him its revenues of Courdemaine and of a manor called La Royère near Filain.[3] Then, in December, the king assigned at farm to Raoul de Presles the *prévoté* of Courdemaine, for which the lawyer was to pay an annual rent of 900 *l. tour.,* and for which he was required, moreover, to give in bond or pledge to Philip 200 *l. tour.* of annual rent on all the possessions which he held in the village and territory of Presles.[4] The revenues of the *prévoté* of Courdemaine were undoubtedly worth more than 900 *l. tour.,* and Presles stood to gain considerably by this assignment. The exact nature and character of the *prévoté* of Courdemaine is a difficult problem. When the commune was originally formed there was apparently territory within its limits and presumably close to the center of the town that was held by seigneurs other than the one who granted the commune. A part of this territory was the *prévoté* of Courdemaine; it contained a population composed largely of serfs who owed rents and other servile dues. Situated within the commune of Vailly, there was undoubtedly commercial activity in Courdemaine which was also taxable by the lord who held the *prévoté*. While the inhabitants of Vailly enjoyed self-government, there remained an island of seigneurial privilege in their midst which now came into the hands of Raoul de Presles.

Courdemaine was a desirable holding that yielded large revenues and its assignment to Raoul de Presles brings up the crucial problem of whether he received compensation for his deposition against the Templars. There are several points of interest in this grant which demand consideration. First of all, the rent involved in the grant was extremely large. Its very size catches the eye, for 900 *l. tour.* of revenue represented an assessed value of approximately 9,000 *l. tour.*

[3] A.N., JJ. 45, no. 185; JJ. 46, no. 114. The abbey's purpose was to recover control of the commune of Corbie.
[4] A.N., JJ. 47, no. 21.

in land holdings. A second point to be noted is that this assignment was the largest recorded grant of revenue ever made to Raoul de Presles by Philip the Fair or any other French king. More than that, it was one of only two recorded gifts from Philip to Raoul. The second and only other grant was made in March 1311, and consisted of 24 *l. par.* of annual rent on the villages of Condé-sur-Aisne and Celles-sur-Aisne, situated about six miles west of Presles.[5] Finally, as we have noted in the grant of Courdemaine, Raoul was required to put up a pledge of bond of 200 *l. tour.* on his possessions in the territory of Presles. The total income which Louis permitted him to transfer from Epernay to the commune of Cys and Presles came to only 60 *l. par.* In some unrecorded way, therefore, Raoul de Presles had acquired far more than 60 *l.* of revenues in the region of his native village. But all efforts to determine how he acquired these rents are frustrated by the lack of information. And the evidence which we can adduce to show that Courdemaine was Presles' reward for his deposition is as circumstantial as the testimony he gave against the Templars. Still, Courdemaine constituted an impressive and unusual grant and we must look for an impressive and unusual service worthy of such financial reward. No matter how the problem is appraised, Raoul de Presles' deposition seemed to be linked with the grant of Courdemaine. It is possible, on the other hand, that Courdemaine was only part of his reward, and that the king gave him further compensation in the form of cash. To pursue this line of investigation, we must examine several financial transactions of Raoul de Presles that took place in 1311. The size and extent of these transactions dwarfed the Courdemaine grant.

One of the outstanding phenomena of economic activity in the early fourteenth century was an inflationary trend

[5] A.N., JJ. 47, no. 99; Archives départementales de l'Aisne, G. 253, fol. 132 v.

that sapped the money reserves and reduced the purchasing power of royal establishments, monastic and episcopal households, and noble families. The result of this trend was the growth of indebtedness, which led sometimes to impoverishment and more often to sudden demands for large quantities of cash. One would suspect offhand that a French baron like Gaucher de Châtillon would never accumulate any serious debt. As constable of France he received a salary and also a portion of spoil and booty taken in battle. He was moreover a powerful seigneur and his land holdings were spotted over a large part of northern France. But he seemed no more immune to the erosive effects of inflation than the lesser nobles. Of course, we do not know definitely that he owned any great indebtedness but the evidence points in that direction. Three events within four years clearly indicate the constable's need of large sums of money. In December 1308, he sold to Enguerrand de Marigny the château and lands of Champrond-en-Perchet for the price of 24,000 *l. par.* of *forte monnaie.*[6] This is the single largest financial transaction to be found in the Chancery Registers of Philip the Fair. Only a month later, in January 1309, he arranged a marriage agreement whereby his daughter, Marie de Châtillon, would become the bride of Guichard, seigneur of Beaujeu. Although the family of Beaujeu was a cut below the house of Châtillon in prestige and lineage, the marriage was an advantageous one for the constable's daughter. But the dowry was heavy, for the father gave to the daughter an annual rent of 500 *l.* of *bons petits tour.* and a lump sum of 8,000 *l.* of *bons petits tour.*[7] The sale of Champrond may have been sufficient to meet the dowry of his daughter, but Gaucher de Châtillon obviously had debts elsewhere for he proceeded in 1311 to obtain additional cash in a negotiation with Raoul de Presles.

Only two months before the sale of Champrond, Gaucher

6 A.N., JJ. 40, no. 86.   7 A.N., JJ. 40, no. 142.

de Châtillon received from the king a money fief (or *fief-rente*) of 1,000 *l. tour.*[8] This was an annual income to be taken upon the royal treasury, and in return the constable gave liege homage to Philip the Fair. It was a large money fief which placed a heavy burden upon the king's cash receipts and must have been given to Gaucher at his special request. It would have permitted a lesser noble with ordinary expenses to escape serious financial trouble, but Gaucher held the revenue for a little over two years and in January 1311 arranged to sell it to Raoul de Presles. By the terms of the agreement, Presles received the 1,000 *l. tour.* of income on the royal treasury and in turn contracted to pay to the constable the sum of 10,000 *l.* of *petits tour.*, 2,000 *l.* at the moment and the remaining 8,000 *l.* by Ascension.[9] The lawyer's policy of localizing his revenues and converting them into landed rents received further expression when, within a few days, he gave back to the king the 1,000 *l.* of rent on the treasury and obtained remission of the farm of Courdemaine.[10] This was not an unusual operation; many clerks and lawyers of the king had money rents transferred to landed rents. What is striking in this instance are the large sums involved. We may be a little surprised that Gaucher de Châtillon had again liquidated some assets in order to obtain ready cash. But what is astonishing is the fact that Raoul de Presles was able to lay hands on 10,000 *l.* within a short time. He was obliged to give Gaucher the remaining 8,000 *l.* within three or four months. In further exploring Raoul's business affairs, we may see how he acquired part of this sum and also how bizarre elements began to creep into his financial negotiations.

The later documents on Courdemaine present confusing evidence on its appraised value but at the same time serve

---

[8] A.N., JJ. 40, no. 180.
[9] A.N., JJ. 47, no. 52; A.N., J. 383, nos. 65, 66.
[10] A.N., JJ. 47, nos. 86, 88.

to itemize the appurtenances of the *prévoté*. In the negotiations with the king, Raoul de Presles freed the royal treasury
of 1,000 *l. tour.* and was himself exempted from 900 *l.* of obligation for Courdemaine, thereby losing in the process 100 *l.*
of rent. That Presles was willing to take this loss is easily
understood; he seemed bent on converting his wealth to
negotiable assets. He proceeded immediately to sell part of
the income of Courdemaine, presumably to obtain cash to
meet his obligations toward Gaucher de Châtillon. In March
1311, he arranged articles of sale with the cathedral chapter
of Laon for 100 *l. par.* of his Courdemaine rent. The price
which the chapter was to pay him for this income was not
mentioned. The *bailli* of Vermandois blocked the transaction
because it involved amortization, and so the problem was
brought before the king. In the discussion which followed,
we are given several important pieces of information. The
king announced that his agents had appraised Courdemaine
at an annual income value of 500 *l. tour.*, and had further
reported that the exchange of this rent for Raoul de Presles'
rent of 1,000 *l.* on the treasury was a good bargain since
the king was receiving more than a double return.[11]

Several items in this discussion touch on an important
question of Philip's reign and on the character of his civil
servants. Did the king always know what his servants were
doing? Was the king ever deceived by his agents? There was
a noticeable discrepancy between the original assigned
value of 900 *l. tour.* and the appraised value of 500 *l. tour.*
on Courdemaine. So far as we know, only one appraisal was
made, and we do not know that this appraisal was made in
1310 when the *prévoté* was first given to Presles or in
1311 when he asked for permission to sell parts of it. In common practice the king usually exacted in rent a sum equal
to the appraised rent of a particular holding, and Philip

[11] A.N., JJ. 47, no. 95.

should have therefore required in farm of Raoul de Presles not 900 *l.* but 500 *l.* What probably happened was this: In making the original grant of Courdemaine to Raoul, Philip did not have an appraisal made but used a sum of rent roughly equal to that which the abbey of Corbie had been receiving from the lands. The official appraisal took place later, possibly when Raoul first tried to sell some of the rent to the chapter of Laon. Even so, this would have taken place within a period of four months and will not explain the remarkably low appraisal. We must therefore ask if Raoul de Presles conspired with the two appraisers, Guillaume de Marcilly and Frémin de Cocquerel, to appraise Courdemaine at a figure so low that the king would be more easily persuaded to let him sell the rent in amortization. The question would be a startling one if we did not have evidence for similar incidents and notably from the career of Enguerrand de Marigny. The document which announced the appraisal of 500 *l.* contains only one other figure—the 1,000 *l.* that Raoul de Presles remitted to the king on his treasury. No mention was made of the original 900 *l.* demanded of Presles in farm from Courdemaine. Presles never made such a payment, for he held the land under farm conditions for only about eight weeks before obtaining it as free income. The evidence, while inconclusive in this case, makes the question of deceit, connivance, and malfeasance an honest and pertinent one.

Once Raoul de Presles received royal permission to amortize his rents on Courdemaine as he saw fit, he completed the sale of rent to the dean and chapter of Laon. In letters dated April 2, 1311, the cathedral chapter agreed to pay to the lawyer 3,000 *l. par.* for an annual rent of 100 *l. par.*, to be taken on Raoul's holdings in Vailly, Filain, Condé-sur-Aisne, and Presles. The assessment would be made by two men chosen by both parties, and would be based on a me-

dian revenue over a period of ten to twenty years.[12] This was
an unusual condition, for most charters on land evaluations
appraised the land at its immediate value. Raoul therefore
stipulated that the sale price be based not on what the lands
had yielded in years past, but on the anticipated yield during
a future period. He argued in effect that the cathedral chapter would receive an increased return from the 100 *l.* of rent
within the next decade or so. The 3,000 *l. par.* was an extraordinary price for 100 *l.* of revenue. The ordinary exchange rate was 100 *l.* of appraised land value for 10 *l.* of
appraised annual rent and was the basis of Raoul's transaction with Gaucher de Châtillon. But in the case of the dean
and chapter of Laon, Presles was able to extract a return of
30 to 1 in place of 10 to 1.

Of Raoul's holdings on which rent was to be levied, Vailly,
Filain, Condé-sur-Aisne, and Presles, the only new item is
Filain, which was attached to the royal grant of Courdemaine. Acquired by the king from the abbey of Corbie,
Filain actually consisted of a small manor or farm called
La Royère and may be considered an appendage to the
prévoté of Courdemaine even though it was located several
miles to the north of Vailly. What appears to have been a
second sale of rent to the chapter of Laon took place in July
1311, when the appurtenances of Courdemaine were further
clarified. The chapter again purchased 100 *l. par.* of rent
from Raoul de Presles for the price of 2,500 *l.* of *bons petits
par.* Part of the rent was to come from the revenues of the
bridge at Vailly; another part was to be taken on the grain
at La Royère or, in default of this, on the mill of Saint Pierre
at Vailly.[18] The Pont de Vailly and the Moulin-Saint-Pierre
were clearly parts of the *prévoté* of Courdemaine, and simply illustrate the diversified nature of the rents included in

[12] A.N., JJ. 47, no. 100. A copy of the transaction is in B.N., Collection Dom Grenier, Vol. 54, fol. 283 r.-v.
[13] A.N., JJ. 46, no. 72.

the *prévoté*. Although the documents do not say so, there is a question of whether this was actually a second sale of rent or a readjusted settlement of the first sale. If two separate transactions were involved, Raoul de Presles accumulated 5,500 *l.* within three months by the sale of 200 *l.* of rent. And if only one sale was involved, he still brought off a spectacular negotiation.

The most impressive financial gain of Raoul de Presles in 1311 was made at the expense of the powerful abbey of Prémontré. Like other monastic houses Prémontré had, in the course of several years, accumulated an oppressive indebtedness. We are concerned here only with the debt which the abbey had contracted with Baudouin Crespin of Arras. Of an original loan of 14,400 *l. tour.*, 9,500 *l.* of *bons petits tour. forts* remained to be paid to its creditor, and the abbey was pressed in 1311 to make final settlement. Unable to pay the debt from their own reserves, the abbot and general of the Premonstratensian Order, Adam de Crécy, turned for help to Raoul de Presles. The lawyer agreed to satisfy Baudouin Crespin for the remainder of the debt, and the abbey in turn contracted to pay Raoul an annual sum of 1,300 *l.* of *bons petits tour. forts* for the rest of his life. Raoul had already delivered 4,500 *l.* to the creditor, and was careful to stipulate that if he should die before the total sum was paid, his heirs and executors would not be held for the remainder. Finally in the same transaction, Raoul promised to serve throughout his life as legal aid to the chapter and Order of Prémontré in return for an annual fee of 100 *l.* of *bons petits tour. forts.*[14] The significance of Raoul de Presles' relations with Prémontré cannot be over-estimated. He was legal counselor not only for the mother house of Prémontré but for the entire Premonstratensian Order, and this speaks eloquently of his immense stature as a lawyer by 1311. This is the only instance in which he is portrayed as a money-

[14] A.N., JJ. 46, no. 147.

lender, but the evidence is impressive enough to justify conjecture on similar operations elsewhere. The oddity, the peculiar nature, and conditions of this charter are reinforced by the fact that this document is one of only two of its kind in the Chancery Registers of Philip the Fair.[15] Three miles to the southwest of Prémontré stood the château of Coucy. Perched above the Ailette on heights that commanded a view of Laon to the east, Noyon to the west, and Soissons to the south, it reflected the qualities of the family that held it. Arrogant and rebellious, the lords of Coucy alternately terrorized and protected the countryside surrounding their château. From his royal domains the king of France kept a wary eye on these fierce barons who fought him as often as they obeyed him. For two hundred years the seigneury was held by the male side of the family but the luck of the house played out in 1310 when Enguerrand IV died without direct heirs. One of his sisters had married Arnoul, count of Guines; two of her sons, Enguerrand and Jean, came forward to claim their uncle's barony. Enguerrand de Guines was brought up at the Scottish court of Alexander III. His aunt had married into the French Bailleul family which became the Scottish Balliol, and Enguerrand in turn took his wife from this family and brought her back to France with him. His younger brother, Jean de Guines, made an equally impressive alliance when he married Jeanne de Chantilly.[16] Several legal problems had to be resolved in establishing the second house of Coucy. The late lord's widow relinquished her rights over the movable goods, assignment of her dowry was made, and the lands were partitioned between the two brothers. All of this was done at Paris in May 1311 with Gaucher de Châtillon and other

[15] The other charter concerns the arrangement between Pierre de Latilly and the abbey of Saint Médard (A.N., JJ. 46, no. 152).

[16] André Duchesne, *Histoire généalogique des maisons de Guines, d'Ardres, de Gand et de Coucy, et de quelques autres familles illustres* (Paris, 1631), pp. 253ff., 283.

nobles presiding.[17] But the lawyer who served the two brothers and arranged the technicalities of the settlement was not mentioned in the legal documents. We discover, when the brothers paid his fee, that he was Raoul de Presles. The letters which stipulated the lawyer's reward were drawn up in May 1311 when the general settlement was made of Enguerrand de Coucy's estate. Raoul de Presles was expected to continue throughout his life as legal counselor for Enguerrand and Jean de Guines. In return for the help which he had already given, and in expectation of future service, the brothers gave him handsome compensation when they assigned to him the seigneury of Lizy-sur-Ourcq.[18] The seigneury lay astride the small stream that cuts through the pleasantly rolling country north of Meaux, and was taken out of Jean de Guines' inheritance. Because it was dependent upon the younger brother's holding of La Ferté-Ancoul, Raoul de Presles owed homage for the fief to Jean de Guines and not to his older brother who became seigneur of Coucy. Unfortunately, we have no clear picture of its size or value; it had all the physical appurtenances of a large seigneury, including hundreds of acres of woods, and must have yielded an annual income in the neighborhood of 1,000 *l.*[19] Beyond its economic value, the grant of Lizy-sur-Ourcq further enlarges the portrait of a lawyer who had powerful feudal lords for clients and who, rising from obscurity, had himself become an important seigneur. Although he owned large rents along the Aisne and around his native village of Presles, the acquisition of considerable domain in the valley of the Ourcq made him a landed gentleman and gave him the title that he would carry for the rest of his life—master

[17] A.N., JJ. 46, nos. 17, 18; JJ. 47, no. 28.
[18] A.N., JJ. 46, no. 10.
[19] For a brief essay on the seigneury of Lizy and the various families through which it passed, see L. Benoist, *Notice historique et statistique sur Lizy-sur-Ourcq* (Meaux, 1889).

Raoul de Presles, seigneur of Lizy, clerk and councillor of the king.

The financial transactions which Raoul de Presles made in 1311 constitute, for the historian, a difficult problem in his life and career as a lawyer. Never again was he to engage in such large scale negotiations and never again was he to experience such overwhelming success. All of his later acquisitions put together would not equal any one deal that he made in 1311. And there is good reason to believe that we do not have a record of everything that he acquired during this short period.[20] But the documents which we do have stand out from the pages of the Chancery Registers and defy adequate analysis or explanation. Of some two thousand letters contained in these registers, those that record Raoul de Presles' operations in 1311 are in a class by themselves. The sums of money involved were exceeded only by certain high-level negotiations of royalty and nobility, such as marriage dowries, money fiefs, maltotes, and a few confiscations. In the area of land transactions, only the exchanges made by persons like the count of Valois, the countess of Artois, the duke of Burgundy, and the constable of France surpass them in value.[21] Certainly no man of Presles' social status or professional class acquired so much wealth in so short a time. Guillaume de Nogaret was an immensely wealthy man, but his holdings had accumulated across the

[20] Presles also held 140 *arpents* of woods, called the "Lus," situated in the *prévoté* of Château-Thierry which he acquired from Louis in exchange for similar acreage in woods located above Chacins. See Longnon, II, 518. When Louis was count of Champagne, he gave to Presles a fief which Adam de la Pierre held at Plessis-l'Evêque. We do not hear of this grant until after the death of Raoul de Presles when the lands became involved in litigation. Included in the fief was a windmill located between Yverney and Villeroy. The land was just west of Meaux. See A.N., JJ. 64, no. 718; B.N., Collection Moreau, Vol. 226, fol. 133-135 v.; Furgeot, no. 1,675.

[21] See for instance A.N., JJ. 49, no. 58 (55,000 *l.*), no. 59 (40,000 *l.*). These involved the duke of Burgundy and Charles de Valois. See also A.N., JJ. 38, no. 201 (200,000 *l.*); JJ. 40, no. 12 (100,000 *l.*). These concerned Mahaut d'Artois.

years, and the same may be said for other lawyers such as Guillaume de Plaisians and Philippe de Villepreux. No matter how we measure the operations of Raoul de Presles in 1311, they were nothing less than stupendous. And because of the proximity of two events, the road of inquiry leads back to the deposition against the Templars.

One is impressed by the fact that, of Presles' negotiations in 1311, all but two were private arrangements that did not directly involve the king. On the face of the matter, Raoul de Presles was simply achieving success as a lawyer and financier. So far as the sequence of acts is concerned, the first question centers around the 10,000 *l.* with which he bought the constable's money fief. Through the earlier grant of Courdemaine, he was able to acquire 5,500 *l.* in successive sales of rent to the cathedral chapter of Laon. At the same time however, he assumed, and immediately paid half of, the debt of Prémontré. This still left him with a short-term obligation of about 10,000 *l.* In all fairness, we must countenance the possibility that he had amassed a small fortune through his earlier legal practice at Laon and elsewhere. But the sequence of events which were crowded into the year 1311 and which came only eight months after the deposition, continues to cast a long shadow over his denial of compensation for his testimony. This shadow grows darker when we recall that, while Raoul de Presles remained in the royal service throughout his life, there are only two instances of payment made to him by Philip the Fair. These were the grant of Courdemaine and the 24 *l.* of rent on Condé-sur-Aisne. One final point should be noted. Apart from the general management of the process by Nogaret, Plaisians, Gilles Aicelin, and Philippe de Marigny, the only royal servant who actually testified during the trial of the Templars was Raoul de Presles. The evidence suggests that Philip the Fair rewarded him for that service and that the pay consisted not only of Courdemaine, but also of a large sum of money.

By 1311 Raoul de Presles had acquired four groups of rents near his native village of Presles. These were the small rent on Condé-sur-Aisne, the extended holdings of Courdemaine in Vailly, the rent on the commune of Cys and Presles, and the large but undetermined holdings around Presles valued at more than 200 *l.* The first two had come from the king, the third from the king's eldest son, and the fourth he acquired by unknown means. Many of the acquisitions which Raoul de Presles made after 1311 serve simply to throw additional light on his constant drive to construct a small personal empire in the valley of the Aisne. Our evidence on these matters is never as full as we would like it to be. Sometimes the exact extent or value of the holdings or from whom and how they were acquired cannot be known. His rents located in Condé-sur-Aisne and Celles-sur-Aisne were probably larger and more varied than Philip's grant would indicate. He also acquired some revenue in these towns from the church of Notre Dame of Compiègne.[22] Across the river from Presles was the village of Chavonne, and here Raoul bought several small rents from a squire by the name of Gérard Boquet.[23] In the forest of Boves just outside the village of Presles, the lawyer bought additional rents from Boquet and other nobles.[24] We are justified in saying that by 1313 Raoul de Presles was the largest landholder in the lower valley of the Aisne. He had pieced together by pur-

[22] B.N., Collection Dom Grenier, Vol. 54, fol. 285. This same document informs us that Presles had a house at Celles and was obliged to pay *taille* to the commune for all that he held in Celles and Condé.

[23] *Ibid.* fol. 283 v.-284 v. The rent amounted to 30 *muids* of wine, 4 *s.* 6 *d. par.* and 4 *sétiers* of grain.

[24] A.N., JJ. 47, no. 153. The local name of the forest was *La Bos-la-hors.* There is also the notice of acquisition by Presles of 145 *arpents* at Crogy and Asy in compensation for similar acreage in woods at Treson which he supposedly transferred to the king about 1313 (*Livre Rouge,* no. 562).

chase and grant lands, mills, manors, forests, and all kinds of appurtenances which formed a continuous strip of territory some six or seven miles in length and which ran west from the hamlets of St. Mard, Rhu, and Boves through Cys, Presles, Chavonne, Vailly, and Celles to Condé-sur-Aisne. The bridge he held at Vailly was probably the only one within twenty-five miles and for that reason afforded him particular power and prestige. But even this enumeration of his landed rents is a moderate one; he undoubtedly held more than is shown in the documentary evidence.

Outside the valley of the Aisne, the seigneur of Lizy followed a similar policy of increasing his landed wealth by purchase or grant. Some of the grants are clear indications of a large private law practice. Enguerrand de Guines scarcely succeeded to his uncle's barony of Coucy before he died; his lands went to his son, Guillaume de Coucy. Cordial relations continued between the new seigneur and Raoul de Presles, and the latter continued to serve as legal counsel to the seigneur of Coucy. Because of this arrangement, Guillaume permitted the lawyer to acquire 105 *l. par.* of rents within Coucy's lands and to assign them as he wished to ecclesiastical houses. Taking advantage of this concession, Raoul secured 60 *l.* of land at Amigny, which was held in fief of Coucy by the lord of Blérancourt. In exchange for Amigny, Presles gave to the lord of Blérancourt an identical amount of land in the territory of Arcy-Sainte-Restitue, which he held in fief of the count of Soissons.[25] Amigny was not a gift from Coucy; it was a favor insofar as Raoul was permitted to acquire feudal holdings and to amortize them without paying a fine. The point of the ex-

[25] A.N., JJ. 49, no. 158. The document consists of a series of four letters which record the various stages of this transaction. There is unfortunately no record of how and when Presles acquired Arcy-Sainte-Restitue from the count of Soissons. Near this village was the *prévôté* of Rugny, which had either been given or sold to Presles by the abbey of Saint Médard (A.N., JJ. 62, no. 267).

change became clear when Presles gave Amigny to the cathedral chapter of Laon and took back the manor of La Royère which he had earlier sold to them.[26] La Royère was much closer to the valley of the Aisne and to Presles' native territory.

From this dizzy round of negotiations several interesting facts emerge. Raoul de Presles continued as the legal counsel of the lords of Coucy, and he appears to have acquired a new and powerful client, Hugues de Nesle, count of Soissons and lord of Chimay, from whom he held land in fief. One other highly placed noble can be counted as a legal client of Raoul during these years. Robert, count of Dreux, gave 140 *arpents* of wood in the forest of Dole to the lawyer and, as we have seen, such gifts were usually made not only for some particular legal service but also in expectation of future counsel.[27] By the end of Philip's reign Raoul de Presles had become the highly esteemed legal counselor of the abbey and order of Prémontré, the lord of Coucy, the count of Soissons, the count of Dreux, the king of France, and his son Louis, count of Champagne and king of Navarre. Furthermore, his land acquisitions kept to a consistent pattern. The new holdings of Arcy-Sainte-Restitue and the acreage in the forest of Dole were located between the Aisne and the Marne. His most distant holding was Amigny and he got rid of that as quickly as possible.

The man who became a wealthy lord through his legal prowess inherited the troubles common to great seigneurs. He became involved himself in litigation over questions of rights, privileges, revenues, and homage. Within a few weeks after he acquired Lizy, his seigneury was invaded by armed men sent from Simon Festu, bishop of Meaux, who claimed that Raoul de Presles owed him homage for the fief because Lizy depended upon the viscounty of Meaux, which in turn depended upon the bishopric of Meaux. The suit was

[26] A.N., JJ. 49, no. 158.   [27] A.N., JJ. 49, no. 188.

brought to the Parlement de Paris but we do not know its ultimate outcome.[28] South of the Marne was the village of Sancy, dependent on the *châtellenie* of Provins but attached to the seigneury of Lizy-sur-Ourcq. A question of seigneurial rights over the high justice of Sancy arose between Presles and the king. Once more the case came to the Parlement de Paris, where the lawyer won a favorable decision.[29]

The thorniest problem of all came out of the relations between the commune of Vailly and Raoul de Presles. This was to be expected for the men of Vailly were fiercely jealous of their communal liberties and resentful of the rival seigneurial jurisdiction represented by Courdemaine. The nature and character of Courdemaine became even clearer in the agreement reached in December 1311 between the lawyer and the commune.[30] Raoul surrendered all rights of justice over the population of Vailly and agreed that his five *échevins* would become in effect the *échevins* of the commune. On the other hand, the bourgeoisie of Vailly would continue to pay Raoul the dues which they had formerly paid. The commune relinquished its claim on the "house" of Courdemaine, but was to receive in compensation another house where it could hold its court. And finally Raoul agreed never to let the house of Courdemaine serve as asylum to fugitives from the justice of the commune. But that was not the end of the matter, and conflict persisted between the seigneur and the commune.

One other aspect of Raoul de Presles' activity during Philip the Fair's reign deserves notice. With his accumulated wealth he turned to philanthropy in the field of education. Many Capetian clerks contributed to poorhouses, monastic houses, and churches. Presles also indulged in this sort of charity, but his financial support of education stands out

[28] *Olim,* III, 687; Boutaric, no. 3,984.
[29] *Olim,* III, 967; Boutaric, no. 4,391.
[30] A.N., JJ. 46, no. 176; JJ. 48, nos. 6, 7.

and provides striking evidence of his interest in that particular field. Of all the better known lawyers of Philip the Fair, Raoul de Presles and Gilles Aicelin were the only two whose philanthropic impulse led them to endow educational institutions. It may be that the college founded by the late queen Jeanne de Navarre inspired Presles to similar work. But it is more likely that he had a deep desire to provide for others the sort of educational opportunity which had enabled him to rise so high in the world. Gui de Laon, treasurer of the Royal Chapel in Paris, had the same desire, and the two men pooled their resources to establish in January 1314 a college in the University of Paris where poor students from the dioceses of Soissons and Laon could come to study. If this house of scholars had any official name in the beginning it was the "College of Laon and Soissons." It was the only instance in medieval college-founding in which two men came together to set up an educational institution. Gui de Laon was interested in educating the young men of the diocese of Laon; Raoul in those of Soissons. The joint enterprise was ill-fated, and the one house later became two separate colleges as a result of quarrels and differences over the endowment. Gui de Laon contributed 100 *l.* of annual revenue and also provided a house in the vicinity of Mont-Sainte-Gèneviève. Presles endowed his part of the college with 200 *l.* of annual income drawn from his woods at Lizy and his mill at Iverny. The college which became a living monument to the memory of Raoul de Presles was not the last of his ventures in educational philanthropy.[31]

In February 1315 while the storm clouds gathered over Enguerrand de Marigny, Raoul de Presles extended his philanthropic activity in education to his native village of Pres-

<hr />

[31] The charter of foundation can be found in A.N., JJ. 49, no. 257; A.N., M. 185, no. 1; A.N., M. 140, no. 2; A.N., MM. 418, fol. 7-8. See also Matton, "Le Collège de Laon et ses bienfaiteurs," *Bulletin de la société académique de Laon*, III (1853), 239-254.

les and arranged for the revival and reform of the school that was formerly in the commune of Cys and Presles. This was presumably a low-level grammar school that gave rudimentary training to the children of the commune. Attached to the village church of Presles, it had fallen on bad days and had either declined or totally ceased its operations. Raoul de Presles provided it with a new endowment of a house situated next to the church and of certain unstipulated revenues amounting to about 10 *l.* of annual income. He also procured from Louis X the right, during his life, to name the rector of the school, who had to take an oath to make personal residence in the school.[32]

Raoul de Presles' educational philanthropy was made possible by his phenomenal acquisition of wealth. Much of that wealth was accumulated by questionable means. But Presles' methods of gaining wealth, and particularly the implicit perjury in his deposition against the Templars, should not subvert the image of an able lawyer and man of finance. The fact remains that he acquired sometime between 1300 and 1310 a tremendous reputation as a legal practitioner and his services were sought by noble and religious houses in Vermandois and Champagne. With his reputation he gained prestige and influence in high circles. His energy and talent in law were supplemented by a driving hard-headedness and opportunism which enabled him to extract from every negotiation the greatest advantage for himself if not always for his client. These characteristics showed up also in his financial dealings. His arrangement with Prémontré represented an extremely hard bargain for the abbey and an impressive benefit for himself. The same was true of his relations with the chapter of Laon. While his service to the Guines brothers and his acquisition of Lizy-sur-Ourcq had nothing to do with

[32] A.N., JJ. 52, no. 10. See also the comment on this act in Stanislas Prioux, "Biographie de Raoul de Presles," *Bull. Soc. Arch. Soissons,* XI (1857), 86-94.

his testimony against the Templars, they do amplify his unique qualities as a lawyer. The same may be said of his service to the count of Soissons, the count of Dreux, and his other highly-placed clients. But talent, hard-headedness, and opportunism needed sponsorship in the fourteenth century as in all centuries. When we have identified Raoul de Presles' friends and patrons, we will better understand his rise to power.

CHAPTER SEVEN

The Origins and Rise of
Raoul de Presles

T HE communal movement that began in the eleventh century and spread rapidly through northern France in the twelfth formed the background of the social and economic environment that produced Raoul de Presles. The example of the large towns, such as Laon and Soissons, was soon followed by neighboring agricultural villages, which also acquired charters of commune from their seigneurs. The charter of Soissons served as a model for liberties which Louis VI granted sometime before 1137 to Vailly, Condé, Chavonne, Celles, Pargny, and Filain. These villages, which lay to the east of Soissons, formed a federated commune with the communal administration centered in Condé and Vailly.[1] Three miles to the east of Vailly on the left bank of the Aisne lay the cluster of agricultural villages which included Presles, Boves, Cys, le Ru, and Saint Mard. Until Jeanne de Navarre married Philip the Fair in 1284, these villages were in the domain of the counts of Champagne. At some undetermined date—1225 or earlier—these same counts had given to the five villages a communal charter based upon that of Meaux, which in turn had been taken from the Soissons charter.[2] The charter granted by the counts

---

[1] Georges Bourgin, *La Commune de Soissons et le groupe communal soissonnais* (Paris, 1908), pp. 79-89, 217-223; Louis Carolus-Barré, "La commune de Condé et Celles-sur-Aisne des origines à la suppression de la commune fédérative de Vailly," *B.E.C.*, cxiii (1955), 75-110.

[2] A copy of the 1225 confirmation is found in B.N., Collection Moreau, Vol. 136, fol. 33-35 v., and another copy with slight variants is in E. Bouchel, "Essai historique sur Presles-et-Boves," *Bull. Soc. Arch. Soissons*, iii (1893), Part 1, 33-38. See also Bourgin, *La Commune de Soissons*, p. 306f.

made a federated rural commune of the five villages and was confirmed on several occasions, by Jeanne de Navarre and Philip the Fair in 1292 and again by Louis, count of Champagne, in 1312.[3] By the late thirteenth century, the lower valley of the Aisne east of Soissons was composed of villages which belonged to federal communes, and the dominant influence in their development had been that of Soissons. It was in this region and in this atmosphere of rural self-governed communes that Raoul de Presles was born and grew to young manhood.

Most scholars have maintained that Raoul de Presles came from humble and obscure origins. The same has been shown to be true of Guillaume de Nogaret, Guillaume de Plaisians, Philippe de Villepreux, and other lawyers of Philip the Fair. Proof in these cases often consists of royal charters permitting the person to hold fiefs, although not of noble birth. Another kind of evidence is the charter of ennoblement, which also proves that the person concerned came from non-noble origins. But to say that a man came from non-noble origins does not specifically describe his origins. Such a person could be of bourgeois birth, which means in a general way that his parents were free and not serf. At the same time, bourgeois birth was a clear indication that at some point in the recent or remote past, the family had come from serfdom to bourgeois status. In the case of Philip the Fair's lawyers who were of non-noble origins, it is sometimes difficult to say much about their parents, their brothers and sisters, or their children. There is none of this vagueness and obscurity about Raoul de Presles. The conditions of his birth are a matter of record and his family is clearly enumerated. We owe this detailed information to the lawyer himself and to his legal-mindedness in putting on record every concession or right that concerned him. Furthermore, this information is not found in any obscure manuscript source or

[3] *Ibid.*, p. 306.

provincial archives but is contained in a Chancery Register of Philip the Fair.

The documents providing information on the origins of Raoul de Presles are found in Chancery Register JJ. 40, a volume containing 183 letters. Except for two or three letters of 1303, the letters of this register are dated during 1307-1309. One of the charters is a *vidimus* by Philip the Fair of a letter of Rénaud Giffard, abbot of Saint Denis:

"Rénaud, by divine mercy, humble abbot of the church of Saint Denis in France, and all those of the same convent, eternal greeting in the Lord. Since Jean, Raoul and Robin, brothers, and sons of Pierre dit Adounard le Jeune de Presles-sur-Aisne, and of the deceased Eudeline our serf, formerly wife of the said Pierre, have been subject to us and our church in servile condition by reason of the said Eudeline, mother of the aforesaid brothers, we and our church by unanimous consent, having considered our best interests, have freed the said Jean, Raoul and Robin, brothers, and all the posterity which will be born to them in free marriage. And we manumit and bestow upon them forever the benefit of liberty, for 60 *l. par.* already received and held by us to be converted as we wish suitably to the utility of our church. We do not remit to the same brothers the reverence and honor which all those manumitted are held to exhibit to those who manumitted them. All of which things we signify by these present letters provided with our seals. Done in the year of our Lord 1299, in the month of March (1300)."[4]

Philip the Fair's *vidimus* of the abbot's letter was dated March 1309, about a year before Raoul de Presles delivered his deposition against the Templars.

A second and third charter in the same register give added interest to the letter of Rénaud Giffard. In January 1307, Gilles de Pontoise, successor to Giffard as abbot of Saint Denis, issued a letter in which he stated that "we manumit,

---

[4] A.N., JJ. 40, no. 152.

absolve and totally free from the servile condition in which they are held by us and our monastery, Marguerite and Marie, daughters of Pierre dit Adounard de Presles, and of Eudeline our serf, formerly the wife of the same Pierre."[5] The royal confirmation of this letter was dated March 1309. The third letter is different in its source and circumstances:

"Philip, by divine permission, humble abbot of the monastery of Saint Médard of Soissons, and all the convent of the same place, eternal greeting in the Lord. Let everyone know that, considering the liberalities and free services which the discreet man, our beloved and faithful master Raoul de Presles, clerk, has rendered to us in times past and which he proposes to render to us in times to come, in remuneration of the aforesaid things and moved by pity . . . we manumit and free forever from all yoke of servitude, without any retention whatever, Gile de Vasseny our serf, widow of Pierre dit Adounard de Presles. . . . In testimony of which things we have been led to place our seals on these present letters. Given in the year of our Lord 1307, in the month of February (1308)."[6]

The king's *vidimus* of this letter was again dated at Paris in March 1309.

It is my contention that Rénaud Giffard's letter of 1300 concerns the lawyer of Philip the Fair and is, in fact, a record of Raoul de Presles' manumission from serfdom. The evidence is overwhelmingly in favor of this view. First of all, there are only three letters of manumission in Chancery Register JJ. 40. This in itself is not curious; in many of the fourteenth-century Chancery Registers there are no charters of manumission, and sometimes as few as one or two. The curiosity in JJ. 40 is that these three manumission charters are registered in a group, the second being separated from the third only by a charter in which Enguerrand de

Marigny received lands in Normandy.[7] Furthermore, all three letters were confirmed by Philip the Fair in March 1309. I suggest that they were confirmed on the same day and were delivered by Presles or one of his servants to the Chancery for immediate registration. In this way they were kept together as a group and were so registered. On the other hand, there was no particular reason why these letters should have been registered in the Chancery. A bare minority of manumission letters ever found their way into the Chancery Registers, and they give evidence of the fact that the person who owned them had an unusually keen sense of legal surety. Only the person who felt that he ought to have the highest legal sanction and insurance in the land would go to the trouble and expense of having letters which recorded his manumission registered in the royal Chancery. Raoul de Presles was such a person. Always eager to have his rights and possessions put beyond all legal dispute, he had his lands and wealth acquired in 1311 registered in the Chancery. After his release from prison in 1315, he made sure that the letters recording his innocence and ordering the restoration of his lands were put in the registers. In 1320, to make doubly sure that his restored lands were secure, he had copies made of the original grants and registered them in the Chancery. The registration of his manumission letters in 1309 was only the first instance in which he manifested this legalistic impulse.

The conditions of Raoul de Presles' birth, childhood and manumission from serfdom may be reconstructed. Much of this reconstruction is admittedly conjecture. But it is con-

---

[7] A.N., JJ. 40, no. 154. L. Douët-d'Arcq, "Inventaire de Jeanne de Presles, veuve de Raoul de Presles, fondateur du collège de ce nom," *B.E.C.*, xxxix (1878), 81-109, was aware of the charter in A.N., JJ. 40, no. 152, but he attached no importance to it, and felt that the persons referred to in it were agricultural laborers with no relation to such a powerful person as Raoul de Presles. Douët-d'Arcq used the faulty index to this particular Chancery Register and was unaware of the other two charters.

jecture based on available evidence and on what we know about the general practice of the time. His father was Pierre de Presles, and we may assume that he was a free man since there is no evidence to the contrary. About 1270 when Raoul was born, the village of Presles and the surrounding territory were in the hands of the count of Champagne. Pierre could have been a bailiff, steward, or serjeant in the count's service, or he could have been a farmer and member of the commune of Cys and Presles. Eudeline, his wife and the mother of Raoul, was a serf of the powerful abbey of Saint Denis. There is no way of determining her residence and, so far as is known, the abbey held no lands at Presles. Therefore, the question of Raoul's birthplace and his residence during childhood cannot be answered. But we must assume that he grew up at Presles or spent considerable time there. Otherwise he would not have taken the name of Presles. He felt for some reason that Presles was his native village.

Raoul's servile status, which he inherited from his mother, was a strictly legal condition. He probably never paid *mainmorte* or tallage or any other such dues, for he undoubtedly left his servile condition while an adolescent. The manumission charter of Rénaud Giffard was dated in 1300 and Raoul de Presles was then thirty years of age. It is unlikely that he would have waited so long to be free from serfdom. In his deposition against the Templars he remarked that he had known Brother Gervais in Laon for four, five, or six years before the arrest of the Templars. Six years before the arrest would mean that he was resident in Laon in 1301. Since he seemed already well settled and knew many people at that time, it is probable that he had settled in Laon by 1295 or earlier. Many sons and daughters of serfs were manumitted by their lords on the promise that they would enter clerical life. This was one of the ordinary avenues to freedom throughout the later middle ages, and it usually opened up opportunities for education. Many young men who were manumitted in this way took first tonsure, became clerks, and later returned to secular life. Quite frequently, as did Raoul de Presles, they carried the title of "clerk" with them throughout their lives. One can cite numerous instances of clerks in Philip the Fair's service who were married and who held no prebends or benefices.[8] They had never proceeded beyond minor orders and in most cases had done nothing more than receive first tonsure.

This explanation seems to fit the childhood and early career of Raoul de Presles. It is the only logical one that agrees with all of the known circumstances in Presles' life. Let us say that Raoul de Presles was freed by the abbot of Saint Denis, perhaps about 1285, on condition that he enter the clerical life. He did so and, during the next ten years, received something of an education in, among other things, law. After taking up residence at Laon, he showed an unusual talent in legal practice and decided not to proceed to higher orders. In surrendering further advancement in an ecclesiastical career he was simply following a path which many other young men of the day followed. However, one difficulty lay in this line of action. When sons of serfs were freed to enter clerical orders, a clause was invariably inserted in the manumission charter to the effect that if the person so manumitted ever returned to secular life he would be reduced to serfdom.[9]

Perhaps Raoul de Presles was pursued by agents of Saint Denis and therefore arranged for final manumission in 1300.

[8] The most famous instance was Nogaret, who was a clerk in his earlier career. Jean Rousselet, clerk of Louis d'Evreux, who received some of Presles' lands in 1315 was married. Many of the notaries in the royal service were married clerks. One well-known instance is that of Jacques de Vertus, who rose from serfdom, married, and served as a notary under five kings. When he died in 1335, the question of his serfdom came up with respect to his will (A.N., JJ. 70, no. 111).

[9] For one example out of many, see A.N., JJ. 62, no. 268, in which Charles IV freed two brothers that they might receive clerical tonsure. The conditional clause provided that if they did not take clerical tonsure, they would return to "pristine servitude."

An explanation which is more plausible would say that Raoul de Presles was not pursued by the abbey. But having determined to return to secular life and having already accumulated some wealth, his legal mind calculated that if he ever were pursued by the abbey and reduced to serfdom, whatever wealth and career he had would be destroyed. Rather than live with this dreadful possibility, he determined to go to the abbot and to arrange final and complete manumission for a sum of money. And he decided to include his two brothers in this final settlement. In this way, Rénaud Giffard made out the manumission charter of 1300. There is nothing ingenuous in this explanation; it is based on what we know was common practice in the late thirteenth century. It is almost the only explanation that will account for the manumission of Raoul de Presles at the advanced age of thirty, when he was already well established as a lawyer in Laon.

One fact not mentioned in the manumission charter calls for further comment. Why was the name of Raoul's brother, Girard de Presles, omitted from that document? We are told that three brothers—Jean, Raoul, and Robin—were freed. In 1307, two sisters, Marguerite and Marie, received their manumission from the same abbey. Pierre de Presles and Eudeline had these five children. Girard de Presles may be identified with either Jean or Robin, for no mention of these two brothers exists outside of Giffard's charter, and manumitted serfs frequently changed their names after they took up new residence and new occupations. If, however, Girard is not to be identified with Jean or Robin, he may have secured his freedom in another unrecorded charter. Girard de Presles rose to some prominence as the civil provost of Laon. At an undetermined date he was sent with the *bailli* of Vermandois to Châlons-sur-Marne to restore order when the townsmen rioted.[10] This could have been in 1306 when much

---

[10] Boutaric, nos. 3,884, 5,089, 5,295. The inhabitants of Châlons were condemned in 1311 to pay an indemnity of 2,000 *l.* to Girard

of the urban population at Châlons revolted against the new change in currency. The provost of Laon was injured in this fracas and the law suit over indemnity dragged on for seven or eight years. Girard was undoubtedly one of Raoul's brothers who accompanied Jeanne de Chastel to the tents at Bondues. He was definitely identified as Raoul's brother in a civil accord of 1321 which concerned business with the cathedral chapter of Laon.[11]

One final piece of evidence offers convincing proof that Raoul de Presles was the person referred to in the 1300 manumission charter of Rénaud Giffard, and this evidence concerns his stepmother and his half-brother. Raoul's mother, Eudeline, was deceased by 1300. For his second wife, Pierre de Presles chose a woman from the village of Vasseny which lies four or five miles southwest of Presles on the left bank of the Vesle. The Soissons abbey of Saint Médard held lands at Vasseny and Gile de Vasseny was a serf of that abbey. In 1308 Raoul de Presles secured from Saint Médard the manumission of his stepmother, who was named as the widow of Pierre de Presles; her manumission charter was one of the three for which Presles obtained royal confirmation in March 1309. No mention was made of the fact that her children would also be free by virtue of this manumission.

We do not know how many children Pierre de Presles had by this second marriage; the records speak of only one. In December 1314, a month after Philip the Fair's death, Jean de Vasseny, son of Gile de Vasseny and Pierre de Presles, obtained his freedom from Saint Médard, and there is a faint hint that Raoul de Presles may have had something to

---

for having injured and maltreated him in the exercise of his duties. The case ran on to 1318. See P. J. Pelicier, "Une émeute à Châlons-sur-Marne en 1306-1307," *Mémoires de la société d'agriculture, commerce, sciences et arts de la Marne* (1890), p. 117.

[11] A.N., X1c 1a, no. 9. A calendar of this document is in Boutaric, no. 6,547.

do with this.[12] Nothing more is heard of Raoul de Presles'
half-brother until 1348. Raoul de Presles' widow, Jeanne de
Chastel, died in 1347 and it was only natural that, in the
settlement of her estate which was largely a matter of her
late husband's wealth, various legal claims would be made.
Among those who laid claim to Jeanne de Chastel's estate in
1348 were "the children and heirs of the deceased Jean de
Vasseny."[13] The most obvious legal ground for such a claim
was that their father had been the half-brother of Raoul de
Presles.

To discover Raoul de Presles' origins is relatively simple;
to determine the nature of his rise to power and to identify
those who assisted him is a more difficult matter. He was a
native of Champagne and the first important person with
whom he was associated was the king's eldest son, Louis,
count of Champagne and king of Navarre. This association
gives the initial direction to our search for there is the distinct possibility that Presles not only served the prince but
may also have risen through earlier service to Louis' mother
in the administration of Champagne. No special study has
ever been made of Jeanne de Navarre's household. Yet there
is some reason to believe that she and the personnel who
served her influenced to a great extent the nature of her
husband's reign. The queen's household was a likely avenue
of approach to offices in the central government and to further prominence and wealth. Two financial agents who
worked for her before 1285 became servants of Philip the
Fair after he married her. These were the Italian banker
Renier Accorre and Michel de Morienval. Accorre became

---

[12] A.N., JJ. 60, no. 21. The abbot's letter was confirmed by Philip
V in 1321. The abbot referred to "free services, counsel and aid
which the friends" of Jean de Vasseny had rendered to Saint Médard,
leading us to believe that perhaps Raoul de Presles also had something
to do with this manumission.

[13] A.N., X1a 12, fol. 107 v. Unfortunately, we are told nothing
about the nature of the claims. The two parties were given license
by the court to reach a settlement among themselves.

royal receiver of Champagne after 1285, and Morienval served as the financial manager of the queen's household as late as 1300.[14] The best known instance of a man who began his career in the queen's household and rose to power in the king's service was Enguerrand de Marigny. Great-grandson of Hugues le Portier, who was keeper of the ducal château of Lyons-la-Forêt in Normandy, Enguerrand de Marigny was born about 1280 and married Jeanne de Saint-Martin whose godmother was Jeanne de Navarre.[15] Some historians have insisted that this marriage was arranged for Marigny by the queen.[16] For a few years at the end of the century, Marigny was the queen's pantler. He moved into the king's service and became a royal chamberlain almost at the moment of the queen's death.[17]

Simon Festu was born at Fontainebleau and was possibly the son or most certainly the relative of Jean Festu, who was a *fourrier* of the royal household with special attachment to the château of Fontainebleau. Just as Philippe de Villepreux seems to have risen through the household at Saint Germain-en-Laye, so perhaps did Simon Festu gain the notice of the king and queen in the household at Fontainebleau. Festu's position in the queen's service cannot be determined, but he

[14] F. Bourquelot, "Renier Accorre, financier et grand propriétaire au treizième siècle," *B.E.C.*, xxviii (1867), 64-81. This study was based on Accorre's cartulary which Bourquelot discovered in the Bibliothèque Nationale. For Accorre at work, see his financial account in Jubainville, *Histoire des ducs et des comtes de Champagne*, ii, lxiii ff. For Morienval, see *H.F.*, xxii, 491; *Journ. Philippe IV*, nos. 24, 33, 105, 254, 290, 1,299, 5,748. He was a canon of Laon and of Soissons (B.N., Collection Moreau, Vol. 213, fol. 200).

[15] The factual information on Marigny's career may be found in the *précis* of Jean Favier's thesis in *P.T.É.C.* (1956), pp. 39-43.

[16] P. Clément, *Trois drames historiques*, p. 11.

[17] For Marigny as the queen's pantler, see *Journ. Philippe IV*, nos. 890, 1,968. He was a chamberlain of Philip the Fair in 1304. While the queen undoubtedly helped him in his advancement, he owed much to the influence of two cousins, Guillaume de Flavacourt, archbishop of Rouen, and Nicholas de Fréauville, confessor of the king. See Favier in *P.T.É.C.* (1956), p. 40.

was at one point called "clerc de madame la reine," and seemed to be engaged in the queen's financial business.[18] At the same time he sponsored the career of Raoul de Préaux in the queen's household and evidently remained Préaux's patron throughout his life. Préaux later became a royal notary and has often been confused with Raoul de Presles. Festu and Préaux are also good examples of agents who did not pass directly from the queen's service to that of the king but remained for awhile in the service of Louis and his wife Marguerite and then moved into the central government.[19] So the household of the queen's eldest son also became a means of introduction to the royal service. How many other agents and lawyers came up through the queen's household cannot be determined, but there were some who worked occasionally for her and enjoyed her favor. These were Aicelin and Flote, who were her proctors, and Nogaret, who executed the commission of 1296 for the reform of Champagne.[20]

Not only did the queen's household furnish agents for the central government but the atmosphere of conspiracy which characterized the queen's service seems also to have passed into later Capetian government. Simon Festu was the person most prominent in the trial of Guichard de Troyes. Guichard himself was a former queen's agent who entered the central government. Just before Jean de Calais died he signed a confession in which he insisted that Festu had perpetrated

[18] Abel Rigault, "Simon Festu: un conseiller de Philippe le Bel, originaire de Fontainebleau," *Annales de la société historique et archéologique du Gâtinais,* xxii (1904), 331-338. Festu's influence over the queen is best shown by the fact that he was named with Marigny among the executors of Jeanne de Navarre's will.

[19] On Préaux and Festu in the service of Louis and Marguerite, see *Journ. Philippe IV,* no. 5,846, and *Clement V,* no. 673, in which Festu was given a prebend at Sens in 1306 at the request of Louis, count of Champagne.

[20] *H.L.,* ix, 171; *Olim,* ii, 408; A.N., J. 206, no. 1.

all of the intrigue against Guichard.[21] There is good evidence
for the view that Jeanne de Navarre's household was composed of men who were accomplished informers, masters of
intrigue, persons or factions working against each other for
promotion, favor, and wealth. So many men who were tried
or who fell from favor under the last Capetians—Renier Accorre in 1288, Guichard in 1302, Marigny in 1315, Raoul de
Préaux in 1319—were or had been agents in the queen's
household. Something of this sinister atmosphere passed into
the household of the queen's eldest son who, at the age of
sixteen, became count of Champagne and king of Navarre.
His wife, the tragic Marguerite de Bourgogne, became a part
of this court intrigue and fell victim to it when, after being
convicted of adultery, she met a mysterious death as a prisoner in the Norman stronghold of Château Gaillard.

How did Raoul de Presles fit into this scheme of things?
No direct evidence exists to show that he came out of the
queen's household. But one stage of his career is clear: he
came to Philip the Fair's service from that of the count of
Champagne. Is it possible that like Festu and Préaux he
also came from the queen's household into the service of
Louis? Far less is known about the advisors of Louis than
about those of his mother. A charter of 1308 mentions that
his chancellor was Pierre de Grez, brother of a marshal of
France, and soon to become bishop of Auxerre.[22] It is in this
same charter that Raoul de Presles appears for the first time
as a clerk of Louis when the count permitted him to transfer
the rent on Epernay to the commune of Cys and Presles for
the purpose of founding two chaplaincies in his native village. These chaplaincies were founded for the soul of the

[21] Rigault, *Ann. de la soc. hist. arch. du Gâtinais*, XXII (1904), 344.
Jean de Calais was the prisoner entrusted to Guichard. See also
Rigault, *Le procès de Guichard, évêque de Troyes (1308-1313)*.

[22] AN., JJ. 41, no. 21; JJ. 42B, no. 21. Pierre de Condé was a clerk
in Louis' *chambre aux deniers* in 1310 (Fawtier, *Comptes du trésor*,
no. 1129).

late Queen Jeanne and for those of the king's predecessors. Presles was again called the clerk of the prince Louis in 1311, and one other charter, concerning an exchange of woodlands, linked him with the king's eldest son.[23] How long before 1308 had Presles been in the service of Louis?

Two other documents show Presles at work before 1308, but they do not link him directly to the service of Louis. In 1306 Philip the Fair granted to Raoul de Presles the privilege of acquiring up to 500 *l. tour.* of landed rents in the fiefs and arrière-fiefs of the county of Champagne, "although he is not procreated of nobility."[24] The amount of land concerned was large; few letters permitting non-nobles to hold noble land contained such a large figure. Only a year after the death of Jeanne de Navarre, Presles was in the royal service and obviously in the service of the prince Louis. Can it be that permission to hold so much noble land was given to Presles in reward for services which he had rendered to the recently deceased queen? An interesting comparison is the case of Enguerrand de Marigny; he appeared in the king's service just about the time of the queen's death. This letter of 1306 and Rénaud Giffard's manumission letter of 1300 are the two earliest documents on Raoul de Presles.

In a very real sense, however, the earliest evidence on Presles is his deposition against the Templars in 1310. The comments he made in his testimony clearly place him in Laon by 1301 and, by direct inference, place him there much earlier. Brother Gervais asked him to speak on his behalf to the great officers of his Order so that Gervais might be called to the General Chapter. This can only mean that Pres-

[23] For the exchange of woodlands, see Longnon, II, 518. The charter of 1311 is in A.N., JJ. 47, no. 153. There was also the matter of Adam de la Pierre's fief at Plessis-l'Evêque, which was given to Raoul while Louis was still count of Champagne. Raoul was also called the clerk of Louis in this charter (A.N., JJ. 64, no. 718).

[24] A.N., JJ. 48, no. 24. The letter was a *vidimus* of 1312 in which Philip extended the earlier privilege to include the kingdom of France.

les continued to reside in Laon after he had acquired some influence and power. In the early years of the fourteenth century, the king maintained three advocates in the ecclesiastical court at Laon. He also had a proctor and an advocate for the *bailliage* of Vermandois both of whom normally resided in Laon.[25] In 1305 he added a fourth advocate for ecclesiastical cases.[26] The proctor and advocate for the *bailliage* were more important persons than those in the ecclesiastical court. Each of the former received 40 *l.* annual salary while the Church advocates were given only a nominal retaining fee of 60 *s.* each. Raoul de Presles' residence in Laon after he had acquired such importance points to a connection with the *bailliage* of Vermandois, and most likely to a position as advocate in the administration of the *bailliage*.

In the late thirteenth century a large part of the county of Champagne, together with the counties of Rethel and Porcien, were dependent in cases of litigation upon the *bailliage* of Vermandois.[27] That is to say, persons holding lands in these territories would bring law suits to the assises of Vermandois at Laon. As a royal advocate of the *bailliage* and also as a private practitioner, Raoul de Presles came to know all of the important people in Vermandois and in a large part of Champagne. In this way he could have come into the service of the queen, the king, and their eldest son by prosecuting their cases that came before the *bailli* of Vermandois. But this does not answer the question of how he acquired his position in the administration of Vermandois or how he gained his introduction to the service of the queen or of Louis. Marigny came to their service through the help of his powerful kinsmen; Festu gained his introduction through a relative who served in the royal house-

[25] Jules Viard, "Gages des officiers royaux vers 1329," *B.E.C.*, LI (1890), 243.

[26] *Comptes royaux*, Part 1, p. 239.

[27] Henri Waquet, *Le bailliage de Vermandois aux XIIIe et XIVe siècles* (Paris, 1919), pp. 10, 14.

hold. Most often, we can not say who introduced men to the royal service, and there is no direct evidence that permits us to determine Presles' patron. But what evidence there is guides us in every instance to a man who was one of the four or five most powerful nobles in Champagne and who played, year after year, a most important role in the government of the last Capetian kings.

The house of Châtillon had long been one of the most prominent in Champagne and one of the oldest in France. The paternal grandfather of Gaucher de Châtillon was *bouteiller* of Champagne, and his mother's father was a marshal of Champagne. Gaucher was born about 1250 and was a household knight in 1270.[28] He inherited from his father the seigneury of Crécy-en-Brie and was named constable of Champagne in March 1285 before Philip the Fair actually assumed control of the county.[29] Gaucher de Châtillon's reputation as a military leader and administrator was already established for he succeeded to an office which had been held by some of the most famous warriors of medieval France. As constable of Champagne he was associated with Jean de Joinville, seneschal, and with Hugues de Conflans, marshal of Champagne.[30] In 1290 he exchanged with the king his seigneury of Crécy for that of Châtillon-sur-Marne.[31] In 1302 when Raoul de Clermont was killed at Courtrai, Philip made Gaucher de Châtillon constable of France. At that moment when he came to the highest military office in

---

[28] The standard work on the house of Châtillon is that of André Duchesne, *Histoire de la maison de Châtillon-sur-Marne* (Paris, 1621). A more recent study on the constable is André Legoy, *Gaucher de Châtillon, comte de Porcien et connétable de France (1250-1329)*, *P.T.E.C.* (1928), pp. 49-56. This latter work contains good factual information but is disappointing because it fails to treat the constable's role in the government of France.

[29] Jubainville, *Histoire des ducs et des comtes de Champagne*, IV, 498. For his part in the crusade of Aragon, see *H.F.*, XXII, 576, 495, 685.

[30] Longnon, III, 47.

[31] Legoy in *P.T.E.C.* (1928), p. 50.

the kingdom, Philip made one last exchange with him. In return for the seigneury of Châtillon-sur-Marne, the king gave to the constable the seigneury of Porcien and elevated it to the status of a county. Appended to it were the seigneuries of Gandelus and Rozoy-en-Thierasche.[32] From that time, Gaucher de Châtillon carried the titles of count of Porcien and constable of France.

There is good reason to believe that Gaucher de Châtillon had authority and power in the king's council before he became constable of France in 1302. And he enjoyed a close relationship with the young queen. As constable of Champagne after 1285, he may be considered as a member of the queen's household although he was paid by the king and received his orders from the king. In protecting the lands of Champagne, he was in effect protecting the domains of Jeanne de Navarre. Furthermore, he and his ancestors had long been vassals of the count of Champagne. One additional fact is worthy of mention: when Philip became king he was only seventeen years of age and his queen was thirteen. Philip was therefore a much younger man when he came to the throne than any of his three sons when they acquired the crown. It was most natural that such a young monarch would look to older and trusted leaders for direction. Such men were the venerable Joinville, who had fought at the side of Saint Louis, and Gaucher de Châtillon, who at thirty-five was a seasoned warrior and governor. The recently published accounts of Philip the Fair portray the constable as perhaps the most important overseer of royal administration in the county of Champagne before the end of the century.[33] There can be no doubt that, in the last fifteen years of the century, Jeanne de Navarre leaned heavily upon the man who had the responsibility of protecting her ancestral lands.

[32] *Ibid.*, p. 51. For appraisal of these lands, see Longnon, I, 217.
[33] *Comptes royaux*, Part 2, p. 95.

While no information is available on the matter, we have every reason to suspect that in 1302 Jeanne de Navarre had much influence on Philip's selection of Gaucher de Châtillon as constable of France. Like Marigny and Festu, the constable owed his advancement to the queen who was his junior by twenty-three years.

Gaucher de Châtillon could have made the acquaintance of Raoul de Presles in many ways. His lands, scattered across the *bailliage* of Vermandois, and his official duties in Champagne brought him on many occasions to Laon for purposes of litigation and administration. As a great baron he himself had a large household organization composed of bailiffs, lieutenants, serjeants, receivers, and lawyers, and Presles could have served him often as a legal counselor.[34] One incident, although inconclusive, points to an interesting connection with the territory of Presles. About 1280 Châtillon married Isabelle de Dreux, daughter of Robert, count of Dreux and of Braine. At that date, the count of Braine held from the count of Champagne large sections of lands in and around the village of Presles. In 1288, Gaucher de Châtillon and his wife sold to the commune of Cys and Presles all of the serfs and lands that they held in the commune for

[34] A good study of Gaucher's household organization as count of Porcien is found in the introduction to Gaston Robert, *Documents relatifs au comté de Porcien (1134-1464)* (Paris, 1935), in Collection de documents historiques publiés par ordre de S.A.S. le Prince Louis II Prince Souverain de Monaco. In October 1310, Louis, king of Navarre and count of Champagne, confirmed for Gaucher de Châtillon some sixteen charters which concerned the regulation of conflicting rights between him as count of Porcien and the abbey of Signy. The oldest of the letters went back to 1158. Most of them had been extracted and made into a legal document. At the end was the notation: "Signata: Per magistrum R. de Praellis." This is the only letter in the Chancery Registers of Philip the Fair signed in this manner. Raoul de Presles had either prepared the document for Gaucher de Châtillon or had examined it for Louis. If the former is true, it is the only overt instance of Presles acting as a legal assistant to the constable (A.N., JJ. 47, no. 16).

the price of 2,000 *l. tour.*[35] These serfs clearly belonged to the inheritance of his wife. At an unknown date, probably after 1300, Raoul de Presles became the legal counselor of another Robert, count of Dreux and of Braine. It is possible that Raoul de Presles came to the attention of Gaucher de Châtillon through the constable's wife, whose family had been for decades lords of the lands from which Presles drew his origin.

Three other incidents occurred after 1300 that brought together Gaucher de Châtillon and Raoul de Presles, and one of these events placed Presles specifically in the service of the constable. In the act of 1311 by which Gaucher de Châtillon sold to Raoul de Presles 1,000 *l.* of rent on the royal treasury, he referred to him as "our beloved and faithful clerk, master Raoul de Presles."[36] Such language invariably meant that the person referred to was in the service of the donor. The very fact of the sale speaks of a close friendship or relation between Châtillon and Presles. If the constable had put the rent on the open market he would have found many buyers. In selling the rent to Presles the constable did him a favor, and a particular one since the price of 10,000 *l.* was a simple exchange of 10 to 1 for the rent. Raoul de Presles obtained a much higher exchange on several of the rents which he sold. The second incident was the settlement of the estates of Coucy in the same year. Châtillon presided over that settlement, and Presles was the lawyer used by the Guines brothers.[37] Perhaps the constable recommended Presles to the new heirs as their legal counsel. The third and most notable instance was the affair of Bondues wherein Gaucher de Châtillon played intermediary for Jeanne de

[35] Duchesne, *Histoire de la maison de Châtillon-sur-Marne,* p. 333. As late as 1318, the constable had to obtain the confirmation of the count of Dreux for manumission of serfs (A.N., JJ. 56, no. 568).

[36] A.N., JJ. 47, no. 86.

[37] A.N., JJ. 46, nos. 10, 17, 18; JJ. 47, no. 28.

Chastel in obtaining royal acquittal of her husband.[38] But an interesting question arises from what happened in the tents at Bondues. Did the constable use his influence primarily for the lawyer or because of some attachment to Jeanne de Chastel?

Jeanne de Chastel provides the most interesting link between Raoul de Presles and Gaucher de Châtillon. She first appeared in 1311 as the lawyer's wife when Presles sold a rent to the cathedral chapter of Laon.[39] In 1315 she appeared in the tents at Bondues as a woman who was almost desperate to secure her husband's freedom, and on that occasion she knew whom she must use. Throughout the rest of the lawyer's life, Jeanne de Chastel's name was placed beside her husband's name in numerous charters of gifts and business transactions. She was willing in 1315 to let Presles sell her land of Montglas in order to meet his debts. But the land of Montglas does not help us to establish her identity for it had evidently been given to her by her husband at an earlier date.

The key to Jeanne de Chastel's identity and the most startling revelation of any connection between her and Gaucher de Châtillon are furnished by a preliminary will which she drew up in 1337 ten years before she died. In that will Jeanne de Chastel stated that all of her property had come to her by acquisition and not by descent, except that which she had in the town and territory of Château-Porcien.[40] Toward the end of the will, she bequeathed to her brothers, nephews and nieces all of her property and this included "all that had come to her by descent from Jean Chauchier, her father, and which she holds in the town and territory of Château-Porcien."[41] Jeanne de Chastel was a

---

[38] A.N., JJ. 53, no. 43.
[39] A.N., JJ. 46, no. 72: "maistre Raoul de Presles, clerc et conseiller nostre seigneur le roy, et Jehanne sa fame."
[40] A.N., M. 185, no. 14.
[41] *Ibid.:* "Avecques tout ce qui li avint par descendue de Jehan

native of the administrative seat of Gaucher de Châtillon's county.

What relation could there have been between the count of Porcien and the wife of Raoul de Presles, who came from the town in which the count's château was located? There is never a hint in any of the documents that Jeanne de Chastel was noble. She did not refer to her father or brothers as being of the knightly class. We are led by the general practice of the time to speculate that her father or some relative was in the service of the constable as a *bailli*, serjeant, receiver, or some other official. Her father can be traced back to 1296. In that year a royal subsidy was collected throughout Champagne. One of only two subsidies registered for the town of Château-Porcien was the large sum of 250 *l.* from "Johannes dictus Chauciers."[42] The name with its *dictus* speaks of a person from obscure origins; the sum of money indicates a well-to-do merchant. It is safe to say that Jeanne de Chastel's immediate family was of respectable middle-class status.

In her preliminary will, Jeanne de Chastel named her father and two brothers, Jean and Pierre de Chastel, and referred to some unnamed sisters. But she furnished another possible clue to her connection with the constable when she mentioned a deceased uncle, master Guillaume Morel, who may have been her mother's brother.[43] We know the names of only a few officials who served the count of Porcien and administered his estates. But among the names we have is that of a *bailli* who served him in 1313-1314. The scholar who edited the document containing the name was uncertain of its exact spelling. He gave it as Jean de Mourel or Moreuil.[44] It is the slenderest sort of thread, but it is pos-

---

Chauchier son père, et que elle tient en la dicte ville ou terroir de Chastel en Porcien et es appendences."

[42] *Comptes royaux*, Part 2, p. 420.   [43] A.N., M. 185, no. 14.

[44] Robert, *Documents relatifs au comté de Porcien*, p. 124. In 1325, a "Gautier du Castel" was a knight of Gaucher de Châtillon, but

sible and even probable that the name was Morel and that Gaucher de Châtillon knew Jeanne de Chastel because her family served in his household.

But whether or not Châtillon's *bailli* was related to Jeanne de Chastel makes little difference. There can be no doubt that the constable knew and favored Jeanne, and this acquaintance and favor came from more than the fact that she was a native of his county seat. The best explanation lies in some family service to Châtillon personally or to his household in general. But let us not mistake her role in the constable's patronage of Raoul de Presles. There is no reason to believe that she introduced Presles to Châtillon for this would imply a prior acquaintance with the lawyer. We do not know the date of their marriage, but since Jeanne de Chastel's home was in Château-Porcien, the evidence suggests that Presles came to know her through his service to the constable. And the fact that Presles came to know Jeanne de Chastel implies visits to Château-Porcien and enlarges the portrait of him as the constable's lawyer. Not only did Gaucher de Châtillon introduce Jeanne de Chastel to Raoul de Presles, but he probably had something to do with arranging their marriage. As Gaucher de Châtillon was the factor common to both Jeanne and Raoul, so the valley of the Aisne was common to all three. Château-Porcien was situated some forty miles east of Presles on the upper reaches of the Aisne and near the northeastern frontier of Champagne.

Throughout this study of Raoul de Presles' origins and rise, we have had to deal with evidence of fact and with evidence of direction or circumstance. Evidence of fact says that Raoul de Presles was manumitted from serfdom by the abbot of Saint Denis in 1300. Inferences from evidence must be used to reconstruct his early years and the background of

there is no reason to believe that he was related to Jeanne de Chastel (*ibid.*, p. 137).

his manumission. Evidence of fact says that he was in the service of Gaucher de Châtillon, and he could not have had a more powerful sponsor. It is curious that the ultimate proof of both his manumission and of his relation to Gaucher de Châtillon was furnished by Jeanne de Chastel, in the one case by the suit brought against her by the heirs of Jean de Vasseny, and in the other case by the information contained in her preliminary will of 1337. But evidence of direction and circumstance must be used to establish Raoul de Presles' connection with the queen's household. Three circumstances point in this direction: his work in the service of the prince, Louis, which implies an earlier connection with Louis' mother; Philip's permission of 1306 to hold noble lands in Champagne; and the patronage of Gaucher de Châtillon. The most cogent argument is probably found in Châtillon's patronage. The constable, who was the military commander of Champagne and a man respected and honored by the young queen, either introduced Presles to the queen's service or found him there. Not only did the constable sponsor Raoul de Presles' rise, but he introduced him to Jeanne de Chastel, saved him from disaster in 1315, and finally outlived him.

The debts which Raoul de Presles incurred as a result of his trial, his indemnity to the king, and the legal costs of recovering his lands continued to plague him after 1320. Not only did he sell some of his holdings to meet his obligations but he turned to a new type of activity, the manumission of serfs. There was perhaps some charitable impulse involved in the freeing of serfs, but most persons, including kings, abbots, bishops, and nobles, freed serfs as a means of obtaining funds to pay off indebtedness and to meet the inflated cost of living. Financial compensation was never mentioned in any of the manumission charters that Presles granted to his serfs, and it was notably absent in most of such charters in the fourteenth century. But what we know of manumission practices during this period leads us to conclude that monetary arrangements were usually involved although such matters were not noted in the charters of formal manumission. Raoul de Presles began freeing his serfs individually in 1317, and this activity reached its peak in 1320, when he issued letters which freed all of his serfs in the *prévoté* of Courdemaine.[45] Despite this general manumission, he still issued individual letters of freedom as late as 1325, which indicates that the document of 1320, like Louis X's charter of 1315, was a general invitation to freedom with financial compensation to be made individually.[46] The fact that Presles did not engage in manumission activities until 1317 supports the view that he used manumission money to pay off his debts.

Raoul de Presles' relations with the commune of Vailly came to an end during these last years of his life. In the manumission charter of 1320 he gave to the commune the rights of *échevinage* which belonged to Courdemaine. This was tantamount to surrendering his right of high justice to the men of Vailly.[47] But the federative commune was beginning to have its troubles with the king, and in 1323 Charles IV decreed the abolition of the commune.[48] At this point, Presles delivered into the king's hands his *échevinage* and high justice which he held by right of Courdemaine. Such an act seems to contradict the document of 1320, and it is difficult to make a coherent story out of these events. Presles made it clear that he surrendered only his rights of high justice and retained all other rights together with his landed holdings.[49] For his part, the king promised that no commune

[45] A.N., JJ. 56, no. 76; JJ. 59, no. 415. The important charter of 1320 is in JJ. 59, no. 607.

[46] A.N., JJ. 60, no. 190; JJ. 62, nos. 284, 285. Most of the serfs whom he freed were from Vailly.

[47] A.N., JJ. 59, no. 607; Boutaric, no. 5,124.

[48] L. Carolus-Barré, *B.E.C.*, cxiii (1955), 102-105.

[49] A.N., JJ. 61, no. 402: "... sauf ce que il nest mie lentencion dou dit maistre Raoul quil donne au roy nulles de ses rentes, de ses hommes

would ever be reestablished in Vailly. There is a hint that Presles was still paying off his debt to the crown and therefore made it possible for Charles IV to obtain complete control of the federated commune. In one way or another, Raoul de Presles played an important role in the destruction of communal liberties at Vailly.

Other activities of Raoul de Presles during his last years merit some attention. Even while he was paying off his debts, he managed to make at least one new acquisition. In 1322 the abbey of Vaucelles near Cambrai let Presles have at farm some of its lands and rents in Vailly, Celles, and Condé.[50] These were small rents but they show that the lawyer continued to increase his landed holdings in the valley of the Aisne. At the same time that the commune of Vailly was abolished, the joint educational enterprise of Presles and Gui de Laon came to an end, and the college they had founded at Paris split into two separate institutions.[51] And

---

et fames de corps, et de chevelise, ne de ses autres droiz quiex quil soient ne comment quil soient nommez quil a en la dicte ville de Vailly mais que tant seulement de leschevinage et iustice dessus diz. . . ."

[50] The first notice of this acquisition comes from A.N., JJ. 61, nos. 52, 55. In November 1328, after the death of Raoul de Presles, the holdings of Vaucelles were the subject of litigation between the abbey and his executors. See Archives départementales du Nord, 28 H 75, no. 1535. Two other documents tell the earlier history of the abbey's rents at Vailly (Archives départementales du Nord, 28 H 75, nos. 1,527, 1,531). During his last years, Presles was frequently engaged in litigation over lands which he had acquired earlier. This was especially true of the rent he had sold to the chapter of Laon. See Comte Maxime de Sars, *Le Laonnois féodal*, v, 666, which concerns the holdings at Amigny which Presles had ceded to the chapter of Laon in return for La Royère. More on the matter is found in A.N., X1c 1a, nos. 9, 10, in which Girard de Presles joined Raoul in making settlement with the chapter. See also Boutaric, nos. 6,228, 6,538, 6,547.

[51] For the documents on the separation, see A.N., M. 185, no. 5; MM. 418, fol. 9 r.-13 v. The two colleges continued to have much litigation over the rents given to them, respectively, by Gui de Laon and Raoul de Presles. From the lands which Raoul had formerly acquired from the lord of Blérancourt at Amigny, he granted a considerable portion to his college and these lands became known as the

finally in 1321, Presles and his wife undertook a pilgrimage
to Saint James of Compostella. Royal letters ordering protection, during his absence, of his lands in Vermandois were
issued in February 1321.[52] As was usually the case, he and
his wife went in company with other pilgrims and an ironic
twist is provided by the fact that Charles de Valois also
made the pilgrimage at this time.[53] In view of their earlier
careers, it is interesting to speculate on the spiritual motives
that prompted these two men to visit one of the great shrines
of western Christendom.

In concluding our comments on Raoul de Presles, we
come to the great question of his public career. Aside from
his deposition against the Templars, what was his role and
what did he do as a lawyer of the last Capetians? The evidence before 1314 portrays him as a private lawyer, a landholder, and a philanthropist. We have only the bare statements that he was in the royal service during this time.
After his acquittal he returned to the government and was
repeatedly referred to as *clerc et conseiller du roi* under the
last two Capetians. We even catch glimpses of him at work
in judicial affairs, which is more than we have for the period
before 1314.[54] This lack of activity gives a strange aspect to

---

"fief of Presles." See Maxime de Sars, *Le Laonnois féodal*, v, 666, 677,
681; A.N., X1c 1a, no. 22. For another gift by Presles, see *Livre Rouge*,
no. 563.

[52] Boutaric, no. 6282. Only the year before, Raoul and his wife had
given to Notre Dame de Laon 100 *s*. of rent on their farm at La
Royère for their anniversary in the cathedral church. Perhaps Raoul
had a serious illness at this time and felt that the end was near.

[53] *Chronique parisienne anonyme*, p. 59. The count of Valois died
in December 1325.

[54] Boutaric, nos. 5,929, 6,501. We must be wary of Boutaric on
this point for he sometimes mistook Presles for Préaux. *Chronique
parisienne anonyme*, p. 61, pictures Presles with Gaucher de Châtillon
and Rénaud de Lor counselling with the bourgeoisie of Paris on the
king's need for a subsidy in 1321. It seems that Presles was never sent
on any commissions or embassies. Fawtier, *Comptes du trésor*, no. 845,
has a "Raoul de Praelis" going with Philip V to the pope. But Fawtier
noted that the manuscript said "Parelis," and this is almost certainly

Raoul de Presles' career and makes him either an invisible agent or a man who did nothing. The latter alternative will not stand up for we do know that he was a *clerc et conseiller du roi* under Philip the Fair. The key to his work is probably to be found in the characterization given him by the chroniclers who called him the "principal advocate of the king."[55] He is never seen in the records as a "master" in the Parlement, and he never received wages for such work as did Latilly, Villepreux, and Mauconduit. Neither did he receive a salary, which was the manner of paying men like Flote and Cuignières.

Lawyers who acted as pleaders or advocates in the Parlement de Paris were not referred to in the records of the Parlement until the later fourteenth century. And those who pleaded for the king did not appear in the financial records until the reign of Philip VI. This is the best reason why the evidence does not portray Raoul de Presles at work as a lawyer. Pleaders or advocates simply did not get their names into legal records and were therefore invisible agents.[56] This principle is no less true of the lawyers who served as royal proctors and advocates in the *bailliages* and *sénéchaussées*. Their names can often be determined; their work remains obscure. The famous Pierre Dubois held the post of royal advocate for ecclesiastical cases in the *bailliage* of Coutances, but scarcely a word can be said about his work for the king. A better example is the case of Pierre de Chalon, who began his career as a royal proctor in the

---

Préaux (see Appendix). *Mignon,* pp. 357, 362, 364, 365, also has Presles making trips on the king's business from 1311 to 1320. Once again, he probably confused the two men. The person referred to in *Journ. Charles IV,* no. 2,375, was probably Presles, who accounted in 1321 for expenses in the business of the king. The entry does not refer to travel.

[55] Contin. de Nangis, *H.F.,* xx, 613; Chroniques de Saint Denis, *H.F.,* xx, 696.

[56] This was also true of English serjeants-at-law during this period. Their names rarely appear in the official plea rolls of the English law courts.

bailliage of Macon.[57] In 1311 he was called to Paris and was
made a *conseiller* in the *hôtel du roi*.[58] We have the actual
letters of his appointment—something that is missing for
Presles and most of the other lawyers. While we know that
Pierre de Chalon was a royal lawyer in the central government during the remainder of Philip the Fair's reign, there
is no evidence of his role or contribution with the exception
of one commission.[59] Like so many of the lawyers who assisted the king in Paris or in the provinces, Pierre de Chalon
was an invisible agent, and Raoul de Presles must unfortunately be placed in this group.

Apart from his deposition in 1310, we can say absolutely
nothing about Raoul de Presles' work or influence in Capetian government. This puts him in a class by himself for
we can usually determine the roles of the other lawyers who
managed the Parlement, acted as judges, formulated policy,
and performed multiple services for the Capetian kings.
Raoul de Presles put most of what we know of his private
life into the Chancery Registers and into other state documents, but not one item on his governmental career found
its way into the records. Yet everything about him spoke of
a man who had power and influence in government; his
trial alone sufficed to put the stamp of importance on him.
He was remembered by historians not as a man who came
out of serfdom and gained great landed wealth but as a
powerful and influential lawyer of Philip the Fair who was
prosecuted after his master's death. Like Villepreux, he did
not live to see the end of the era. He died on the morrow
of Saint Vincent, January 23, 1327, and was entombed in
the parish church of Presles.[60] So he returned to the valley

---

[57] *Comptes royaux*, Part 1, p. 284.
[58] A.N., JJ. 42A, no. 133.   [59] A.N., JJ. 42A, nos. 90-92.
[60] That Presles died on January 23 is made clear by A.N., M. 140,
no. 6, in which the scholars of the Collège de Laon agreed to sing a
mass for Raoul each year on the "lendemain de feste Saint Vincent,
le quel jour li diz maistre Raoul trespassa de cest siècle." He was still

of the Aisne where he had accumulated his earthly treasures and there, twenty years later, his wife who had meant so much to his career was laid beside him.

---

living in 1326 (A.N., MM. 418, fol. 181 r.-v.) and he was dead by October 1327 (A.N., JJ. 64, no. 718). Remnants of the sepulchral statues of Raoul and Jeanne still existed in the church at Presles as late as 1882. But the soft stone had deteriorated so that the features were scarcely visible. See Edouard Fleury, *Antiquités et monuments du département de l'Aisne,* IV (Paris, 1882), 192.

CHAPTER EIGHT

The New Generation

HISTORIANS have for the most part scorned the reigns of Philip the Fair's three sons although Paul Lehugeur gave detailed attention to Philip V. This neglect can be largely understood, for the last fourteen years of the Capetian era were unproductive of great issues and dramatic episodes. The energy of the tremendous offensives mounted in so many directions by the lawyers of Philip the Fair seems to have dissipated after his death. But this is appearance rather than reality. The two celebrated affairs that have given so much publicity to Philip the Fair's reign were settled; there was no longer any need for struggle with the papacy, and the Templars were destroyed. The fourteen-year period of the three sons has suffered, therefore, mainly as a result of contrast with the turbulence and violence of their father's reign. So far as the other incidents that made Philip the Fair's reign famous are concerned, these were repeated although less strikingly under his three sons. The Jews were again persecuted in 1321, when they were held guilty of complicity in the lepers' plot to poison streams and fountains in southern France. They were put to a ransom of 150,000 *l.* The Lombards were again charged with usury in 1320, and Charles IV proceeded to new money alterations after 1322.[1] And as for Flanders and Gascony, this

---

[1] For the affairs of the lepers, the Jews, and the Lombards, see *H.L.*, IX, 409-412, 415-416; Langlois in Lavisse, *Histoire de France*, III, Part 2, pp. 221, 229; *Journ. Charles IV*, nos. 28, 96, 105, 374, 434. The period of Philip V has been fruitful ground for studies of representative assemblies by C. H. Taylor, "An Assembly of French Towns in March, 1318," *Speculum*, XIII (1938), 295-303; "Assemblies of French Towns in 1316," *Speculum*, XIV (1939), 275-299; "The Composition of Baronial Assemblies in France, 1315-1320," *Speculum*, XXIX (1954), 689-711. See also Armand d'Herbomez, "Notes et documents pour servir à l'histoire des rois fils de Philippe le Bel," *B.E.C.*, LIX (1898), 497-532, 689-711.

entire period formed the background to the beginning of the Hundred Years War.

The era of the three sons was also similar to their father's reign in that administrative persecutions or state trials continued with almost as great a frequency. The brief reign of Louis X Hutin, aside from the revolt of the barons, was a continuous process against the favorites of Philip the Fair, and we have already noted the trials of Raoul de Préaux and Béraud de Mercoeur under Philip V. The provost of Paris, Henri de Taperel, was charged in 1320 with various malefactions by the count of Valois and the king's brother. Despite the queen's plea, he was found guilty by a panel of great nobles and was hanged.[2] Perhaps the most impressive trial took place in 1322 after Charles IV came to the throne. Géraud Gueite was a member of the wealthy banking and merchant family of Clermont. He had served as master of the Chamber of Accounts under Philip V after a career as royal receiver for Beaucaire, Champagne, and Auvergne. His brothers, Jacques and Mathieu, had also been receivers of Auvergne and Toulouse, and the entire family had served as bankers to the French crown. A curious prelude to the trial of 1322 occurred in 1318, when Géraud and his brothers were found guilty of undue speculations on the variations in money. For this misconduct they were pardoned by Philip V. But Charles IV had second thoughts on the matter, and perhaps Géraud's pardon encouraged him to more serious malfeasance. Géraud was found guilty but died shortly after he was imprisoned.[3] Another celebrated trial of Charles IV's reign involved the southern baron,

---

[2] A. Hellot, *Chronique parisienne anonyme* in *Mémoires de la société de l'histoire de Paris et de l'Ile de France*, XI (1884), 51ff.

[3] For Philip V's pardon for money speculations, see *Livre Rouge*, no. 1,083. The most extensive study of the Gueite family is M. Boudet, "Les Gayte et les Chaucat," *Revue d'Auvergne* (1911), pp. 1, 146, 238, 379; (1912), pp. 43, 116, 260. No one has ever determined the correct spelling of the name. The three brothers were ennobled in 1319 (A.N., JJ. 59, nos. 270, 272).

Jourdain de l'Isle, who was accused of sundry crimes including murder. He was hanged in 1323 at Paris.[4] The longest
and most tedious process came to an end in 1319 when
Bernard Délicieux, the Franciscan of Carcassonne, whose ordeal had run on for some fifteen years, was sentenced to imprisonment.[5]

Just as the period of the three sons had neither the bril-
liance nor the drama of their father's reign, so did their lawyers fail to develop the historical personality or the administrative drive that characterized the lawyers of Philip the
Fair. Perhaps strong personalities produced important
events, or perhaps it was the other way around. Flote, Nogaret, and Plaisians had passed from the scene, and Philip the
Fair's lawyers who continued to serve his sons became weary
with age or bored by inactivity. While one can speak of a
new generation of lawyers under Philip V and Charles IV,
there is little of importance to be said about these men who
came into view between 1316 and 1328. They performed
their work dutifully and made their contributions to the
formulation of policy quietly and without ostentation. Few
survived after 1328 or continued in their posts under the
first of the Valois kings.

So far as can be determined, the four chancellors who
served Philip V and Charles IV came from noble families
and were lawyers and ecclesiastics. When Philip V became
regent in the summer of 1316 he removed Etienne de Mornay
from the Chancery and replaced him with Pierre d'Arrabloy,
who had been his chancellor when he was count of Poitiers.
The orthography of this man's name is controversial and
most historians have spelled it "d'Arrablay." But Henri Stein
maintained that he was a member of the family whose home
was Arrabloy near Gien in the Gâtinais, and who gave so

---

[4] *H.L.*, ɪx, 418. The Picard noble, Ferry de Picquigny, was also tried
and his property confiscated in 1325 (A.N., JJ. 64, no. 75).

[5] Langlois in Lavisse, *Histoire de France*, ɪɪɪ, Part 2, pp. 201-207;
H.L., ɪx, 389-393.

many high-ranking officers to the service of the last Capetian kings.[6] Pierre d'Arrabloy was probably the son of Jean d'Arrabloy, who served Philip the Fair at various times as seneschal of Périgord, Quercy, Carcassonne, Beaucaire, and Nîmes. Jean d'Arrabloy the younger was Pierre's brother and seneschal of Cahors in 1316. Another brother was Guillaume, who obtained a university education and entered the service of the Church. Pierre d'Arrabloy had worked in the Parlement under Philip the Fair and remained in Philip V's Chancery for only a few months. Although he was made a cardinal and surrendered the post of chancellor in 1317, he was retained as a member of the king's council and was one of his executors in 1322. There can be no question of patronage with Pierre d'Arrabloy; his family had long been in Capetian administration.[7]

Pierre de Chappes succeeded d'Arrabloy as chancellor and held the office until he obtained the bishopric of Arras in 1321. His name indicates that he may have come from the village or territory of Chappes in Champagne, north of Château-Porcien. The canonry that he held in Reims substantiates this view. One of his patrons was Louis de Clermont, seigneur of Bourbon, who helped him to obtain a canonry in Châlons in 1316.[8] At that moment he was a clerk and councillor of Philip the regent. Chappes had been a doctor of law since 1309.[9] His career in Capetian government was calm enough but his ecclesiastical career was stormy. As treasurer of Laon he had so much trouble keep-

---

[6] Henri Stein, "Recherches sur quelques fonctionnaires royaux des XIIIe et XIVe siècles originaires du Gâtinais," *Annales de la société historique et archéologique du Gâtinais*, XXXII (1914-1915), 203-212.

[7] For Pierre d'Arrabloy, see Père Anselme, *Histoire généalogique*, VI, 306-309; Lucien Perrichet, *La Grande Chancellerie de la France des origines à 1328* (Paris, 1912), pp. 533-534. Pierre d'Arrabloy was given a study permit in 1314 (*Clement V*, no. 10,111), or perhaps it was nonresidence permission for teaching purposes.

[8] *Jean XXII*, nos. 177, 202, 257, 346, 7,673, 12,897-12,906.

[9] For Chappes as a doctor of laws in 1309, see *Clement V*, no. 4,379.

ing control of his benefice and property that the pope assigned the abbot of Saint Germain des Près and other high ecclesiastics to adjudicate for him in his land disputes. When he was named bishop of Arras in 1320, he could not even take possession of his see because the heirs of his predecessor stirred up trouble and appropriated the episcopal lands.[10]

For his third chancellor Philip V chose Jean de Cherchemont, who had been in the service of Charles de Valois since 1316. A lawyer by training, he became Valois' chancellor in 1316 and served him in various capacities until the count's death.[11] Cherchemont's career as chancellor was interrupted briefly when Charles IV came to the throne in 1322. Like his brother before him, Charles replaced Cherchemont with Pierre Rodier, who had been his chancellor when he was count of La Marche. Père Anselme called Rodier a gentleman of Auvergne. There is a greater likelihood that he was a native of the Limousin. Most of his prebends were in and around Limoges, and this would easily account for his introduction to Charles' service while the latter was still count of La Marche. Rodier was a canonist and one of the few to become prominent among the Capetian lawyers. He surrendered his governmental office in 1323, when he became bishop of Carcassonne.[12]

Jean de Cherchemont returned to the Chancery at Rodier's resignation and remained there until his death in October 1328. He derived from a noble family of Poitou, several of whose members distinguished themselves in the service of the Church. He was so well known as a lawyer that John XXII committed to him in 1317, in company with the arch-

[10] *Jean XXII*, nos. 7673, 12,897-12,906.
[11] *Ibid.*, nos. 329, 966.
[12] Père Anselme, *Histoire généalogique*, vi, 310; Perrichet, *La Grande Chancellerie*, p. 536. He took part in peace negotiations with Flanders in 1319 (A.N., JJ. 58, no. 390). See also *Mignon*, p. 364. Information on his prebends is in *Jean XXII*, nos. 382, 6,037, 10,512, 13,659, 13,661, 13,154.

bishop of Bourges, the task of reforming the law school at Orléans.[13] In his ecclesiastical career he became dean of Poitiers, canon of Paris, and finally treasurer of Laon. His personality stands out from those of the other three chancellors, and he seems to have had something of the force, arrogance, and drive of Pierre de Latilly. Cherchemont was one of the few Capetian lawyers who served, but only for a brief period, under the first of the Valois kings. He made enemies and his administration of the Chancery came into question after his death when it was discovered that he had charged too much for the issuance of certain types of letters.[14] All four of the last Capetian chancellors used governmental service as an avenue for advancement in the Church. One became a cardinal, two became bishops, and Cherchemont, like Etienne de Mornay, was thwarted in his desire for a bishopric. Three of them—Chappes, Rodier, and Cherchemont—were probably university professors before they became chancellor.

The outstanding example of the lawyers who came into the royal government at the end of Philip the Fair's reign and served to the end of the dynasty was Michel Mauconduit. Born of a noble Norman family whose lands lay on the Channel coast between Fécamp and Dieppe, he appeared in January 1306 as a witness to a charter in which Guillaume Mauconduit, *vicomte* of Blosseville, founded a chaplaincy in his manor house at Blosseville. Another member of the family, also named Guillaume, was then dean of Canville-les-Deux-Eglises, and a third person, Jean Mauconduit, was named in the charter.[15] The relationship between these four

[13] *Ibid.*, no. 5,378.
[14] For comment on Cherchemont, see Père Anselme, *Histoire généalogique*, vi, 309f.; Perrichet, *La Grande Chancellerie*, p. 535; Raymond Cazelles, *La société politique*, p. 57f. For the investigation after his death, see Furgeot, nos. 3,424, 3,708. For two grants to him by Charles IV, see A.N., JJ. 64, nos. 87, 713.
[15] A.N., JJ. 45, no. 205. In 1312 Guillaume Mauconduit was still dean of Canville. Another member of the family, Robert Mauconduit,

persons cannot be determined, although one is led to suspect that the *vicomte* was the father of the others. The family name came from the two villages of Saussetôt-le-Mauconduit and Criquetôt-le-Mauconduit. Michel Mauconduit was qualified in the charter as *legum professor*. He had already reached the height of his teaching career as professor of law in the school at Orléans. One year earlier, he and Etienne de Mornay had pleaded with Clement V to grant new privileges and immunities to the law school.[16] Mauconduit, therefore, falls into the class of Mornay, Pierre de Belleperche, and Guillaume de Nogaret, whose professorial careers preceded their entry into Capetian government.

Michel Mauconduit came to the service of Philip the Fair at the moment that Nogaret and Plaisians passed from the scene. He came immediately into the king's council, for during the remaining months of Philip's reign Mauconduit ordered some half-dozen letters out of Chancery, two of them in company with Philippe de Villepreux.[17] His first assignment came under Louis X when in July 1315 he and Villepreux were dispatched into Vermandois to sell freedom to the royal serfs. During the reign of Philip V he was present in council more often than anyone with the exception of Villepreux and Pierre de Chappes.[18] Yet it is difficult to describe his contributions to policy-making or to the machinery of government during these years. By his very presence in council one must presume that he had influence in decisions of state. But his career was a quiet and uneventful one and was, in this respect, similar to those of Pierre and Philippe de Mornay.[19] His ecclesiastical advancement

---

was the rector of the parish church of Criquetôt-le-Mauconduit (*Clement V*, nos. 8,940, 8,941).

[16] *Ibid.*, no. 359.

[17] A.N., JJ. 49, nos. 75, 209, 220; JJ. 50, nos. 88, 97, 98.

[18] Lehugeur, *Philippe le Long: le mécanisme du gouvernement*, p. 31.

[19] He made peace with the dean and chapter of Tournai in 1324 (A.N., JJ. 62, no. 401), and, with Cherchemont, Guillaume Flote, and

also moved along unspectacular lines. He held the parish church of Saussetôt-le-Mauconduit by family inheritance, obtained the archdeaconry of Pont-Audemer, the treasurership of Saint Frambald in Senlis, and prebends in Paris, Rouen, and Lisieux. In 1318 he was offered the bishopric of Pamplona in Navarre but declined and became dean of Chartres in 1326.[20] Mauconduit represents the lawyer of Philip V and Charles IV who, after the great battles had been fought, dedicated himself to the calm and undisturbed administration of government. He died in 1328 shortly after Philippe de Valois came to the throne.

Three other men who rose to prominence after 1314 represent the lawyers who began their careers under the last Capetians and continued in government well into the reign of the first Valois. More than anyone else they showed that the new generation was not at all new, for they displayed the same penchant for embroiling themselves in celebrated affairs that characterized Nogaret, Plaisians, and Presles. Jean d'Asnières made his name in 1315 when he delivered the king's case against Marigny. He again achieved notoriety in 1322 when Charles IV chose him to prosecute Géraud Gueite.[21] He was called "advocate in Parlement" at that moment, but we know nothing about his origins or family. It has been assumed that he was Charles de Valois' agent, and Joseph Petit identified him with the provost of Orléans

---

Pierre de Cuignières, negotiated with the Flemish towns in 1326 (A.N., JJ. 64, no. 154). He can be seen at work in the Parlement in Boutaric, nos. 4,482, 7,666, 5,727. For his wages in the Parlement, see *Journ. Charles IV*, nos. 1,521, 2,438, 4,432, 6,745, 8,585.

[20] Glimpses of his ecclesiastical career can be seen in *Jean XXII*, nos. 393, 6,177, 7,903, 27,330. His philanthropic activity included the hospital of Bringuedale which he founded in the parish of Saussetôt (A.N., JJ. 64, no. 849).

[21] *Journ. Charles IV*, no. 115. Very little information is found in B. Hauréau, "Jean d'Asnières, avocat," *Histoire littéraire de la France*, xxviii, 456-459. See also Roland Delachenal, *Histoire des avocats au Parlement de Paris, 1300-1600* (Paris, 1885), p. 356f.

in 1308 and with the *bailli* of the county of Valois in 1323.[22] But we are not even sure that his name was d'Asnières or Hanière. The lawyer who prosecuted Marigny and Gueite was the same person, and he was in the service of Philip VI as late as 1347 when he was associated with such famous Valois lawyers as Jacques la Vache and the younger Simon de Bucy.[23]

The second of these lawyers was Pierre de Maucreux, who sprang into notice in 1323 when he was selected to handle the king's case against Jourdain de l'Isle.[24] He must have been in the royal service for some time before this date for Charles granted nobility in 1326 to "our beloved advocate, master Pierre de Maucreux."[25] If he came from the hamlet of Maucreux, situated between Neuilly-Saint-Front and Villers-Cotteret, he may have risen under the auspices of Charles de Valois. He was constantly present in Parlement during the first decade of the Valois dynasty and was associated with such notables as Jean l'Orfevre, Jacques la Vache, and the notorious Guillaume du Breuil.[26] His biographer claimed that he was not only in the service of Mahaut d'Artois but also helped Guillaume du Breuil to defend the former's adversary, Robert d'Artois.[27] His association with du Breuil lends an unsavory taste to his character and career for the latter, while never a royal lawyer, represents the worst possible ethical tradition in the practice of fourteenth-century French law. Like du Breuil, Maucreux was an author and has been given credit for a short law tract on pleading which was composed sometime before 1334.[28] Maucreux died

[22] Petit, *Charles de Valois,* pp. 343, 346.
[23] Furgeot, nos. 3768, 7817; Journ. Philippe VI, no. 1651.
[24] *Journ. Charles IV,* no. 4,836.
[25] A.N., JJ. 64, no. 166.
[26] Furgeot, nos. 1190, 2876; A.N., X1c lb, nos. 179, 218.
[27] Paul Fournier, "Les deux Maucreux, jurisconsultes," *Histoire littéraire de la France,* xxxvi, 596. A short notice of Maucreux is in Delachenal, *Histoire des avocats,* p. 365.
[28] Fournier, *Histoire littéraire de la France,* xxxvi, 597.

about 1340 and left a son and a daughter, Jeanne, who married into nobility.[29]

The best known lawyer of the new generation was Pierre de Cuignières. Although d'Asnières and Maucreux took part in important cases, they never achieved the fame which Cuignières gained when he represented the royal view in the debate at Vincennes in 1329. As for his biography the account by Carlier deserves mention for there is little in it that has been contradicted. He came from a noble family of the Beauvaisis whose origins have been explored back to the twelfth century. During an earlier ecclesiastical career he presumably obtained a formal education in law. But like many other clerks he surrendered his career in the Church and married Jeanne de Néry, a member of the illustrious house of Nanteuil-le-Haudouin and granddaughter of Guillaume de Crépy, lawyer and chancellor of Philip the Fair. Carlier believed that Crépy not only introduced Pierre de Cuignières to the court but sponsored a friendship between him and the Flotes. In 1311 the Cuignières family obtained the seigneury of Saintines on the southern border of the Forest of Compiègne, and Pierre became lord of Saintines after his brother's death.[30]

The only trouble with Carlier's story is that we cannot find Cuignières in the royal service until 1322, and after that point he was much in evidence. He was not an ordinary member of the Parlement for his salary was much larger than that paid to Mauconduit or to d'Asnières and Maucreux. He received 500 *l. par.* every year and seemed to be used by Charles IV in special work, often on secret business and sometimes on embassies.[31] It is possible that he was used against Robert d'Artois in 1329 and that he profited from

[29] Furgeot, no. 2,886.

[30] Claude Carlier, *Histoire du duché de Valois* (3 vols.; Paris, 1764), II, 234-246.

[31] *Journ. Charles IV*, nos. 2,971, 3,727, 5,331, 5,561, 9,544.

the count's fall.[32] In any event he obtained a secure niche in the tradition of Gallican lawyers when in 1329 at the Assembly of Vincennes he defended royal rights over ecclesiastical justice against such churchmen as Pierre Bertrand and Pierre Roger. Pierre de Cuignières continued in the Valois government until his death about 1347. Tradition says that he had one son and two daughters. One of these daughters, Marguerite, married Pierre de Sermoise, and when she died in 1369 she founded a chaplaincy at Saintines for her father "Pierre, seigneur of Cuignières," and for her brothers. No mention was made of sisters and this seems to contradict tradition. Her daughter, Marie de Sermoise, married into the Bouteiller de Senlis family, and so the alliances with powerful noble houses continued.[33]

What did the new generation prove? The few lawyers whom we have treated here behaved much as had Flote, Nogaret, and Presles under Philip the Fair. They were willing to do their king's bidding in every instance. The lawyers of Philip the Fair prosecuted Saisset, Guichard, Boniface, and the Templars. The lawyers of the three sons managed the cases not only against Philip the Fair's favorites but also against Géraud Gueite, Béraud de Mercoeur, Jourdain de l'Isle, and Robert d'Artois, although this last case came

[32] Carlier, *Histoire du duché de Valois*, II, 240; Cazelles, *La société politique*, p. 90.

[33] A.N., JJ. 102, no. 327. For his performance at Vincennes, see Olivier Martin, *L'Assemblée de Vincennes de 1329 et ses conséquences* (Rennes, 1909). For additional comment on Cuignières, see Félix Aubert, "Notes pour servir à la biographie de Pierre de Cugnières," *Bulletin de la société de l'histoire de Paris et de l'Ile de France* (1884), pp. 134-137, and the vicomte Amaury de Caix de Saint-Aymour, "Additions aux notes pour servir à la biographie de Pierre de Cugnières," in the same journal (1885), pp. 50-53. For Cuignières at work, see Furgeot, no. 2,995; A.N., X1c 1b, nos. 195, 228; X1c 2a, no. 161; L. H. Labande, *Trésor des chartes du comté de Rethel* (Paris, 1916), IV, 201. The name of this lawyer has usually been spelled "Cugnières," but the name of the village is spelled "Cuignières." Delisle lists him as *bailli* of Sens in 1322 (*H.F.*, XXIV, Part 1, p. 43).

after the end of the Capetian period. While Cuignières and the chancellors came from nobility, the example of Pierre de Maucreux proved that lawyers could still rise from the middle class or even from recently manumitted serfs. As a group or as individuals these lawyers were not as impressive as their predecessors, but one suspects that if the cases of Boniface and the Templars had been given to them, they would have conducted themselves much as had Nogaret and the others.

Perhaps the most interesting fact about this new generation was its connection with Charles de Valois. D'Asnières, Cherchemont, and Etienne de Mornay, who really belonged to the new generation, owed their advancement to Valois. Since Mauconduit knew Etienne de Mornay and was his academic colleague, it is possible that Mornay introduced him to the count, who in turn obtained his entry into government at the very end of his brother's reign. One scholar who has studied Cuignières suggested that he had connections with the house of Valois, and if Pierre de Maucreux actually derived from the village near Villers-Cotteret he quite possibly came up under the tutelage of Charles de Valois. In effect, Charles de Valois prepared in some measure the foundations of his son's reign by bringing into the government of his nephews lawyers who owed loyalty to the house of Valois.

CHAPTER NINE

The Legacy of the Capetian Lawyers

NOTHING is so impressive about the end of the Capetian era as the disappearance of so many lawyers in such a short time. Raoul de Presles, Pierre de Latilly, Philippe de Villepreux, Michel Mauconduit, Jean de Cherchemont, and Philippe de Mornay, all died in 1327 and 1328. Etienne de Mornay followed them in 1332. Even within the new generation, only Cuignières, d'Asnières, and Maucreux continued for any length of time into the age of the Valois. All of the lawyers who had gained any significance or importance under the last Capetians vanished with their kings. But this phenomenon was true only of the lawyers. In the Chancery, Pierre Barrière and many of the notaries remained in service. A large group of financial personnel, including Jean de Saint-Just and the Mignon brothers, was active for some time after 1328. Most of all, the machinery, traditions, and practices of French governmental administration continued with no great changes.

More than the passing of the lawyers, the death of Gaucher de Châtillon symbolized the end of the Capetian era. During his life he represented the forces of stability in French government, and the essence of his career was loyal service to the French crown. This loyal service carried with it authority and influence. The venerable status of his house and his position as a military commander and constable of France made his a power to reckon with. In giving him the county of Porcien, Philip the Fair picked Châtillon as the man best qualified to guard French interests on the northeastern border of Champagne and to watch over developments in the empire that lay beyond those borders.[1] When Châtillon was not on military campaigns, he sat almost constantly in the Parlement de Paris and in the king's council. In this way, he came to know all of the lawyers. His sponsorship of Raoul de Presles illustrated his close ties with the Capetian lawyers.

Still, as constable of France, it is Châtillon's military exploits that are best known. No one has ever determined how many military campaigns he executed, but Robert Mignon's inventory gives some idea of their number and variety.[2] Although most of his fighting and military administration took place in Flanders, his greatest strategic value was proved in Champagne, which he constantly protected from the count of Bar. He even led an army in 1309 against his colleague the unruly Béraud de Mercoeur, and he spent most of 1317 fighting the rebellious nobles in Artois and Champagne. In short, his military expeditions took him from Aragon and Navarre to the North Sea, and from Gascony and Normandy to the Rhone and the Meuse.

While Châtillon exercised tremendous influence in the government of Philip the Fair, his contributions to political stability and to the formulation of policy are best illustrated

[1] Châtillon made many expeditions into the county of Bar to restore peace or to exact retribution for invasions of Champagne. One of these is described in Lehugeur, *Histoire de Philippe le Long*, pp. 235ff. His third wife was Elizabeth de Rumigny, dowager duchess of Lorraine, and mother of Ferry, who succeeded to his father. The marriage may have been prompted by Philip the Fair, who wished in this way to establish stronger contact with the lands to the east. See Duchesne, *Histoire de la maison de Châtillon-sur-Marne*, p. 344.

Next to the county of Porcien lay the county of Rethel, held by the counts of Flanders. Especially after 1318, Châtillon was constantly involved in the affairs of Rethel. (*Trésor des chartes du comté de Rethel*, I, 663, 692, 697, 715; IV, 236f.). For Châtillon and the events of the summer of 1316, see G. Servois, "Documents inédits sur l'avènement de Philippe le Long," *Bulletin de la société de l'histoire de France* (1864), pp. 44-79.

[2] *Mignon*, pp. 340-343.

by his conduct in the reign of Louis X and during the months just after Louis' death. The counsel of Châtillon can be seen in Louis' approach to the settlement of the baronial complaints and in his behavior in the tents at Bondues.[3] In the days after Louis' death, Châtillon virtually ran the government, sometimes in conjunction with and sometimes in opposition to the count of Valois. He had as great a voice as anyone in the decisions to give the regency and then the crown to Philip V.[4] During the remaining twelve years of Capetian rule, Châtillon continued to defend the realm, to counsel the kings, and to help in the everyday administration of the government.[5]

The end of the Capetian house came with the death of Charles IV on February 5, 1328. Gaucher de Châtillon survived the Capetians, and we have one last glimpse of him in the council of the new Valois king debating another campaign against the Flemish. Most of the barons were disposed to put the matter off, but Philip VI asked Gaucher his opinion and the constable replied, "Qui bon cuer à la bataille, touz jours treuve-il temps convenable."[6] The battle of Cassel was fought in August 1328 and Châtillon, now some eighty years of age, rode in the vanguard of the attack. But this was his last battle and his last victory for death took the old warrior in May of 1329. The aged Joinville had died ten years earlier; thus Gaucher de Châtillon was the last of the great nobles who had "known" Saint Louis. He had served seven kings and five of them as constable of France. It was fitting that he fought at Cassel, for Cassel was the last victory of the French feudal army before the terrible defeats suffered

---

[3] Artonne, *Le mouvement de 1314*, p. 56f.

[4] Lehugeur, *Histoire de Philippe le Long*, pp. 28ff.

[5] Under the reign of Philip V, Châtillon was present in the Great Council more often than any noble with the exception of Rénaud de Lor, Henri de Sully, and Anseau de Joinville (Lehugeur, *Philippe le Long: le mécanisme du gouvernement*, p. 30). He had usually sat in the Parlement since the beginning of the century.

[6] Viard, *Les Grandes Chroniques*, IX, 79.

during the Hundred Years War. In this respect, the passing of Gaucher de Châtillon signified the end of a military era as well as the end of Capetian France.

The Valois were simply Capetians under another name. The break in line of descent which occurred in 1328 was not much greater than that of 1316 when Philip the Fair's second son mounted the throne. To the question, "What did the Capetians leave to France?" one may answer, "The Valois kings." In the same spirit we must now ask, "What did the lawyers of the last Capetians leave to France?" Unlike the lawyers of Saint Louis and Philip III, the lawyers of the last Capetians gave to France their sons, nephews, and cousins, and thereby established a tradition of civil service by descent, the origins of which cannot be traced back earlier than Philip the Fair's reign. The first faint evidence of this new development can be found in the reigns of the last Capetians, but the expansion and maturity of the tradition came under the Valois kings.

The Flote family is a good example of service dynasties in the fourteenth century. Guillaume Flote was the elder son of Pierre Flote. He decided upon a clerical career at an early date, and Boniface VIII heaped favors upon him because his father was chancellor of France and his first cousin was Gilles Aicelin. Guillaume Flote was engaged in university studies in 1298 when Boniface permitted him to hold the archdeaconry of Brabant without necessity of taking priestly orders.[7] By 1299 Guillaume was provost of Normandy in the church of Chartres, archdeacon of Brabant, treasurer of Saint Frambald of Senlis, and held prebends in Cambrai, Paris, Chartres, Lyons, Vienne, Macon, Le Puy, and Clermont.[8] He could easily have acquired a bishopric and perhaps a cardinal's hat within a short time if relations between his father and Boniface had not suddenly deteriorated. In November 1302, Boniface damned the memory of Pierre Flote,

---

[7] *Boniface VIII*, no. 2,420.   [8] *Ibid.*, no. 2,857.

deprived his two sons of all their prebends and offices, and disqualified his descendants up to the fourth generation from holding ecclesiastical office.[9] Although Benedict XI revoked Boniface's sentence in 1304, Guillaume Flote never resumed his clerical career.[10] His brother, Artaud, who was formerly a monk of Cluny, did otherwise and eventually became abbot of Vézelay and councillor to the count of Flanders.[11] Perhaps Guillaume felt that he wanted to live as a lay seigneur. He inherited his father's estates at Ravel, and Philip the Fair gave him a pension of 400 *l.* in 1303, not only in memory of his father's service but also for that which the son had rendered.[12] There was therefore the hint that Flote was already working for Philip the Fair in 1303. Shortly after 1307 he was managing, with Raoul Rousselet and Philippe de Mornay, the *requêtes de la langue d'oc* in the Parlement.[13] While his career under the last Capetians cannot be filled in completely, the evidence says that he was constantly engaged in the work of the Parlement.[14] Guillaume Flote represented the lay lawyer who had a university education and a former clerical career. He belongs to the group which included Nogaret, Cuignières, Presles, Préaux, and many others who returned to secular life after service in the Church.

Under Philippe de Valois, Guillaume Flote continued to sit in the *grand'chambre* and was also used as an ambassador.[15] He briefly disappeared from service in 1332, but was active

---

[9] *Ibid.,* no. 4,847.

[10] Charles Grandjean, *Les registres de Benoît XI* (Paris, 1883), no. 1260.

[11] For the early clerical career of Artaud Flote, see *Boniface VIII,* nos. 2,673, 2,732, 3,664. For his later career, see Cazelles, *La société politique,* pp. 83, 93.

[12] *Livre Rouge,* no. 349.

[13] Langlois, *Textes relatifs à l'histoire du Parlement de Paris,* p. 179.

[14] Petit, *Essai de restitution,* p. 210; *Olim,* ii, 660; iii, 1,049, 1,052; Boutaric, nos. 4,754, 7,666.

[15] Cazelles, *La société politique,* has good coverage of Guillaume Flote's career under Philip VI.

again in 1335 and was made chancellor of France in 1338. The following decade was the period of Flote's greatest influence and power in French government. With Mile de Noyers and Jean de Marigny, he seemed to control the work of the Great Council, and for a while after 1345 he actually ran the government in company with the bishop of Laon and Jean de Nesle. After the defeat of Crécy, an assembly of estates was called in 1347 and several changes were made in the government. One of these concerned Guillaume Flote, who was removed from the Chancery; almost at the same time his son, Pierre Flote, was removed from his post as admiral of France.[16] But this was not a matter of disgrace for Flote. He continued to appear in the council and was still at work in government when John the Good came to the throne in 1349. There can be no doubt that Guillaume Flote was one of the five most important men in government under Philip VI and certainly after 1338, when he became chancellor. He left his imprint on the history of the Valois kings just as his father had done on that of Philip the Fair.

Other lawyers of Philip the Fair contributed relatives to the civil service of the Valois kings. Little can be said about the nephew of Gilles Aicelin. He was a president in the Parlement about 1320 and was active in the reign of Philip VI although his career has never gained great publicity. It is uncertain whether it was this same Gilles Aicelin de Montaigu or his son who served as chancellor for a brief period in 1357, but the family continued to be prominent in both Church and state throughout the fourteenth century.[17] We know of no relatives of Plaisians, Villepreux, or d'Aumelas who served under the Valois kings. There was a Pierre de Latilly who appeared in 1347 collecting the biennial tenth

---

[16] *Ibid.*, pp. 219-222.

[17] A.N., JJ. 59, nos. 114, 567, show Aicelin as president in the Parlement in 1320. His later career is mentioned in Cazelles, *La société politique*, pp. 37, 70, 289, 347.

in the diocese of Soissons, and he could well have been a relative of the former bishop of Châlons, but there is no evidence to support this view.[18] Enguerrand de Marigny was not a lawyer but one of his brothers, Jean de Marigny, did study law, became bishop of Beauvais, and, with Guillaume Flote and several others, played a prime role in the government of Philip VI.[19] Furthermore, there is reason to believe that other kinsmen of Marigny showed up as Valois lawyers and servants. In 1312, Marigny obtained a benefice for a Pierre de Villaines who was then a canon of Auxerre and only fifteen years of age.[20] One of the more prominent lawyers of Philip VI was Pierre de Villaines, who eventually became bishop of Auxerre.

The one lawyer of the early Valois kings who has received more attention than any other, with the possible exception of Robert le Coq, is Simon de Bucy. He is also the best representative of the tradition wherein descendants of Capetian lawyers continued to serve French kings throughout the fourteenth century. His father was a professor of law and the *procureur* of Philip the Fair, who took clerical orders late in life after the death of his wife. The younger Simon de Bucy appeared in Parlement in 1332 and had risen to the position of third president by 1335.[21] He also began as a clerk who probably received no more than first tonsure and a university education during his clerical career. In 1339 he

[18] *Journ. Philippe VI*, nos. 316, 1,274, 2,354, 4,496.

[19] Cazelles, *La société politique*, also covers the career of Jean de Marigny in some detail.

[20] *Clement V*, no. 9,197.

[21] Much has been written on the younger Simon de Bucy. See Félix Aubert, "Un grand magistrat au XIVe siècle," *Revue des questions historiques*, xciii (1913), 250-261; Nöel Valois, "Le gouvernement représentatif. Etude sur le conseil du roi pendant la captivité de Jean le Bon," *Revue des questions historiques*, xxxvii (1883), 63, 115; N. Valois, *Le conseil du roi aux XIVe, XVe et XVIe siècles. Nouvelles recherches suivies d'arrêts et de procès-verbaux du conseil* (Paris, 1888), pp. 5-9. Cazelles, *La société politique*, follows his career in some detail throughout the reign of Philip VI.

was given nobility by Philip VI, and his clerical life was abandoned.[22] When he became first president in the Parlement de Paris in 1345 one may say that he had already enjoyed a decade of power and influence in Valois government. Yet, the height of his career lay ahead of him. He was increasingly associated with the duke of Normandy, who became king as John the Good in 1349, and, during the turbulent and tragic years of that monarch's reign, Bucy became one of the two or three most important lawyers in French government. He moved through the violent years of 1356-1358 with the agility of a ballet dancer, always keeping to his role as a royalist lawyer. The influence and favor which he enjoyed with John the Good resembled that of Marigny with Philip the Fair. His strong personality and his forceful and often high-handed actions recalled Nogaret and Latilly. He died in 1368 after having served for a short time under Charles V.

At least two of Simon de Bucy's children rose to positions of prominence in church and government during the latter part of the fourteenth century. His namesake became bishop of Soissons and another son, Rénaud de Bucy, enjoyed a dual career.[23] In 1353, Rénaud was given a prebend in the church of Saint Quentin. Seven years later he held a prebend in Cambrai and by 1376 was *clerc et conseiller* of Charles V. His career spanned at least a quarter of a century for his will was dated in 1398.[24] He probably died shortly thereafter. The Bucy family, therefore, played an important role in French politics across a period of one hundred years, and the street in the Latin Quarter that still bears their name

[22] A.N., JJ. 73, no. 295.

[23] Litigation on the execution of his will mentioned his three sons. Simon was bishop of Soissons. The other two sons were simply listed as Rènaud de Bucy and Jean de Bucy (A.N., X1a 23, fol. 65 r.-v.).

[24] For the prebends and the will of Rénaud de Bucy, see A.N., L. 739, no. 94 bis; L. 938, no. 30. Some trouble had arisen between Rénaud and his brother Jean for he excluded Jean from his will.

is one of the lesser marks of their position and influence in fourteenth-century French society.

Raoul de Presles and Jeanne de Chastel had no children for whom there is any record. After her husband's death, Jeanne continued his charitable work, particularly in the field of education, and made several grants of rents to the Soissons abbey of Saint Jean-des-Vignes.[25] The executor of Raoul de Presles' will was his nephew, Robert, canon of Laon and Soissons, to whom he had sold some holdings at Vailly in 1315. Robert inherited the seigneury of Lizy but he was dead by 1333 and his brother Raoul became executor and inherited Lizy.[26] These two men were probably the sons of Girard de Presles, and their sister was a Jeanne de Presles who married Mathieu Chambellan.[27] We know nothing about them beyond the fact that the second Raoul was something of a scoundrel. In 1346 he was put in prison for counterfeiting the seal of his aunt, Jeanne de Chastel.[28] He and a daughter, Jeanne, were dead by 1365 when his son-in-law, Garin de Giffosse, brought legal suit on rents at Courdemaine.[29] One other nephew of Raoul de Presles cannot be accounted for. He appeared in 1323 when Raoul transferred to him the *prévoté* of Rugny.[30] His name was Jean de Presles, and he was the son of Hernart Berthemet de Presles and

---

[25] In May 1330 Jeanne de Chastel gave to the abbey of Saint Jean-des-Vignes rents which Raoul de Presles formerly held at Chavonne, across the river from his native village. Notices of this grant are found in A.N., L. 1008, no. 20, and B.N., Collection Dom Grenier, Vol. 54, fol. 183 v.-184 v. In 1335 and 1336 she arranged to give to the same abbey a rent of 30 *l. par.* which she inherited from her husband and which was located in Vailly and on the Moulin Saint-Pierre. This was to be used by the abbey to support students who were sent to study at Paris. See A.N., L. 1008, nos. 22, 23, and B.N., Collection Dom Grenier, Vol. 54, fol. 286 v.-289.

[26] A.N., MM. 418, fol. 13 v.-22 r.

[27] B.N., Collection Dom Grenier, Vol. 54, fol. 285 v.-286 v. Jeanne de Presles and her husband were living in Presles in 1348.

[28] A.N., JJ. 75, no. 118.

[29] A.N., X1c 16a, no. 8.

[30] A.N., JJ. 62, no. 267.

of a woman named Héloise. At that moment he was a clerk living at Orléans, which hints at his engagement in legal studies. He appeared again in 1339 in a law suit over Rugny, and on that occasion stated that the late Raoul de Presles was his uncle.[31] The vast landed holdings that Raoul de Presles accumulated during his life were dispersed and dissipated within forty years of his death. Vailly and Lizy moved out of the family after the death of the second Raoul de Presles and the holdings in the village of Presles which were inherited by Jeanne de Chastel cannot be traced beyond her death in 1347. Reference to other lands formerly held by Raoul occurred as late as 1376 but they had long since passed out of the family.[32]

Although Raoul de Presles had no children by Jeanne de Chastel, he did have a son who became one of the four or five most important literary figures during the second half of the fourteenth century. For the modern historian, there are many secrets or mysteries in the life and career of Raoul de Presles which can be solved only through careful attention to the documents. The problems of his origins, his rise to power, his landed acquisitions, his trial and acquittal have the elements of mystery and secretiveness about them. But in every instance the lawyer left clues to the solution of these problems in the letters which he placed in the Chancery Registers. The matter of his son was the only instance in which he failed to leave a clue, for he never made any mention of a son during his lifetime. On the other hand, the document which may have furnished such information— Raoul de Presles' will—is missing. But the son inherited his father's penchant for putting things on record and in his legitimation letter of 1373 carefully but briefly stated the

---

[31] Furgeot, no. 2428. Furgeot transcribed his name not as Jean de Presles but as Jean Bartholomei.

[32] A.N., L. 734, no. 76, in which a canon of Laon had acquired lands at Filain from the heirs of Raoul de Presles.

circumstances of his birth.[33] According to his account, during the summer of 1315 while Raoul de Presles was in prison, he had an affair with a woman by the name of Marie de Portes, who gave birth to his illegitimate son in the early months of 1316.

Whether Marie de Portes was a woman of the streets whom Presles found in prison, or whether she was his mistress cannot be determined. If she was simply an abandoned woman, it would seem that he would never have seen or heard of her again. This was not the case, for Raoul de Presles knew that the illegitimate child was his and he went to some trouble to provide for the financial support and education of the boy. Ironically enough, Jeanne de Chastel provided the earliest mention of her husband's illegitimate son and did it in the same document which gave a clue to her relationship with Gaucher de Châtillon. In her preliminary will of 1337 she stated that there was a house in the Cité at Paris which formerly was owned by her and her husband and which presently belonged to "Raoulin de Praelles."[34] After the name "Raoulin," someone inserted above the line the words "le petit." The identity of this person became clear a year later when Jeanne de Chastel became involved in litigation with the Collège de Laon, which laid claim to certain rents formerly held by her husband. In the lengthy document of settlement, Jeanne appeared with "Raoulin de Praelles, filz et heritier seul" of the late Raoul de Presles.[35] He appeared several times in the document and was usually styled as the son and heir of Raoul de Presles. Despite the problem of how an illegitimate son could inherit, there can

[33] A.N., JJ. 105, no. 63.

[34] A.N., M. 185, no. 14: " . . . et à la maison qui fu aus diz maistre Raoul et damoiselle, et qui est à présent à Raoulin (le petit) de Praelles. . . ."

[35] A.N., MM. 418, fol. 23 v. At another point (fol. 24 r.): ". . . la dicte damoiselle Jehanne de Praellez et le dit Raoullin filz et heritier comme dit est dudit feu Raoul de Praelles. . . ."

be no doubt that this young man was the son of Raoul de Presles and Marie de Portes. He carried the diminutive form of the name Raoul and was never referred to as the son of Jeanne de Chastel. Raoul de Presles had made legal provisions for his son, and had presumably provided for his education.

Raoulin de Presles dropped the diminutive form of his name later in life, probably after the nephew and namesake of his father died. He thereby became the third Raoul de Presles of the fourteenth century. Like his father, he became a lawyer but did not appear in the royal service until the reign of Charles V. He had already begun, before that date, the activity which was to give him far greater fame than his work as a lawyer. In 1363 he produced the *Compendium morale de re publica,* which he dedicated to the bishop of Chartres.[36] Three years later he presented the *Musa,* an allegorical Latin tract, to Charles V. He was a *conseiller du roi* in 1371 when he began, at the request of his king, his best known and most laborious work, the translation with commentary of Saint Augustine's *City of God* which was completed in 1375.[37] Other work included some historical writing which has been lost and an attempted translation of the Bible.[38]

Fifty years separated this *homme littéraire* and lawyer of Charles V from the men of his father's age, the lawyers of the last Capetians. But the bridge between the two was

[36] Jacques Decanter, *La muse de Raoul de Presles. Etude et édition,* *P.T.E.C.* (1954), pp. 37-41, discussed the *Compendium morale* and Presles' other works. He made several errors in his biographical comment on the first Raoul de Presles.

[37] The story of how Presles came to translate the *City of God* is told in the florid introduction to the work. He also mentioned his public office as an advocate, and many of his other literary works. See, for instance, B.N., MS. 170 (Fonds français), fol. 2 v.-3 r. See also Henri Vallet, *La culture classique dans Raoul de Praelles d'après sa traduction avec commentaire de la Cité de Dieu de Saint Augustin,* *P.T.E.C.* (1913), pp. 99-102.

[38] Decanter, *P.T.E.C.* (1954), p. 39.

established when the illegitimate son translated into French the *Rex pacificus,* a monarchical tract on the struggle with Boniface VIII. Not content with this contribution, he turned to the Vincennes debate of 1329 and translated Pierre de Cuignières' argument into French. One other short tract, the *Discours de l'oriflamme,* portrays him as a publicist who developed the theme of sacred kingship.[39] The questions of Philip the Fair's reign were still alive in 1375, and either Charles V or his lawyers felt that the Latin of Philip the Fair's age should be put into French to reach a wider audience. The legal career of the third Raoul de Presles was swallowed up and lost in his literary activity. We know of nothing that he did as a lawyer of Charles V, but as a literary figure he took his place beside the other French writers of the late fourteenth century such as Philippe de Mézières, Christine de Pisan, and Guillaume Machault. He was a part of the budding humanism which appeared in the court of Charles V and which finally bloomed a hundred years later.

One final aspect of the legacy of the Capetian lawyers must be mentioned. Not only did their sons, nephews and cousins help to establish the tradition of civil service by descent, but these same descendants put a firm foundation under the tradition by marrying whenever possible into noble houses. Marriage alliances between the merchant middle class and the feudal aristocracy began under the last Capetians and the practice became frequent under the Valois kings.[40] There arose alongside this practice the phenomenon of service families marrying into families of the military nobility. Sometimes, through such alliances, the service family ceased its tradition of civil service and became indistinguishable from the established seigneurial families into which they married. Sometimes, through lack of evidence, we cannot pursue the subsequent history of these mar-

[39] *Ibid.*
[40] Cazelles, *La société politique,* pp. 289-296, 389f.

riages. For instance, Guillaume de Plaisians came from non-noble origins, acquired nobility, and married at least one of his daughters to a son of the seigneur of Alais in Languedoc. There is the possibility that his two other daughters also married into landed nobility but the Plaisians name itself died out for he had no sons.[41]

The most complete information on this phenomenon concerns the family of Guillaume de Nogaret. About 1308, Nogaret married his daughter, Guillelme, to the eldest son of Bérenger Guilhem, seigneur of Clermont-Lodève. The conditions of this marriage contract illustrate some of the motives and machinery behind such alliances. The seigneur of Clermont-Lodève was rich in land and poor in currency, a common failing among the fourteenth-century nobility. Bérenger had obtained, for the price of 3,000 *l.*, the royal promise that rights of self-government would never be granted to the inhabitants of Clermont. But he was unable to pay the sum. Nogaret intervened and gave in dowry to his daughter 3,000 *l.*, which would be delivered to the royal treasury to satisfy Bérenger's debt. Nogaret incidentally paid only 1,000 *l.* and was acquitted by the king of the remainder.[42]

But that was not the end of the Nogaret alliances, for the lawyer's elder son, Raymond, married the sister of the younger Bérenger, and the second son, Guillaume, wed a daughter of the house of Montpezat. All three of Guillaume de Nogaret's children, therefore, married into old, established feudal families and assumed the status and appearance of the other great seigneurial families of Languedoc. The second Guillaume had no children, but there is a special interest in examining the progeny of Raymond de Nogaret. Married to Hélix de Clermont, he had seven children and

[41] Henry, *Le Moyen Age*, v (1892), 37.
[42] The affair is covered in Louis Thomas, *Annales du Midi*, xvi (1904), 190. The document on the matter is in *H.L.*, x, 451 (Preuves).

one would think that the future of the Nogaret name would have been ensured on that count alone. But none of the seven children was able to continue the family name.[43]

Still, we must follow one of the seven to the end of the century for his life and career encompassed the end of the Nogaret family. Grandson of the lawyer, Raymond II de Nogaret was the most illustrious member of the clan after his famous grandfather. In his hands were reunited all of the lands that had been accumulated between 1295 and 1310; he acquired, moreover, the lands of his grandfather's brother around St. Félix de Caraman when that branch of the family died out. Raymond de Nogaret probably fought at the battle of Poitiers and, throughout the latter part of the century, was instrumental in organizing military defense in the south against the roving companies of the Hundred Years War. In 1374 he was again summoned as a feudal noble for military service around Toulouse and five years later was lieutenant of the seneschal of Beaucaire. This was the only instance in which any of Guillaume de Nogaret's descendants entered directly into governmental administration.[44]

Although Raymond de Nogaret was successful as a military leader, a great landed seigneur, and a provincial administrator, he experienced no success in perpetuating his family line. Two marriages failed to produce children, but his second wife brings us to the climax of the Nogaret story. Marie de Beaufort was one of thirteen children of Guillaume Roger, count of Beaufort and Alais. The significance of the Roger family scarcely needs elaboration. Marie was the niece of Pierre Roger, who was pope as Clement VI, and her younger brother by the same name became pope in

[43] Louis Thomas, "L'héritage de Guillaume de Nogaret. I. La famille de Guillaume de Nogaret," *Mémoires de la société archéologique de Montpellier*, 2nd ser., ix (1924), pp. 69-72. The article itself is an excellent piece of work on the subsequent history of the Nogaret family.

[44] *Ibid.*, pp. 73-5.

1370 under the name of Gregory XI. Marie had three sons by an earlier marriage to Guérin d'Apchier and, when Raymond de Nogaret realized that he would have no children, he designated one of his step-sons as sole heir to all of his estates. With Raymond de Nogaret's death in 1399, the Nogaret family came to an ironic end. Most of the lands which Guillaume de Nogaret received from Philip the Fair for his work against Boniface VIII descended to the nephew of the pope who took the Avignon papacy back to Rome.[45]

More significant alliances were made by the grandsons and granddaughters of Capetian lawyers in the Valois period. The three husbands of Guillaume Flote's daughter form a veritable roster of powerful feudal barons—Eustache de Conflans, Enguerrand de Coucy, and Gaucher de Châtillon, grandson of the constable.[46] The alliance between the houses of Flote and Châtillon was firmly established when Pierre Flote, Guillaume's son and admiral of France, married Marguerite de Châtillon.[47] There is nothing startling in these marriages for the Flotes were feudal aristocrats by birth and, on the face of the matter, we simply have nobles marrying nobles. But it must be conceded that the Flotes, as feudal nobles, had nothing like the prestige and glory which attached to the houses of Conflans, Coucy, and Châtillon. Their reputation and fame had come, not through military exploits, but through the forensic prowess of the lawyer and the administrator, and therein lay the significance of the Flotes' marriages with great military families.

More unusual was the marriage which another Gaucher de Châtillon made about 1370, when he took for his second

[45] *Ibid.*, p. 78. Thomas also traced the Apchier family and the other families which succeeded to the Nogaret lands in "L'héritage de Guillaume de Nogaret. II. Les familles substituées: Apchier, Murat, Louet. Vicissitudes d'une seigneurie constituée sur l'ancien domaine royal (1318-1483)," *Mémoires de la société archéologique de Montpellier,* 2nd ser., ix (1924), pp. 233-277.

[46] Duchesne, *Histoire de la maison de Châtillon-sur-Marne,* p. 398.

[47] Furgeot, nos. 1,288, 2,143, 2,556.

wife, Jeanne de Bucy, daughter of Simon de Bucy. André Duchesne, in recounting the fact, seemed impressed that Châtillon made a proper alliance with the daughter of Simon de Bucy, *chevalier*, seigneur of Bucy, councillor of the king, and first president in the Parlement de Paris.[48] He was totally unaware that the Bucys had risen from the most obscure origins to a position of power and prestige in the space of forty years, and that the *chevalier* had been granted nobility as recently as 1339. In such an alliance we encounter the phenomenon of service nobility wedding military nobility, and with the Flotes and the Bucys marrying into the ancient and venerable house of Châtillon we have come to an appropriate place to end this study of the lawyers of the last Capetians.

[48] Duchesne, *Histoire de la maison de Châtillon-sur-Marne*, p. 558.

CONCLUSION

The Roles of the Lawyers

HOW did Thierry, Guizot, and Michelet view the lawyers of the last Capetians? They saw them as the unalterable opponents of noble privilege, the legal architects of an undivided public authority, and as men who laid the cornerstone of an egalitarian society. The lawyers played the role of revolutionaries, and it is needless to comment further on the fact that the view of these three historians was determined by the issues of the French Revolution. The essence of the interpretation was contained in the thesis of a struggle between the baron and the legist, and the baron represented both the lay and ecclesiastical nobility. But even Guizot warned against the unqualified acceptance of this thesis for he saw in the events of 1315 the use of baronial lawyers to prosecute royal lawyers. There is more to it than that, however, for in the face of historical evidence the thesis must be completely rejected. Every noble, great or small, and every ecclesiastical house, episcopal or monastic, had an entourage of legal counselors who served them well and faithfully because they were dependent upon their employers for economic reward. The lawyers were not interested in betraying or destroying their noble clients but in extracting from them as much compensation as possible.

The thesis of the struggle between baron and legist supposes, moreover, that a particular group of lawyers served only the king and served him with singleness of purpose. But we have seen that Raoul de Presles had as clients the count of Soissons, the count of Dreux, the lords of Coucy, the constable of France, the abbeys of Prémontré and Saint Médard, the count of Champagne, and probably many others for whom the evidence has been lost. Nogaret, Plaisians, and d'Aumelas served the king of Majorca and various bishops, seigneurs, and communes in the south. Pierre de Latilly had at least one other client in the abbey of Saint Médard, and even a noble lawyer like Gilles Aicelin had clearly given counsel to other persons. The lawyers undoubtedly counted the king as the most important of their employers for he was the greatest of the nobles and offered far greater compensation. But they enjoyed the custom and presumably the right to serve other clients while engaged in the royal service, and this custom remained as prevalent under the Valois kings as it had been under the Capetians.

A graver aspect of the conjectured struggle of the legist against the baron is that it proposes the unmistakable concept of a class struggle in fourteenth-century France, and more especially a class struggle between the nobility on the one hand and the lawyers as representatives of the middle class on the other. Of the lawyers who have been considered in this study, only Nogaret, Plaisians, Villepreux, and Presles were indisputably members of the middle class. But Nogaret and Plaisians acquired nobility, and Villepreux had such important connections with the royal house that he had no need to despise the aristocracy. Only Raoul de Presles remained middle class throughout his life. Flote, Aicelin, the Mornays, Mauconduit, and Belleperche were noble by birth, and we are unsure of the origins or social class of Latilly and d'Aumelas. More of the lawyers were noble than middle class and, on the sheer weight of numbers, the idea of a class struggle between the middle class lawyers and the feudal barons will not hold up. There may have been a class struggle in fourteenth-century France, but it most assuredly was not waged by the lawyers against the nobles.

To say that there was no class struggle is not to say that lawyers of middle class origin had no class-consciousness. But it was the variety of class-consciousness which made them wish to achieve the status of the most socially approved class. We therefore come to the aspirations of the lawyers. If we draw conclusions from what we know of their behavior, we must say that they wanted first of all status and approval, and the first step toward this goal was the acquisition of wealth in land or money. It sometimes appeared that they did not wish to be ennobled but rather to have the wealth and social approval that the nobles enjoyed. There were, for instance, certain advantages in being permitted to hold noble land without becoming noble. Still, most of those who were middle class displayed a drive to achieve nobility. Once again, however, the number that acquired nobility must be reexamined. The early nineteenth-century historians created the impression that Philip the Fair had the habit of ennobling all of his *roturier* staff. Such was not the case. When the careers of the better known lawyers are closely examined, we discover that only Nogaret and Plaisians were given nobility. Pons d'Aumelas was a knight in his later years but there is no proof that he came from non-noble origins. Guillaume de Plaisians did not acquire his nobility from Philip the Fair but rather from Humbert, dauphin of Vienne. That leaves the curious case of Guillaume de Nogaret.

Nogaret was entitled "master" in 1298 and was a *chevalier* in 1300. Tradition holds that Philip the Fair granted him nobility about 1299. But we do not have the document of ennoblement, and no other proof exists that Philip ennobled him at that time. In fact, however, the reign of Philip the Fair was not the great age of ennoblement. That phenomenon came later, under his three sons and more especially under the Valois. Even then, letters of nobility were given more often to the notaries in the Chancery, to financial agents in the Chamber of Accounts, and to provincial lawyers, especially in the south, than to the front-line lawyers who managed the Parlement and had the most important roles in the central government.

The view of the Capetian lawyers as builders of an egalitarian society was an integral part of the concept of the baron-legist struggle and was necessary to the scheme of the post-Revolutionary historians. But little can be said for the Capetian lawyers as egalitarians or defenders of communal liberties. Above all, there is no evidence to show that any of the lawyers identified themselves with the Third Estate or that they even conceived of the Third Estate as a social group or a political force. Nogaret's oppression of the common people of Lunel, Marsillargues, and their neighboring villages, and his disregard of their rights, do not paint a picture of a lawyer bent on the construction of an egalitarian society. Pierre de Latilly's arrogance and arbitrary action against the townsmen of Languedoc in 1298 were not calculated to encourage the growth of human liberty or respect for the rights of man. Even Raoul de Presles, who never achieved noble status but became a great landed seigneur, showed that he could forget his origins. His relations with the commune of Vailly were not those of a man who wished to see communes flourish. In the end, he assisted the king in abolishing communal liberties at Vailly and his activity in serf manumisson can best be explained by his need of money. Aside from personal behavior, one cannot point to legislation or ordinances designed to favor the growth of equality. The mass of common men moved toward freedom through flight or through manumission, but this latter was due to the economic revolution that had brought inflation and had consequently forced the nobles to the practice of manumission in order to satisfy their debts and meet the increased cost of living.

The other element in the supposed baron-legist struggle made of the Capetian lawyers the architects of an undivided public authority. This is perhaps the most popular image of the Capetian lawyer created by the early nineteenth-century historians. Guizot, Thierry, and Michelet were disposed to believe that the shortest route to an egalitarian society was through an authoritarian state. It is a concept that is all too familiar to the twentieth century, and in an earlier age it spoke to the idea of absolute monarchy. For the period of the last Capetians the idea implied the destruction of feudal privilege and the creation upon its ruins of a unified sovereign power vested in the monarch. The Capetian lawyers were uniquely qualified to pursue such an ideal because of their training in Roman law, which played not to feudal particularism but to the concept of absolute power as represented by the ancient Roman emperors.

We know that the noble lawyers, Aicelin, the Mornays, Mauconduit, and Belleperche, were formally trained in Roman law, and, therefore, should have been the proponents of political absolutism, of monarchical sovereignty, of the undivided public authority. Yet these men, all nobles and civilians, were the quiet group who administered the government without fanfare or ostentation. If anything, as in the case of Aicelin, they exercised restraint on royal ambitions. The group consisting of Nogaret, Plaisians, Latilly, Villepreux, and Presles was the driving force in Philip the Fair's government. While all were lawyers, we are unsure of the formal training of any save Nogaret. But let us grant that the education of these men was identical with that of their noble colleagues; then we must ask why their behavior or conduct was so radically different from that of the noble group. Was their energetic prosecution of royal aims born of the conviction that a king ought to be sovereign, or did they serve their master with such force and will so that they might more readily acquire the wealth and status which the nobles had by birth? Their motivation is suspect in every instance.

This view of the lawyers as agents of arrogant force bent

on the destruction of noble privilege leads us to a final comment. Michelet believed that the lawyers suffered because of their role in the creation of a sovereign monarch. In the time of weak kings, the nobles wreaked their vengeance on the lawyers who sought to destroy them. "After Philip III, Pierre de la Broce; after Philip the Fair, Marigny; after Philip V, Géraud Gueite; after Charles IV, Pierre Remi." The interesting point in this quotation from Michelet is that not one of these men was a lawyer. On the contrary, they were all financiers or chamberlains who handled finance. We do not know of a single lawyer who perished under the last Capetians and only two, Presles and Latilly, were prosecuted. On the contrary, financial officers were prosecuted for financial malfeasance, and nobles like Mercoeur, Jourdain de l'Isle, and Robert d'Artois were tried for treasonable conduct. In no instance was the element of the baron-legist struggle present. Raoul de Presles and Pierre de Latilly were caught up in the state trials of 1315 not because nobles wished to destroy them but because they were suspected of financial misconduct that could not be proved.

What does a study of the Capetian lawyers reveal about the nature of Philip the Fair's reign? Their behavior and the work which they accomplished indicate that neither they nor Philip were engaged in a conscious drive toward political absolutism. Philip the Fair was not a power-mad monarch and certainly not a political despot. Everything about his reign points to him as a needy king. He was caught in the grip of the inflationary trend which had come out of the thirteenth century and, ultimately, out of the economic revolution that had occurred in the eleventh and twelfth centuries. His ordinances, his legislation and his commissions scarcely mention the ideal of political absolutism. But they constantly refer to the inflated cost of living and they constantly assert, not his right to legislate for all of France, but his need to tax as widely as possible.

Beyond the matter of ordinary taxation, they give evidence of his desperate need for extraordinary sources of income. This we take to be the sense of Philip the Fair's reign and of the work done by his lawyers. Historians know well that the struggle with Boniface was born of the issue of taxation. The Templars constituted no internal threat to the king's political rule, but they did control an enormous depository of wealth. The alterations of currency and the confiscation of Jewish and Lombard property are too transparent for comment. Far from being the architects and agents of monarchical absolutism, the lawyers advised the king on the acquisition of income, formulated his taxation policy, and then went into the field where they became the agents and executors of a fiscal absolutism.

This fiscal absolutism was one of the lawyers' contributions to the French monarchy. The political position of a Francis I or of a Louis XIV was made possible in part by the early growth of this fiscal absolutism. In the hands of Nogaret, Villepreux, and Latilly, this absolutism sometimes deteriorated into fiscal terrorism. Even at this point, primarily political objectives seemed to be absent. It is true that Philip the Fair issued ordinances in which he repeatedly prohibited the judicial duel, private wars, and tournaments among the nobles. Even here, he usually made it clear that the prohibition applied only when the kingdom was at war. The Baronial Revolt of 1314 arose not so much from the expansion of royal jurisdiction at the expense of seigneurial jurisdiction, but rather from the too frequent subsidies, the incessant alterations of money, and the intolerable behavior of some of the king's favorites. Pierre de Latilly was interested in collecting money in 1297, not in proclaiming or extending royal sovereignty. His heavy hand fell on the common people and scarcely ever on the nobles. There was the constant and natural tendency for nobles and others to encroach on royal rights, and the numerous commissions sent out by Philip the Fair, the commissions on non-noble acquisitions of noble lands, on money, on servile dues, on the "reformation" of various districts, were directed more to the reestablishment of ancient royal rights than to the creation of new ones. In the execution of these commissions, the lawyers and other agents sometimes gave the appearance of extending royal jurisdiction. The essence of Philip's fiscal absolutism lay in his constant and often cruel drive to reestablish, to expand, and ultimately to nationalize, all of the possible sources of royal revenue.

The Capetian lawyers also made a contribution to the formation of French bureaucracy when they realized that in order to profit from this fiscal absolutism they had to insure for their families constant access to the power structure. We cannot say that the Capetian lawyers established the Robe. But they laid its foundations when they developed the faint outlines of the tradition whereby their relatives and descendants would also serve the king in similar positions. We have seen the early history of this tradition which led to the phenomenon of civil service dynasties. The Mornays represent the tendency toward the horizontal dynasty while the Bucys and the Flotes illustrate the development of the vertical tradition. At the same time, the civil service families who were non-noble achieved nobility and then proceeded to strengthen their position by marriage with the old military houses. As the civil service nobility developed the custom of passing public offices on to their children, the Robe came into existence.

It is interesting to note the longevity of the early dynasties that grew out of Philip the Fair's reign. The horizontal dynasties of the noble Mornays and the non-noble Villepreux extended across some forty to sixty years. The vertical tradition of the Flotes ran through three generations and died out about 1360. The Bucy family was the most successful and kept its members in the royal service until the end of the fourteenth century. Raoul de Presles, through his illegitimate son, was more successful than most, for his dynasty lasted about eighty years. As often as not, the failure to maintain a service dynasty was due either to a failure of influence and connections or to the inability to keep the male side of a family going. The Nogaret family, which never set up a service dynasty, still lasted only to the end of the fourteenth century. As these old service families from the Capetian period died out, new ones took their place. The halfway point to the Robe was reached in the late fourteenth and fifteenth centuries with the rise of such families as Dormans, d'Orgemont, and Paillart, but the Robe came only at the beginning of the sixteenth century. However that may be, the development began with the lawyers of the last Capetians.

While it is easy enough to dispense with the dated interpretations of Guizot, Thierry, and Michelet, we are still confronted with the pessimism of Charles Victor Langlois. Can we ever know the lawyers of the last Capetians? Langlois overlooked the possibility that an individual who possesses no personality by himself may acquire one when made to stand beside other men. Nogaret and Plaisians must remain as Michelet painted them, *âmes de plomb et de fer*, men consumed by ambition and even by malice. Nogaret was a phenomenon, a juggler who kept five pins in the air at once. From Anagni to the end of his life, he sought relief from the excommunication placed on him by the pope whose memory he wished to have damned. All the while, he managed a hundred small items of business for the king and directed either the initiation, the progress, or the conclusion of a half-dozen great state affairs. But let us not forget that Nogaret was a university professor. His was not a drive blinded by rage, but molded by calculated objectives; he worked by plan. Plaisians had all of the will, talent, and energy of Nogaret but was never able to play the senior role in any of the great events. There can be no doubt of his importance, but more often than not he implemented what Nogaret devised, and his image has been unfortunately obscured by the shadow of his better known colleague.

Next to Nogaret and Plaisians we must place Pierre de Latilly and perhaps beyond him Philippe de Villepreux. Their contributions to the government of Philip the Fair are clear. Latilly was the architect of fiscal policy, not the only one but perhaps the most important. He executed every kind of mission and was involved, directly or indirectly, in all of the great affairs. He was tax collector, paymaster, ambassador, inquisitor, and policy maker. But his work in the field of royal finance stands out, and he must be regarded as one of the major authors of the fiscal absolutism that marked Philip the Fair's reign. Villepreux's role is even clearer than Latilly's. Philip the Fair never assigned to any other lawyer such a specific field of activity. And he never gave to any other agent such complete authority and responsibility, both in the execution and formulation of the policy that pertained to that field. Villepreux will be remembered as the converted Jew and godson of a great Capetian king, the law student sponsored by a monarch, who became the governor of the royal forests of France.

Professor Fawtier once remarked, "Why study Raoul de Presles? We know nothing of his work." Put in that context, we should not study Presles for scarcely a word can be said about his work for the Capetian kings. But it is what we know of the man, not of his work, that gives Raoul de Presles an importance not possessed by any lawyer of his age. All of the secrets of this man can be unlocked save one. All of the questions for which we want answers about the lives of the other lawyers can be answered most completely for Raoul de Presles. These are, in his case, the questions of origins, family, patrons, clients, rise to power, land acquisitions, trial, acquittal, charities, death, and even illegitimate son. Only his role remains undetermined. Presles is the complete biographical specimen which his colleagues fail to become. A careful examination of the documents on Presles makes his personality as clear as that of any lawyer. Ambitious and grasping, he was a man capable of perjury, usury, fraud, and adultery. No life was filled with more turbulence and peril than his. But he was also capable of the generous impulse, the creation of educational opportunity, the endowment of Christian activity, a solicitous care for his family and relatives, and loyalty to his friends. And we know all of this because the man had an unmatched drive to get everything on record. Any study of the Capetian lawyers would be incomplete without the life of Raoul de Presles.

Gilles Aicelin stands in utter contrast to Raoul de Presles and the other legists. As generous as Presles, he had an incorruptible sense of honor and justice, and this set him off sharply from his colleagues. Most of his associates were *hommes tracassiers*, men hated and feared for their power and their methods. There is none of this in the character or career of Gilles Aicelin. The most dreadful charge that can be made against him is that of naïveté, although some have hinted that he was a coward. But the charge of naïveté explains away the appearance of cowardice, and he certainly was not lacking in moral courage. He recognized perjury and collusion when he saw it, and he would not be tainted or corroded by the methods that others used to acquire fortune and status. If Aicelin's type had prevailed, the history of the last Capetians would have run a different course.

Perhaps Langlois would disagree with this attempt to characterize these men. Or perhaps he would concur in the light of documents and evidence that have been published or otherwise made available since his day. This study of the Capetian lawyers was done with the conviction that if one can see enough of a man's life or activities, one can draw valid conclusions about his role and personality. Others will judge if this is *enfantillage.*

A Case of Mistaken Identity

IN AN age when no rules of orthography had been established for the rising vernacular languages, the written word was initially formed according to sound with the use of Latin characters. Even so, scribes in the late thirteenth and early fourteenth centuries reached a fair amount of agreement in writing the French language. The greatest difficulty came in spelling the names of persons and places, an area in which formal Latin orthography gave little help since so many French place names and personal names had existed for only two or three centuries. The Latin forms for the more obscure French place names often had three or four variants while the vernacular forms were usually more chaotic. This difficulty has constituted a pitfall for historians of medieval Europe and particularly for those who have sought to identify individuals. If two contemporaries with identical Christian names, who came from places with similar names, rose to prominence or engaged in similar occupations, the likelihood of confusing them is great. In such cases the historian must be keenly aware of orthography, onomastics and paleography. Guillaume de Plaisians, Pons d'Aumelas, Pierre de Latilly, and Philippe de Villepreux took their surnames from their places of origin. No other persons with similar names acquired prominence during their time, and their identities have never been confused. Raoul de Presles was not so fortunate. A contemporary with a similar name served in the government of the last Capetians, and historians have invariably confused him with the famous lawyer.

The failure to distinguish between Raoul de Presles and another Capetian clerk with a similar name arose precisely from the problems of orthography and place names. The Latin form of Presles was *Praellis* and sometimes *Pratellis*. The French equivalent ranged from Presles, Prelles, and Praelles to Praières.[1] But the important point is that the Latin form had an *ra* construction after the initial *P* and this was invariably shown by the proper ligature when the Latin form was abbreviated. On the other hand, the Latin for the name of the person who has been confused with Raoul de Presles was *Perellis* and I know offhand of no variation in this form. And when *Perellis* was abbreviated by scribes, the proper ligature showing an *er* after the initial *P* was always used. The French form of *Perellis* also varied from Pereaus to Préaus. On the point of Latin abbreviation alone, the two men should never have been confused. But even the scribes in the royal chancery were careless or absent-minded for on three notable occasions they confused the two men in spelling their names. In 1312 and 1313, three royal grants of land were made to the clerk whom we shall, for the moment, call Raoul de *Perellis*. The title of each of these three letters clearly said that the grants were made to *Radulpho de Praellis*. But in the texts of all three letters the name was spelled *Perellis*.[2]

From the eighteenth century when Lancelot completed his study of Raoul de Presles, historians have constantly mistaken the royal notary, Raoul de *Perellis*, for the lawyer of Philip the Fair. Perhaps we should say that the general confusion has resulted, not from the failure to recognize the orthography of two different names, but from the simple fact that the two names were similar. Occasionally, when a scholar looked critically at the two names, he sometimes recognized that two men were concerned, and then pro-

---

[1] The chronicles usually have the widest variations in orthography. He was called Raoul de Praières in Chronique de Saint Denis, *H.F.*, xx, 696, and Radulfus de Penoariis in Contin. de Nangis, *H.F.*, xx, 613.

[2] A.N., JJ. 47, no. 77; JJ. 49, nos. 9, 140.

ceeded to confuse them. This was the case with Borrelli de Serres. In studying Simon Festu, who was one of the three treasurers in 1308-1309, he found that Festu had several clerks working with him among whom was a man named "Raoul de Perelles." The learned colonel was quick to point out that this treasury clerk must be distinguished from the lawyer who was also a royal notary and a victim of the 1315 reaction. But in calling Raoul de Presles a royal notary, Borrelli de Serres had already confused the two men.[3] As recently as 1931, Paul Lehugeur maintained that there is no need to distinguish between the two names; Raoul de Presles, the lawyer, and the man whom he called Raoul de Pereaus were one and the same.[4] But before either Borrelli de Serres or Lehugeur had published their comment, Auguste Coulon had written a critical note on Raoul de *Perellis* and had clearly separated him from Raoul de Presles.[5] Coulon failed, however, to determine the French equivalent of *Perellis* and consequently could not pin down the geographical origin of this notary.

While the Chancery Registers do not tell us the place from which *Perellis* came, they do provide a good indication of the right answer. The land grants which he received and which are recorded in the registers enable us to trace Raoul de *Perellis* to the general vicinity of Loches and to the countryside between the Indre and the Cher. Not far from Loches, and situated on a small tributary called the Indrois, is the village of Préaux. There can be no doubt that Raoul de *Perellis* was Raoul de Préaux. The comment of Borrelli de Serres links Préaux with Simon Festu, who was a favorite

[3] Leon Borrelli de Serres, *Recherches sur divers services publiques du XIIIe au XVIIe siècle* (Paris, 1909), III, 48, note 13.

[4] Paul Lehugeur, *Philippe le Long: le mécanisme du gouvernement* (Paris, 1931), p. 102.

[5] Auguste Coulon, *Lettres secrètes et curiales du Pape Jean XXII (1316-1334) relatives à la France* (Bibliothèque des Ecoles Françaises d'Athènes et de Rome, Paris, 1900), col. 65-68.

of Jeanne de Navarre. It is quite likely that Raoul de Préaux owed his rise and royal patronage to the archdeacon of Vendôme. He was in the service of the new queen of Navarre in 1307 and 1308 when he rendered account of money spent for "certain secret business" of the queen Marguerite.[6] In the latter instance he was again associated with Simon Festu. The likelihood that he came up through the household of Jeanne de Navarre is strengthened by the fact that he and his wife Eustachie were given lands in 1311 because of Préaux's "services to the late queen Jeanne."[7] This means that he was in the royal service in 1304-1305 if not earlier.

At the moment that Simon Festu became bishop of Meaux, Raoul de Préaux left the service of the new queen of Navarre and entered the central government as a royal notary. He signed his first letter in December 1309, a letter ordered by Nogaret,[8] and he signed intermittently throughout the reign of Philip the Fair. This is the first point on which Préaux has been confused with Raoul de Presles; the latter was never a royal secretary or notary. Under Louis X Hutin, Raoul de Préaux continued in favor and became one of the *clercs du secret*.[9] In June 1315 he was assigned to a judicial commission with the *bailli* of Tours to try cases in the Loire valley.[10] As *clerc du secret* he accompanied the king on the Flemish campaign of 1315 and was very likely in the tents of Bondues when Jeanne de Chastel pleaded for her hus-

---

[6] *Journ. Philippe IV*, nos. 5,846, 5,908. In the latter entry, the account was made "per Radulphum de Perellis clericum, archidiaconum Vindocinensem." There is no evidence that Préaux was ever archdeacon of Vendôme. The entry must have been miswritten or misread; it means that Préaux was either the clerk of Simon Festu or was making his account with Festu.

[7] A.N., JJ. 47, no. 77.

[8] A.N., JJ. 42B, no. 155; JJ. 41, no. 156. See also *Olim*, III, 575, 647 for Préaux at work in 1310 and 1312.

[9] Lehugeur, *Philippe le Long: le mécanisme du gouvernement*, p. 101.

[10] A.N., JJ. 52, no. 218.

band. An ironic twist is provided by the possibility that Raoul de Préaux drew up the letters of Châtillon and Mercoeur which announced the acquittal of Raoul de Presles. In fact, Préaux's presence in the Flemish campaign makes more puzzling the failure of Louis X to issue under his own seal the letters of Presles' acquittal.[11] During the summer of 1316, when the future Philip V was regent, Préaux continued to serve as *clerc du secret,* but in the autumn of that year he was shifted to new functions and was made royal keeper of papal privileges. This office seemed to be a new one, formed within the complex of the royal Chancery.[12] For Raoul de Préaux it meant a new connection with Avignon and Pope John XXII. He was to spend much time during the next few years at the papal court.

The landed rents which Raoul de Préaux acquired were not nearly as large as those of Raoul de Presles, and they were located far away from the valley of the Aisne. Yet, the matter of landholdings is the second point on which historians have mistaken the lawyer for the notary. In March 1312, Philip the Fair gave to Préaux all of the lands and essarts which lay along the road from Le Liège to Montrichard.[13] These landed rents formed a straight line across the country from the Indre north to the Cher. In the following year he received fifty arpents of woods recently acquired by the king

[11] While the army moved through northern France, Préaux signed three letters dated in order at Corbie, Péronne, and Arras. All three were ordered by the king. The letter at Arras was written on September 1, 1315. See A.N., JJ. 52, nos. 229, 231, 232.

[12] Petit, *Essai de restitution,* pp. 57, 168. In September 1316, Préaux received from Felisius Colombi, clerk of the French king, forty-nine papal privileges which were itemized. In the following January, he again took from Colombi additional papal letters. However, in April 1317, it was Pierre de Chappes, chancellor, to whom Colombi delivered papal letters to be deposited in the treasury of the cathedral of Bourges. The keepership of papal privileges was probably annexed to his ordinary duties as royal notary, for he signed letters in the summer of 1318 (A.N., JJ. 56, nos. 248, 453).

[13] A.N., JJ. 47, no. 77.

from the monastery of Grammont near Tours.[14] In the latter
part of 1313 the king granted to Préaux various small rents
which included high and low justice in the parish of Le
Liège, revenues at Hys and neighboring villages, the fief of
La Charproy to be held in fealty and liege homage, some
meadowland outside Loches, and grain revenue in the parish
of Chédigny.[15] Apparently, Préaux never sought rents in
his native village but grouped his holdings closer to Tours.
The location of his lands sets him clearly apart from Raoul
de Presles. The lawyer was a clerk from the valley of the
Aisne and created his landed empire as close as possible to
that region. The notary was a clerk from the valley of the
Loire and accumulated a much smaller estate between the
Cher and the Indre.

Raoul de Préaux came to the height of his career in 1317.
He had only recently been made keeper of papal privileges,
and in the early years of Philip V's reign was treated as gen-
erously as he had been treated by Philip the Fair and Louis
X. Philip V gave him an additional 60 *l.* of landed rents and
assigned to him some of the wealth from the confiscated
property of Jean Chevreux, *viguier* of Toulouse.[16] But the
grandest gesture came when the king granted nobility to
Raoul de Préaux and his children. This is the third point on
which the notary has been confused with the lawyer. There
is no evidence that Raoul de Presles ever received nobility
from any of the Capetian kings. But historians have constantly insisted that he was ennobled and have pointed to the
royal letter of September 1317.[17] That letter clearly states
that nobility was given to *magistro Radulpho de Perellis*.
The orthography says that the man concerned was Raoul

14 A.N., JJ. 49, no. 9.
15 A.N., JJ. 49, no. 140; *Livre Rouge*, no. 924. Langlois transcribed
the name as "Raoul de Presles."
16 A.N., JJ. 53, nos. 313, 327. For other grants, or confirmation of
grants, to Préaux by Philip V, see A.N., JJ. 52, no. 12; JJ. 53, no. 136.
17 A.N., JJ. 53, nos. 314. No mention was made of his wife Eustachie.

de Préaux. Later evidence confirms his ennoblement. But the mere fact that Préaux was ennobled points to a social origin which was similar to that of Raoul de Presles. Both men rose from a non-noble background and it is possible that Préaux or his parents came from serfdom.

As was the case with the lawyers of Philip the Fair, the height of Raoul de Préaux's career was shortly followed by his fall. Only two months after he received his letter of nobility, John XXII wrote a long letter to the king defending Préaux against calumnies and mendacious accusations which had been heaped upon him.[18] For the next three years the pope was Préaux's strongest defender against those who pursued him. This friendship between the pontiff and the notary is difficult to explain. In September 1316, when Préaux became the royal keeper of papal privileges, he was sent to Avignon. This is the fourth point on which Presles has been mistaken for Préaux. Raoul de Presles was never sent to Avignon or anywhere else on royal business. Préaux's entrée at the papal court can best be explained by the patronage of Simon Festu bishop of Meaux. If we accept the premise that Préaux had risen through Jeanne de Navarre's household under Festu's tutelage, it is reasonable to believe that Festu was behind the favors which the pope showered upon the notary. It is also possible that Préaux knew Jacques Duese before he became pope, but there is no evidence for this view. In any event, John XXII issued twelve letters in September 1316 which gave privileges to him, his friends, relatives, and his clerks.[19] He was referred to by the pope as "master Raoul de Préaux, married clerk" (*clericus conjugatus*).[20] He obtained permission to nominate persons to prebends and to the office of tabellion.

[18] Coulon, *Lettres secrètes et curiales du pape Jean XXII*, no. 451.
[19] *Jean XXII*, nos. 31, 90, 99, 126, 865, 1,119, 1,129, 1,193, 1,196-1,199. Letters granting additional favors were written in 1317 (*ibid.*, nos. 2,507, 4,653, 4,674, 4,818).
[20] *Ibid.*, no. 31.

Most of the ecclesiastical livings which he obtained for his friends and relatives were located in the Loire valley.

The causes of Raoul de Préaux's disgrace and fall from royal favor cannot be accurately determined. Court intrigue was clearly one of the factors at work. From the moment that Préaux was absent from Paris on business in Avignon, his enemies went to work. Most of what we know about his downfall comes from the letters which John XXII wrote in his behalf. From November 1317 to January 1319, the pope wrote repeatedly to the king, the queen, Charles de Valois, Louis d'Evreux, and the king's brother, fervently protesting Préaux's innocence in the face of the malicious charges made against him.[21] Gradually, out of this mass of correspondence, arose the indication that much of the intrigue was centered in the queen's household and was promoted by a Dominican, Guido Peregrini, who had the queen's confidence. Peregrini, who was aided by an unnamed monk from the diocese of Troyes, poisoned Jeanne de Bourgogne's mind against Préaux and intimated that the notary had spoken indecent words about her.[22] From that point the rumor grew that Préaux was the author of malicious gossip about several prelates in the royal council.[23] The queen ordered a secret inquest conducted by the bishop of Mende and Henri de Sully, who, more than any other person, played Marigny to Philip V. For his part, the pope questioned two cardinals who knew the most about Peregrini and the unnamed monk,[24] and reported that the Dominican was a man "known for his malicious opinions and grave crimes and was held suspect by many, even in his own order."[25] Peregrini had

[21] Coulon, *Lettres secrètes et curiales du pape Jean XXII*, nos. 452, 517-522, 526-529, 553, 554, 791, 1,205-1,208. A total of about twenty letters were written.

[22] *Ibid.*, no. 553.   [23] *Ibid.*, no. 697.

[24] *Ibid.*, no. 554. The pope questioned the two cardinals in the presence of Henri de Sully and the bishop of Meaux.

[25] *Ibid.*, no. 553.

spoken against Préaux "not from a love for truth or a zeal for justice but rather from hatred and vindictive spite."[26] The persecution of Raoul de Préaux assumed the characteristics of the earlier process against Guichard de Troyes and, like it, was spawned in a queen's household.

Despite all that the pope did and said, Préaux was swept on toward his ruin.[27] A royal inquest, completed in January 1319, put a different light on the charges against the notary. Raoul de Jouy and the *bailli* of Tours had made inquiries in that *bailliage* and had found that Préaux was guilty of extortions, malefactions, criminal deeds, and other excesses.[28] Upon the completion of this inquest, Préaux was presumably dismissed from the royal service. But that was not the end of the affair. John XXII continued his efforts to clear Préaux and from the letters which he wrote after the completion of the royal inquest new and interesting facts emerged. While evidence was amassed against Préaux, Béraud de Mercoeur, constable of Champagne, became entangled in charges of treason for having entered the Franche-Comté with an armed force. His chief antagonist and accuser was Henri de Sully. His lands were seized and a duel was set between him and Sully. But in a meeting at Vincennes in June 1319, the count of Valois delivered testimony which quashed Mercoeur's defense and he submitted.[29] During Mercoeur's

[26] *Ibid.*, no. 554.

[27] An interesting aspect of Préaux's fall is that it coincided with the death of his sponsor and patron, Simon Festu. Festu died on December 30, 1317. The charges against Préaux had begun to accumulate only a month earlier. Presumably, if the bishop of Meaux had lived, he might have been able to give his protégé greater protection than he received.

[28] Boutaric, no. 5647. Raoul de Jouy was the notary who was sent to Toulouse in 1316 to gather evidence on Pierre de Latilly. Actually, Jouy and the *bailli* of Tours made separate inquiries, Jouy being assigned to the case after the *bailli* had uncovered substantial evidence of Préaux's malfeasance. Boutaric mistakenly transcribed Préaux's name as "Presles."

[29] The story of the Sully-Mercoeur struggle was reconstructed by Lehugeur, *Philippe le Long: le mécanisme du gouvernement*, p. 121f. The evidence comes from A.N., JJ. 55, no. 31.

process, the pope sought to reconcile him with Sully through the good offices of the papal nuncio. At the same time, he also attempted a reconciliation between Préaux and Jean d'Arrabloy, a representative of the noble house which rose to administrative prominence under the last Capetians. Finally, in a third letter, John XXII asked the nuncio to intervene between Sully and Mercoeur and between Préaux and d'Arrabloy.[30] There is no indication of the role played by d'Arrabloy in Préaux's trial, but the papal evidence seems to link the notary's trial with Mercoeur's troubles.

Like the lawyer with whom he has been confused, Raoul de Préaux went through a judicial ordeal without being completely destroyed. Coulon insisted that he never came back to the royal service after his trial.[31] But the outcome of his trial is not known. Whether he was proved innocent or guilty, whether his lands were seized, or whether he was actually dismissed from his office are all mute questions. John XXII's support was probably more effective than has been realized, for Préaux reappeared under Charles IV and in his old function of royal representative at Avignon. In 1324 and 1325 he carried out an extensive mission to the papal court.[32] He probably retired from governmental service at the death of the last Capetian, and returned to the valley of the Loire to live out his days as a landed gentleman. He was still living in 1358.[33]

The custom of passing on one's influence and connections at court to sons, nephews, and cousins was not confined to

[30] The papal letters asking for reconciliation in both of these trials are in Coulon, *Lettres secrètes et curiales du pape Jean XXII*, nos. 1,089-1,091, and are vaguely dated between March 20, 1319, and June 14, 1320.

[31] *Ibid.*, col. 65-68.

[32] *Journ. Charles IV*, nos. 7265, 8235, 8245, 8470, 8654.

[33] Louis de Grandmaison, *Cartulaire de l'archévêché de Tours* (Paris, 1892-1894), II, 31 and 51f. The first entry is dated 1335 and mentions a fief which Préaux held in the region between the Indre and the Cher. The second entry is of 1358 when he was cited as holding a fief near Loches from Pierre de Mornay.

the Capetian lawyers. Personnel in the finance departments picked up the habit, and Raoul de Préaux was one of the earliest Chancery notaries to secure a position in the royal service for his son. Guillaume de Préaux first appeared in November 1316 when he was granted a canonry in St. Martin of Tours.[34] His patroness in this case was Jeanne de Bourgogne, countess of Poitiers, and soon to become queen of France. His father had been made royal keeper of papal privileges only two months before. During the following year, Guillaume accumulated ecclesiastical livings until, in the late summer of 1317, the pope gave him a non-residence permit to attend a university.[35] After that, he disappeared from the records until 1333 when he was called "canon of St. Martin of Tours and professor of laws."[36] He probably spent some time teaching in a law school. Guillaume de Préaux was a clerk and counselor of Philip VI in 1345 when the king permitted his father, referred to as "chevalier," to amortize rents for two chaplaincies. In this same letter, Raoul and Guillaume were commended for the services that they had rendered to Philip VI and his predecessors.[37]

Much of the story of Raoul de Préaux has no bearing on the career of Raoul de Presles. But in a general way the life of Préaux amplifies the conditions and atmosphere in which Presles worked. The careers of both men followed a similar pattern—the rise to wealth and success, the fall and disgrace, and the recovery of status. They undoubtedly knew each other, but they were not one and the same. Raoul de Presles was never a notary; he did not hold any lands in the Loire valley; he never received nobility; and he never served as

[34] *Jean XXII*, no. 1,713.
[35] *Jean XXII*, nos. 3,131, 3,204, 4,083, 4,651. In the first two, Guillaume de Préaux was qualified as "in annis teneris existenti."
[36] *Jean XXII*, no. 60,517.
[37] A.N., JJ. 75, no. 583. Raoul de Préaux's wife, Eustachie, was deceased by this date.

royal emissary to the papal court. The confusion which arose from the similarity of the two names may perhaps be excused. But historians should have noticed that there was an entirely different sense in each of the two lives and careers, and this difference in sense or flavor owed more to local history and habitat than to any other circumstance. A notary whose interests lay in the Loire valley should never have been mistaken for a lawyer whose interests lay in the valley of the Aisne.

BIBLIOGRAPHY OF MANUSCRIPT SOURCES

1. ARCHIVES NATIONALES

A. CHANCERY REGISTERS

The Chancery Registers of Philip the Fair and his three sons form the essential foundations of this study. Just after I had completed the research, the long-awaited calendar of Philip the Fair's Chancery Registers was published by Professor Robert Fawtier with the assistance of M. Jean Guerout and M. Jean Glénisson (*Registres du Trésor des Chartes. Tome I. Règne de Philippe le Bel*, in Archives Nationales: Inventaires et documents. Paris, 1958). For this reason I have used the manuscript references rather than the published calendar references in citing the Chancery Registers of Philip the Fair in this study. These can be found easily in the published calendar because the editors used not only their own enumeration but also the manuscript references. At the same time, I have found the published calendar extremely valuable for rechecking references, and for verifying dates, place names, and personal names. There are fourteen Chancery Registers of Philip the Fair of which two, JJ. 41 and JJ. 42B, are duplicates and one, JJ. 39, is missing. They contain approximately 2,300 letters, which cover the period 1302-1314. Part of JJ. 50 contains letters of Philip the Fair and the Registers therefore run in number from JJ. 37 to JJ. 50.

The Chancery Registers of Philip the Fair's three sons begin with JJ. 50 and run through JJ. 64. Chancery Register JJ. 65A has a few letters from the reign of Charles IV. The Chancery Registers of the three sons contain some 5,400 letters. Various Chancery Registers of the Valois kings were also used.

Louis X Hutin (1314-1316)

JJ. 50 (1314-1315) 148 letters.
JJ. 51 (missing)
JJ. 52 (1315) 232 letters.

Philippe V le Long (1316-1322)

JJ. 53 (1317) 364 letters.
JJ. 54A (1317) 701 letters.
JJ. 54B (1316-1317) 84 letters.
JJ. 55 (1316-1319) 160 letters.

JJ. 56 (1317-1319) 623 letters.
JJ. 57 (Household ordinances).
JJ. 58 (1317-1320) 487 letters.
JJ. 59 (1318-1321) 621 letters.
JJ. 60 (1319-1321) 226 letters.

Charles IV le Bel (1322-1328)

JJ. 61 (1322-1323) 496 letters.
JJ. 62 (1323-1325) 531 letters.
JJ. 63 (missing)
JJ. 64 (1324-1328) 756 letters.

B. Parlement de Paris

Much of the material in the records of the Parlement de Paris which concern the last Capetians has been published in its entirety or in calendar form. I have used in manuscript form many of the registers of civil accords which form the series xic, and several of the registers in the xia series which include *juges, lettres, arrêts,* and *conseil et plaidoiries.*

C. Ecclesiastical Institutions

Various cartons (Series L) in the ecclesiastical section have furnished at times valuable information on the identities, families, and ecclesiastical holdings of the lawyers and other civil servants. The registers (Series LL) have been of little help in this study.

L. 733 (Bishopric of Laon).
L. 734 (Bishopric of Laon).
L. 739 (Bishopric of Noyons. Chapter of Saint Quentin).
L. 742 (Bishopric of Soissons).
L. 881 (Monastic Paris—Ste. Gèneviève).
L. 938 (Monastic France—Chartreux).
L. 1008 (Abbey of Saint Jean-des-Vignes, Soissons).

D. Educational Institutions

The charters and registers in the Archives Nationales which bear the designations of M. and MM. contain not only the history of the colleges which were part of the University of Paris but they also provide information on the founders of the colleges and more particularly on the families of the founders. In the case of Raoul de Presles, crucial evidence comes from these sources.

M. 140 (Carton—Collège de Laon).
M. 185 (Carton—Collège de Presles).
MM. 418 (Cartulary—Collège de Laon).

2. BIBLIOTHÈQUE NATIONALE

For information on the Capetian lawyers, the most valuable collection of transcribed charters in the Bibliothèque Nationale is the Collection Moreau. But in most cases the items furnished by this collection duplicate the information which comes from other available sources. Of less use was the Collection Dom Grenier.

Several other individual manuscripts were used and are cited in the study.

3. *ARCHIVES DÉPARTEMENTALES*

The departmental archives of France contain much information on Philip the Fair's civil servants in general, but little of importance on the lawyers who are treated in this study. I have therefore listed only those items which provided concrete information on some particular lawyer. For instance, the Archives départementales de la Marne have many charters on Pierre de Latilly, but they all deal with him after 1320 when he had given up his governmental career.

A. ARCHIVES DE L'AISNE
   (LAON)
   G. 2   (Register)
   G. 13   (Liasse)
   G. 75   (Liasse)
   G. 253 (Register)
   H. 477 (Register)

B. ARCHIVES DE L'EURE
   (EVREUX)
   G. 92   (Liasse)
   G. 122 (Register)

C. ARCHIVES DE LA MARNE
   (CHALONS)
   G. 10   (Probably Latilly's
            Register)
   G. 171 (Liasse)
   G. 198 (Laisse)
   G. 200 (Liasse)
   G. 250 (Liasse)
   G. 406 (Liasse)
   G. 458 (Liasse)
   G. 475 (Liasse)
   G. 484 (Liasse)

D. ARCHIVES DU NORD
   (LILLE)
   28 H. 75 (Liasse)

INDEX